The Son of Man in the Gospel of John

New Testament Monographs, 28

Series Editor
Stanley E. Porter

THE SON OF MAN
IN THE GOSPEL OF JOHN

J. Harold Ellens

SHEFFIELD PHOENIX PRESS

2010

Copyright © 2010 Sheffield Phoenix Press

Published by Sheffield Phoenix Press
Department of Biblical Studies, University of Sheffield
Sheffield S3 7QB

www.sheffieldphoenix.com

A CIP catalogue record for this book
is available from the British Library

Typeset by CA Typesetting Ltd
Printed on acid-free paper by Lightning Source UK Ltd, Milton Keynes

ISBN-13 978-1-906055-99-8

Dedication
This work is dedicated to
Nicholas Robert Kwantes Ellens,
My eldest grandson,
Who encouraged me to persist
When I was at the moment of being
Most ready to abandon this project.
He insisted that I remember well
What I had told him in College:
'Never Give Up!'
He had me!
What could I do but carry on?
I am pleased that I did and thank him heartily.

CONTENTS

LIST OF FIGURES

LIST OF TABLES

ACKNOWLEDGMENTS

Now that I have reached the point of completing this major scholarly endeavor in graduate study, I am aware of my deep indebtedness to more colleagues, friends, and family than it is possible to name here. However, there are a number of key persons and institutions that have made this accomplishment possible. First and foremost I wish to express my appreciation and palpable gratitude to my Advisor, Professor Gabriele Boccaccini. His patience, wisdom, creativity, and scholarship have inspired, encouraged, and led me in this work. His imaginative ideas and illumining insights regarding Second Temple Judaism and a wide range of broader interests, enriched my research, guided its trajectory, and led me to a fruitful outcome.

I first met Professor Boccaccini in 1990 when he lectured at the Gregorian University in Rome. It was an interesting and stimulating experience at that august institution to have the riches of Second Temple Judaism scholarship opened before me in a manner I had hitherto not encountered. It was particularly gratifying, therefore, to discover in the years that followed that he was to be Visiting Professor at the University of Michigan, Department of Near Eastern Studies, where I had undertaken the PhD program. That offered us the opportunity to deepen our scholarly relationship. It has subsequently given rise to a close collegial friendship. We have, with genuine satisfaction, shared the work of a great number of scholarly endeavors.

Some of the richest experiences under the tutelage of and as assistant to Professor Boccaccini were the development and execution of the biennial International Enoch Studies Conferences in Italy and the co-editing of the scholarly papers of those conferences, so proficiently published by Zamorani in 2003 and by Eerdmans in 2005, 2007 and 2009, as well as the launching of the new series of the Journal *HENOCH* in 2005. We traveled together widely through Europe to attend international conferences of the Learned Societies, including the University of Michigan NES Summer Program on Jews and Christians in the Roman World (Rome, 2003). Moreover, together we established The Michigan Center for Early Christian Studies which vigorously supports the work of the division of Christian Studies in our department. We developed in partnership a comprehensive bibliography of Enoch scholarship.

I was privileged to share for a number of years, and to my great profit, the experiences of Professor Boccaccini's numerous seminars in methodology, history of ideas, and trajectories of traditions in Second Temple Judaism. It was in this context that I had the good fortune to receive his inspired and inspiring suggestion that important work could be and needed to be done on the special Second Temple Judaism subject of the Son of Man in John's Gospel. Pursuing that suggestion has proven to be a demanding but enormously enriching scholarly undertaking that has enhanced my understanding of the ancient world, 300 BCE–300 CE, beyond anything I could have anticipated.

My odyssey in pursuit of this second PhD has been a long and demanding journey. When I finished my MDiv at Calvin Seminary fifty-three years ago, I did not anticipate further graduate work. However, after many years as an Army Chaplain I realized that I would feel much more gratification in my work if I could acquire extensive additional training in both biblical studies and in counseling. Therefore, I left active army duty to take a ThM in New Testament and Intertestamental Studies under Professor Bruce M. Metzger at Princeton Theological Seminary. I followed that with a PhD in the Psychology of Human Communications (1970) at Wayne State University.

There followed years of professional work in church ministry, university and seminary teaching, presenting papers at conferences of learned societies, and conducting a private practice in psychotherapy. In 1990 I was pleased with the opportunity to build further on my work under Metzger as a result of being invited by Professor Jarl Fossum to pursue this present PhD in Second Temple Judaism and Christian Origins. Fossum provoked me to study at the University of Michigan by his severe critique of my paper on 'Zoroastrian Influences in Jewish Apocalypticism' at the SBL in 1990. In consequence, I read his meticulous book, *The Name of God and the Angel of the Lord* (Tübingen: Mohr–Siebeck, 1985). That volume and Professor Boccaccini's early work, *Middle Judaism, Jewish Thought 300 BCE to 200 CE* (Minneapolis: Fortress Press, 1991), set me on a more sophisticated course in pursuit of my interests in Second Temple Judaism studies. Fossum's and Boccaccini's lectures were always substantive and interesting and advanced my research significantly.

When Fossum left the university, Professor Boccaccini picked up the pieces of the program, reoriented my project, and guided me through this work to its fruition. It is not possible to express adequate gratitude for my development under such signal scholars.

During this long and arduous process many colleagues shared with me the vicissitudes and gratifications of graduate work. Among those closest to me in this project were Grant Shafer, Mark S. Kinzer, James Waddell, Jason Van Ehrenkrook, Ronald Ruark, and in more recent years, Isaac Oliver and

Pierpaolo Bertalotto. They were humorful, inspiring companions and illumining fellow scholars throughout the years. In the many superb graduate seminars conducted by Professor Boccaccini during our years of work together, these friends and fellow pilgrims in the quest for understanding and scholarly maturity always proved to be generatively instructive in their rich contributions. I will count them as more than colleagues, indeed, as permanent friends for my remaining years. As fellow Graduate Student Instructors we struggled together to measure up to the high performance necessary to match the erudition of Professor Boccaccini and handle the enormous enrollments of students flocking in to hear his lectures. I am sure we will always remember this as a time of demanding and gratifying pilgrimage together.

It is imperative that I also recognize here, with deep gratitude, the financial support for my work in research and writing that was afforded me by the Department of Near Eastern Studies, The Michigan Center for Early Christian Studies, The Frankel Center for Judaic Studies, and the Rackham Graduate School. Without their help and encouragement I could not have completed this challenging undertaking. Through every year of my work at the University of Michigan the efficiency of its administrative processes and student support seems to me to have increased markedly.

With special appreciation, I wish to thank the members of my doctoral committee. In addition to the enormous help, care, and kindness of my Advisor, I am greatly indebted to Professor Phillip B. Munoa III of the Religious Studies Department of Hope College, Professor Raymond Van Dam of the History Department at the University of Michigan, and Professor Brian Schmidt of the Department of Near Eastern Studies of the University of Michigan. Consequent to a number of key personnel changes at the university during my research and matriculation, these gentlemen were called upon relatively late in the process and immediately rose to the demands of the committee work, carefully studying my dissertation, providing an appropriate and useful critique, and executing their response to my defense of it with skill, precision, sophisticated erudition, and grace. I shall always be grateful and joyful about that.

Finally, I thank Mary Jo Lewis Ellens for flagging but not failing in her faith that this project was worthwhile, despite the decade of our lives that it consumed. She encouraged me to the very end with more confidence in the importance and potential gratification of the undertaking, than I often felt myself. Moreover, I am painfully aware of how long and how much my time, energy, and presence was drawn away from my entire family because of the seemingly endless years of my preoccupation with this work. I wish now to express my empathy and gratitude to Deborah, Jacqueline, Daniel, Rebecca, Rocky, Brenda and Brett; as well as my eight grandchildren and one great grandchild. I cannot make up to them the hours, potential memories, family fun, and just plain relaxed intimacies this endeavor has cost us all. I hope they can forgive, forget, and feel some of the celebrative gratification I now have for a task thoughtfully undertaken, carefully seen through to the finish, and done well.

ABBREVIATIONS

AB	Anchor Bible
ABD	David Noel Freedman (ed.), *The Anchor Bible Dictionary*, (New York: Doubleday, 1992)
ABR	*Australian Biblical Review*
ABRL	Anchor Bible Reference Library
ADB	James Hastings (ed.), *A Dictionary of the Bible* (Edinburgh: T. & T. Clark, 1902)
ATR	*Anglican Theological Review*
BETL	Bibliotheca ephemeridum theologicarum Iovaniensium
Bib	*Biblica*
BibSciRel	Biblioteca di scienze religiose
BJRL	*Bulletin of the John Rylands Library*
BR	*Bible Review*
BTB	*Biblical Theology Bulletin*
BZNW	Beihefte zur *Zeitschrift für die Neutesamentliche Wissenschaft*
CBET	Contributions to Biblical Exegesis and Theology
CBQ	*Catholic Biblical Quarterly*
CBQMS	*Catholic Biblical Quarterly*, Monograph Series
CTJ	*Calvin Theological Journal*
EBC	Expositor's Bible Commentary
ExpT	*Expository Times*
EQ	*Evangelical Quarterly*
ETL	Ephemerides theologicae Iovanienses
ETR	*Etudes théologiques et religieuses*
FCJS	Frankel Center for Judaic Studies at the University of Michigan
FOTL	The Forms of the Old Testament Literature
GThJ	*Garret Theological Journal*
HBT	*Horizons in Biblical Theology*
HSM	Harvard Semitic Monographs
ICC	International Critical Commentary
ICCNT	International Critical Commentary of the New Testament
IRT	Issues in Religion and Theology
ITQ	*Irish Theological Quarterly*
JAOS	*Journal of the American Oriental Society*
JBL	*Journal of Biblical Literature*
JBS	*Journal for Biblical Studies*
JETS	*Journal of the Evangelical Theological Society*
JSNT	*Journal for the Study of the New Testament*
JSNTSup	*Journal for the Study of the New Testament*, Supplement Series
JSOT	*Journal for the Study of the Old Testament*
JSOTSup	*Journal for the Study of the Old Testament*, Supplement Series
JSPSup	*Journal for the Study of the Pseudepigrapha*, Supplement Series

JSSR	*Journal for the Scientific Study of Religion*
JTC	*Journal of Theology and the Church*
JTS	*Journal of Theological Studies*
KEK	Kritisch-exegetishcer Kommentar über das Neue Testament
LNTS	Library of New Testament Studies
LTPM	Louvain Theological and Pastoral Monographs
LXX	Septuagint
MCECS	Michigan Center for Early Christian Studies at the University of Michigan
NICNT	New International Commentary on the New Testament
NICOT	New International Commentary on the Old Testament
NovT	*Novum Testamentum*
NovTSup	*Novum Testamentum*, Supplements
NTD	Das Neue Testament Deutsch
NTL	New Testament Library
NTS	*New Testament Studies*
NTSR	New Testament for Spiritual Reading
NTT	*Nederlands theologisch tijdschrift*
OTE	*Old Testament Essays*
ÖTKNT	Ökumenischer Taschenbuchkommentar zum Neuen Testament
OTL	Old Testament Library
OTP	James C. Charlesworth (ed.), *Old Testament Pseudepigrapha*, 2 vols. (New York: Doubleday, 1983)
RBL	*Review of Biblical Literature*
RSR	*Religious Studies Review*
RSV	Revised Standard Version
SBL	Society of Biblical Literature
SBLDS	Society of Biblical Literature Dissertation Series
SBT	Studies in Biblical Theology
SE	Studia evangelica
SNTSMS	Society for New Testament Studies Monograph Series
SL	*Studium legionense*
ST	*Studia theologica*
TANZ	Texte und Arbeiten zum neutestamentlichen Zeitalter
TB	*Tyndale Bulletin*
TD	*Theology Digest*
TDNT	Gerhard Kittel and Gerhard Friedrich (eds.), *Theological Dictionary of the New Testament* (trans. Geoffrey W. Bromiley; 10 vols: Grand Rapids: Eerdmans, 1964–1976)
THAT	Ernst Jenni and Claus Westermann (eds.), *Theologisches Handwörterbuch zum Alten Testament* (Munich: Chr. Kaiser, 1971–76)
THKNT	Theologischer Handkommentar zum Neuen Testament
TLOT	E. Jenni (ed.), with assistance from C. Westermann, *Theological Lexicon of the Old Testament* (trans. M.E. Biddle: 3 vols.; Peabody, MA: Hendrickson, 1997)
TOTC	Tyndale Old Testament Commentaries
TSR	Texts and Studies in Religion
TWNT	Gerhard Kittel and Gerhard Friedrich, *Theologisches Wörterbuch zum Neuen Testament* (10 vols; Stuttgart: Kohlhammer, 1932-1979)
TWOT	R. Laird Harris, Gleason L. Archer, Jr, and Bruce K. Waltke (eds.), *Theological Wordbook of the Old Testament* (2 vols.; Chicago: Moody Press, 1980)

WBC	Word Biblical Commentary
WMANT	Wissenschaftliche Monographien zum Alten und Neuen Testament
WUND	Wissenschaftliche Untersuchungen zum Neuen Testament
ZAW	*Zeitschrift für die altestamentliche Wissenschaft*
ZNW	*Zeitschrift für die neutesamentliche Wissenschaft*
ZTK	*Zeitschrift für Theologie und Kirche*

Chapter 1

INTRODUCTION

A. *Setting the Stage (Defining the Topic)*

Much scholarship has been generated in the study of the Son of Man phrase or title in the New Testament. The modern history of this enterprise started with the very beginning of critical research on the historical Jesus and was fueled by the rediscovery of the *Parables of Enoch* in the early nineteenth century.[1] Ever since, a broad stream of research and publication on the Son of Man in the New Testament proliferated throughout the twentieth century, producing a variety of models that scholars have proposed for understanding the Son of Man logia in the Synoptic Gospels.[2]

In contrast, only a relatively small number of publications had appeared on the Son of Man in John before the last quarter of the twentieth century. Robert Maddox observed in 1974 that 'little research is directed to the Son of Man theme in John, at least by comparison with the flood of studies on the Son of Man in the synoptic gospels'.[3] That sentiment was confirmed by such scholars as Francis Moloney, who expressed surprise at the point of the publication of his dissertation that the use of the phrase or title, Son of Man, in the Gospel of John had aroused so little scholarly attention. It is of interest that recently, however, Moloney declared that 'it can no longer be claimed that there is scant interest in the Johannine Son of Man'.[4] The last quarter of the twentieth century began the process of repairing the former inattention to that gospel with the publication of monographs, articles,

1. Jason von Ehrenkrook, 'The Parables of Enoch and the Messiah Son of Man: A Bibliography, 1773–2006', in *Enoch and the Messiah Son of Man: Revisiting the Book of Parables*' (ed. G. Boccaccini; Grand Rapids: Eerdmans, 2007), pp. 513-39.
2. Delbert Burkett, *The Son of Man Debate: A History and Evaluation* (Cambridge: Cambridge University Press, 1999).
3. Robert Maddox, 'The Function of the Son of Man in the Gospel of John', in *Reconciliation and Hope: New Testament Essays on Atonement and Eschatology Presented to L.L. Morris on his 60th Birthday* (ed. Robert J. Banks; Exeter: Paternoster Press, 1974), pp. 186-204 (186).
4. Francis J. Moloney, *The Gospel of John: Text and Context* (Leiden: E.J. Brill, 2005), pp. 66-67.

and significant reviews by Maddox,[5] Joseph Coppens,[6] Moloney,[7] Peter Borgen,[8] John Painter,[9] Jerome Neyrey,[10] Margaret Pamment,[11] Wolfgang Roth,[12] Wayne Meeks,[13] Robert Rhea,[14] Delbert Burkett,[15] Mogens Müller,[16] Mary Pazdan,[17] John Pryor,[18] Richard Bauckham,[19] Pierre Létourneau,[20]

5.   Maddox, 'The Function of the Son of Man', pp. 186-204.

6.   Joseph Coppens, 'Le fils de l'homme dans l'évangile johannique', *ETL* 52 (1976), pp. 28-81.

7.   Francis J. Moloney, 'The Johannine Son of Man', PhD dissertation at St Mary's College, Oxford, 1975, subsequently published as his *The Johannine Son of Man* (Bib-SciRel, 14; Rome: Pontifical Biblical Institute, 1976); Moloney, 'The Johannine Son of Man Debate', *BTB* 6 (1976), pp. 177-89, a digest of his 1975 dissertation; Moloney, 'A Johannine Son of Man Discussion?', *Salesianum* 39 (1977), pp. 93-102. See also Delbert Burkett, 'Review: Francis J. Moloney, *The Son of Man in the Gospel of John*', *JTS* 44 (1993), pp. 259-61 and Burkett, 'Review: Francis J. Monoley, *The Son of Man in the Gospel of John*', *ABR* 43 (1995), pp. 85-87.

8.   Peter Borgen, 'Some Jewish Exegetical Traditions as Background for Son of Man Sayings in John's Gospel (Jn 3.13-14 and context)', in *L'Evangile de Jean* (ed. Marinus de Jonge; Gembloux: Duculot, 1977), pp. 243-58.

9.   John Painter, 'Review: Francis J. Moloney, *The Johannine Son of Man*', *ABR* 25 (1977), pp. 43-44; Painter, 'The Enigmatic Johannine Son of Man', in *Four Gospels 1992, Festschrift Frans Neirynck* (ed. Frans van Segbroeck *et al.*; BETL, 100; 3 vols; Louvain: Peters, 1992), pp. 1869-87.

10.   Jerome Neyrey, 'The Jacob Allusions in John 1.52', *CBQ* 44 (1982), pp. 586-605.

11.   Margaret Pamment, 'The Son of Man in the Fourth Gospel', *JTS* 36.1 (1985), pp. 56-66.

12.   Wolfgang Roth, 'Jesus as the Son of Man: The Scriptural Identity of a Johannine Image', in *The Living Test: Essays in Honor of Ernest W. Saunders* (ed. Dennis E. Groh and Robert Jewett; Lanham, MD: University Press of America, 1985), pp. 11-26.

13.   Wayne A. Meeks, 'The Man from Heaven in Johannine Sectarianism', in *The Interpretation of John* (ed. John Ashton; IRT, 9; Philadelphia: Fortress Press, 1986), pp. 141-73.

14.   Robert Rhea, *The Johannine Son of Man* (Zurich: Theologischer Verlag Zürich, 1990).

15.   Delbert Burkett, *The Son of the Man in the Gospel of John* (JSNTSup, 56; Sheffield: Sheffield Academic Press, 1991).

16.   Mogens Müller, 'Have You Faith in the Son of Man? (John 9.35)', *NTS* 37 (1991), pp. 291-94.

17.   Mary M. Pazdan, *The Son of Man: A Metaphor for Jesus in the Fourth Gospel* (Collegeville, MN: Liturgical Press, 1991); Pazdan, 'Review: Delbert Burkett, *The Son of Man in the Gospel of John*', *Interpretation* 47 (1993), pp. 312-13.

18.   John W. Pryor, 'The Johannine Son of Man and the Descent-Ascent Motif', *JETS* 34 (1991), pp. 342-51.

19.   Richard Bauckham, 'Review: Delbert Burkett, *The Son of Man in the Gospel of John*', *Evangelical Quarterly* (1993), pp. 266-68.

20.   Pierre Létourneau, *Jésus, fils de l'homme et fils de Dieu: Jean 2,23-3,36 et la double christologie johannique* (Montreal: Bellarmin, 1993).

Jarl Fossum,[21] Clay Ham,[22] and Felipe Ramos.[23] As the twenty-first century opened, these were followed quickly by the work of Markus Sasse,[24] Walter Wink,[25] Moloney,[26] Maurice Casey,[27] Peter Ensor,[28] and Benjamin Reynolds.[29] Nonetheless, the Johannine Son of Man remains largely overshadowed by the Synoptic Son of Man. In what is so far the most comprehensive treatment of the Son of Man in John, Reynolds observes that: 'The Son of Man sayings in John's Gospel are often neglected in the Son of Man debate, mainly because the Gospel of John is not considered historical'.[30] The assumption that the study of the Gospel of John does not have the same immediate impact as the Synoptics on the understanding of the historical Jesus is enough to limit drastically its scholarly interest.

It is my intention in this dissertation to investigate the issue of the Son of Man logia in the Fourth Gospel, as a way of setting forth matters of distinctive interest to the question suggested in my title, What is the Son of Man in John's Gospel? More precisely, I shall attempt to describe the transformation of the Son of Man in the Gospel of John from heavenly eschatological judge, as he is in the Synoptic Gospels, to divine savior, which seems to be the intended outcome in John. I shall achieve that objective by analysis of the relationship between the Fourth Gospel and other Son of Man traditions in Second Temple Judaisms, including comparison of John with the Synoptic Gospels. Hence this study on the Son of

21. Jarl E. Fossum, 'The Son of Man's Alter Ego: John 1.51, Targumic Tradition and Jewish Mysticism', in *The Image of the Invisible God* (Göttingen: Vandenhoeck & Ruprecht, 1995), pp. 135-51.

22. Clay Ham, 'The Title "Son of Man" in the Gospel of John', *Stone-Campbell Journal* 1 (1998), pp. 67-84.

23. Felipe F. Ramos, 'El hijo del hombre en el cuarto evangelio', *Studium legionense* 40 (1999), pp. 45-92.

24. Markus Sasse, *Der Menschensohn im Evangelium nach Johannes* (TANZ,15; Tübingen: Francke, 2000).

25. Walter Wink, 'The "Son of Man" in the Gospel of John', in *Jesus in the Johannine Tradition* (ed. Robert T. Fortna and Thomas Thatcher; Louisville, KY: Westminster/John Knox Press, 2001), pp. 117-23.

26. Francis J. Moloney, 'Review: M. Sasse, *Der Menschensohn im Evangelium nach Johannes*,: *JTS* 83 (2002), pp. 210-15; Moloney, 'The Johannine Son of Man Revisited', in *Theology and Christology in the Fourth Gospel: Essays by the Members of the SNTS Johannine Writings Seminar* (ed. Gilbert van Belle *et al.*; BETL, 184; Leuven: University of Leuven Press, 2005), pp. 177-202.

27. Maurice Casey, 'The Johannine Sayings', in *The Solution to the 'Son of Man' Problem* (LNTS, 343; New York: T. & T. Clark, 2007), pp. 274-313.

28. Peter W. Ensor, 'Glorification of the Son of Man: An Analysis of John 13.31-32', *Tyndale Bulletin* 58.2 (2007), pp. 229-52.

29. Benjamin E. Reynolds, *The Apocalyptic Son of Man in the Gospel of John* (WUNT, 2/249; Tübingen: Mohr–Siebeck, 2008).

30. Reynolds, *Apocalyptic Son of Man*, p. 2.

Man logia in the Gospel of John and in the Synoptic Gospels, in the light of Second Temple Judaism Son of Man traditions.

To that end, I will explore the relationship between the Son of Man of the Fourth Gospel, and of the other Second Temple Jewish Son of Man models reflected in Ezekiel, Daniel (7–9), the *Parables of Enoch* (*1 En.* 37–71), and the Synoptic Gospels. I will also briefly reflect upon the figures of the Son of Man and the Man in the *Testament of Abraham*, and *4 Ezra* regarding their relevance to my theme: *What is the Son of Man in John?* That analysis will provide a basis and method for discerning the influence of Second Temple Judaism Son of Man traditions upon the concept of the Son of Man in the Gospel of John. The issue is framed here in just this fashion to emphasize that in a discussion of the relationship between all these Second Temple Judaism traditions, including John and the Synoptic Gospels, we are dealing with an intra-Judaism dialogue. Christian origins and the formation of the four gospels were processes that took place within the apocalyptic eschatological Judaisms of the Second Temple Period.[31]

A great amount of research, such as that developed by the biennial international Enoch Studies Seminars,[32] has been devoted to *1 Enoch* in recent years, particularly to the Son of Man in the *Parables of Enoch* and the relationship of that apocalyptic figure to the 'one like unto a Son of Man' in Dan. 7.13ff.[33] It is of interest whether the author of the Fourth Gospel was

31. Reynolds's study, cited above, persuasively puts to rest the question whether the Son of Man is an apocalyptic figure in John's gospel. His work challenges Burkett's argument that there is no relationship between the Son of Man in Daniel and in John. Reynolds asserts that Burkett makes his argument 'against the connection between Dan. 7 and John 5.27 in order to refute the apocalyptic nature of the Johannine Son of Man' (Ibid., 10). Reynolds entire volume is devoted to demonstrating conclusively that the Son of Man *logia* in John all present an apocalyptic figure and drama, not just a few of them such as 1.51, 3.13, and 5.27.

32. Beginning in 2001 a series of Biennial International Enoch Seminars was established by Professor Gabriele Boccaccini and hosted in Italy by the University of Michigan. They were planned to run to the end of the decade, and beyond. Five such seminars have been held in Florence, Venice, Camaldoli, and Naples, Italy, in 2001, 2003, 2005, 2007, and 2009. These were initiated and planned by Boccaccini of the Department of Near Eastern Studies of the University of Michigan, and generously supported by the university, the Frankel Center for Judaic Studies, and the Center for Early Christian Studies. See www.enochseminar.org.

33. See the recent publications of the Biennial International Enoch Seminar. Note particularly the proceedings of the conferences in 2003, 2005 and 2007, respectively: G. Boccaccini (ed.), *Enoch and Qumran Origins: New Light on a Forgotten Connection* (Grand Rapids: Eerdmans, 2005); Boccaccini (ed.), *Enoch and the Messiah Son of Man: Revisiting the Book of Parables* (Grand Rapids: Eerdmans, 2006); Boccaccini (ed.), *Enoch and The Mosiac Torah: The Evidence of Jubilees* (Grand Rapids: Eerdmans, 2009).

aware of the Son of Man traditions in Daniel 7, *1 Enoch* 37–71, the Synoptic Gospels, and other late first-century Jewish or early second-century literature. Did these traditions influence the shape of the Son of Man concept in John? There seem to be strong indications that the author of the Fourth Gospel was aware of the Son of Man tradition in Daniel. There are also reasons to suspect that at least the authors of Matthew (19.28; 25.31) and John (3.13; 8.28) were aware of the concept of the Son of Man as used in *1 Enoch.* These issues will be explored in detail.

Thus, the objective of this research project is to focus specifically upon the use of the phrase, Son of Man, in the Gospel of John in the light of its sources and over against the claims of contemporaneous competing traditions. I will argue that in Second Temple Judaism, including the four gospels, there are mainly four types of Son of Man. He is a human prophet (in the tradition of Ezekiel); a heavenly figure (in the tradition of Daniel), a human being ultimately designated by God to be the heavenly Eschatological Judge (in the *Parables of Enoch,* and in the Synoptic Gospels), and a divine figure (in the Gospel of John).

A number of issues remain regarding our question about what the Son of Man is in John, as seen in the light of Second Temple Judaic traditions. These include: (1) the identity of the Son of Man in John compared with that in the Synoptic Gospels, (2) the relationship between the Son of Man in John and in other Second Temple Son of Man traditions, and (3) the nature of the Son of Man in John compared with the traditions of the Son of Man as Judge.

B. *History of Research and* Status quaestionis

The history of research on the meaning of the phrase Son of Man in the gospels, particularly in the highly theological Gospel of John, falls into three discernible phases. We may nominate them as the Ancient Pre-critical Phase, the Modern Critical Phase, and the Contemporary Critical Phase. As we explore each of these, we will notice that the third phase has two trajectories. One, which we will designate as 'The Non-Apocalyptic Son of Man', tends to revert to some of the key tenets of the Pre-critical Phase. The other, 'The Apocalyptic Son of Man', breaks significant new ground by relocating the Johannine Son of Man in its original Jewish apocalyptic context.

1. *The Ancient Pre-critical Phase*

After the gospels were completed, the Church Fathers continued to use the biblical term, 'Son of Man', as well as its corollary, 'Son of God', but with markedly different meanings than one finds in the gospels. In the Patristic literature, it is possible to find the Son of Man occasionally referred to as the Eschatological Judge,[34] but usually the Church Fathers employed the phrase, Son of Man, to indicate the humanity of Jesus Christ and Son of God[35] as reference to his divinity. As regards the former, 'both patristic authors and Gnostics understood the phrase, Son of Man, to identify Jesus as the son of some particular [human] parent, such as Mary, Adam, or the Gnostic god *Anthropos*. This type of interpretation prevailed throughout the Middle Ages'.[36] Thus the Patristic tradition was accepted, largely without significant further analysis, until the Protestant Reformation. Medieval scholars showed considerable interest in the Son of Man, but they offered little that was new, which the Church Fathers had not already set down. In the entire literary corpus, from the second to the sixteenth century, the Son of Man is the human Jesus, that is, *a special designation for the human nature of Jesus Christ* as defined in the historic creeds.

The sixteenth-century Reformation in northern Europe brought the text of the Bible into center focus in the church and academy. The quest for discerning the meaning of the phrase, Son of Man, resurged with a new breadth of inquiry. Beza examined the question in 1557,[37] initiating a discussion that has steadily grown for four and a half centuries. Burkett observes that the expression, Son of Man, 'has been a central issue in New Testament studies since the beginning of modern scholarship… The Gospels never explain the phrase, and though it has been the object of intensive study since the Protestant Reformation, scholars have come to no agreement on even the most basic questions concerning it'.[38]

Ulrich Zwingli insisted that the term Son of Man indicated that Jesus was truly human in every way.[39] His contemporary, Martin Bucer agreed, but was at pains to emphasize that it referred to the lowliness of the person that

34. Irenaeus, *Contra haereses* 3, 18, 6; 5, 40, 2; This usage also appears in *The Revelation of Saint John the Theologian*. Cf. also the *Epistle of Ignatius to the Magnesians*, 13, 1. Origen seems to have in mind a thorough-going Synoptic Gospels' image of the Eschatological Son of Man as Judge, in his *Commentary on Matthew*, 12, 29.

35. Tertullian, *Contra Praxeas* 18, 23. Cf. also Iranaeus, *Contra haereses* 3, 18, 6; *Epistle of Ignatius to the Magnesians* 8, 2; *Epistle of Ignatius to the Ephesians* 20, 2. For further references to the divinity of the Son of God see the *Epistle to Diognetus* 7, 4; *Epistle of Ignatius to the Smyrneans* 1, 1. See also *Encyclical Epistle of the Church at Smyrna concerning the Martyrdom of the Holy Polycarp* 17, 3; *Epistle of Polycarp to the Philippians* 12, 3; and Origen's *Commentary on John* 1, 17-32 and 2, 5.

36. Burkett, *Son of Man Debate*, pp. 3, 6-13.

37. Theodore de Beza, Annotations in Volume 3 of *Novum D. N. Iesu Christi Testamentum* (Geneva, 1557).

38. Burkett, *Son of Man Debate*, pp. 1-2. See also Burkett, *The Son of the Man in the Gospel of John*.

39. Ulrich Zwingli, *Annotationes in quatuor evangelia ac epistolas* (Tiguri: Froschover, 1531).

Jesus saw himself to be.[40] Heinrich Bullinger declared that the term signifies that Jesus was truly human, born of human origin, participating in the misery of human nature, and thus in solidarity with humanity.[41] Benedict Aretius[42] and Cornelius Jansen[43] saw the designation as a reference to Jesus' unhappy and miserable experience of being human, while Henry Hammond[44] and J.L. von Wolzogen[45] thought it described the fragile infirmity of human nature which Jesus shared with all humankind.

Jacob Alting perceived that Jesus wished by the use of this term to tell his followers that he was not ashamed of his lowly human condition.[46] Sebastian Münster,[47] Hugo Grotius, and most scholars after them, down to the end of the eighteenth century, thought the term Son of Man as applied to Jesus, meant that he saw himself as one of the common people.[48] This view of the lowliness or commonness of the Son of Man was severely critiqued by Johann David Michaelis, a scholar of Hebrew and Aramaic, claiming that to so interpret the phrase indicated unacceptable ignorance of Oriental, particularly biblical, languages. After his critique was published the interpretation of the Son of Man as a lower class designation for Jesus virtually disappeared.[49]

40. Martin Bucer, *Ennarrationum in evangelia Matthaei, Marci, et Lucae* (Argentorati: Hervag, 1527). See also Wessel Scholten, *Specimen hermeneutico-theologicum: De appellatione tou huiou tou anthropou, qua Jesus se Messiam professus est* (Trajecti ad Rhenum: Paddenburg und Schoonhoven, 1809).

41. Heinrich Bullinger, *In sacrosanctum Iesu Christi Domini nostri evangelium secondum Matthaeum, commentariorum libri xii* (Tiguri: Froschover, 1542).

42. Benedict Aretius, *Commentarii in quatuor evangelistas* (Lausanne, 1597); reprinted as part 1 of *Commentarii in Domini nostri Jesu Christi Novum Testamentum* (Bern: Le Preux, 1607).

43. Cornelius Jansen, *Tetrateuchus, sive commentarius in sancta Iesu Christi evangelia* (Louvain: Zeger, 1639). See also Jansen, *Commentariorum in suam concordiam, ac totam historiam evangelicam partes quatuor* (Louvain: Sangrium, 1576).

44. Henry Hammond, *A Paraphrase and Annotations upon All the Books of the New Testament* (1639; repr., Oxford: Oxford University Press, 1845).

45. Johan L. von Wolzogen, 'Commentaria in evangelium Matthaei', in *Opera omnia, exegetica, didactica, et polemica* (Irenopolis, 1656).

46. Jakob Alting, *Comm. in loca quaedam selecta Novi Testamenti* (1685–87), cited in Scholten, *Specimen hermeneutico-theologicum*, pp. 203-204; and in Burkett, *Son of Man Debate*, p. 15.

47. Sebastian Münster, *Torat hammashiach: Evangelium secundum Matthaeum in lingua hebraica, cum versione latina aeque succinctis annotationibus* (Basel: Petrus, 1537).

48. Hugo Grotius, 'Annotationes in libros evangeliorum', in *Opera omnia theologica* (Amsterdam, 1679; repr. Stuttgart/Bad Cannstatt: Frommann, 1972).

49. Johann D. Michaelis, *Anmerkungen fur Ungelehrte zu seiner Uebersetzung des Neuen Testaments* (4 vols.; Göttingen: Vandenhoeck & Ruprecht, 1790–92). This work is a publication of select comments from Michaelis, *Deutsche Uebersetzung*

Johann Christoph Wolf,[50] in his commentary on the gospels and the Acts of the Apostles, and Johann Christoph Kocher,[51] in his exegetical work on the four gospels, surveyed medieval and early modern uses of the term Son of Man demonstrating that the Patristic perspective still dominated biblical studies up to the eighteenth century. The nineteenth century opened with Scholten's[52] exhaustive analysis of the influence of Patristic interpretations of the Son of Man concept down to the end of the eighteenth century.

A lead figure in the eighteenth century, Gabriel Mosche, believed that the title, Son of Man, designated 'the most eminent man, the noblest, most excellent man, the man without equal', but nonetheless, Jesus as human being.[53] This set in motion the nineteenth-century humanist perspective about the Son of Man as the ideal human. Friedrich Schleiermacher held this view, but suggested that Jesus' use of the designation for himself indicated solidarity with humans, while it expressed his ideal humanity. Nonetheless, Jesus wanted to emphasize that there was a difference between himself and other humans. Schleiermacher said that Jesus could not have named himself in this way 'if he had not been conscious of sharing completely in the same human nature as others; but it would have been meaningless to claim it specially for Himself, if He had not had a reason for doing so which others could not adduce—if, that is, the name had not had a pregnant meaning, which was meant to indicate a difference between Him and all others'.[54]

2. *The Modern Critical Phase*

a. *Part I: The Nineteenth Century*
The first modern scholarly address to the question of the meaning of the Son of Man logia in the Fourth Gospel was produced by William Ainger in Cambridge in 1822.[55] Though it was presented before the Cambridge University Assembly as a sermon on Commencement Sunday (June 30), it was officially published by the university as a scholarly paper. Ainger reflects a

des Alten und des Neuen Testaments, mit Anmerkungen fur Ungelehrte (Göttingen: Dieterich, 1773–90).

50. Johann C. Wolf, *Curae philologicae et criticae in IV. ss. evangelia et actus apostolicos* (2 vols.; Hamburg: 1725).

51. Johann C. Kocher, *Analecta philologica et exegetica in quatuor ss. evangelia* (Altenburg: Richter, 1766).

52. Scholten, *Specimen hermeneutico-theologicum.*

53. Gabriele C.B. Mosche, *Erklarung aller Sonn- und Festtags-Episteln* (2nd edn; 2 vols.; Frankfurt: Fleischer, 1788–90).

54. Friedrich Schleiermacher, *Die christliche Glaube* (2nd edn; Halle an der Saal: Hendel, 1830–31). English version: *The Christian Faith* (Edinburgh: T. & T. Clark, 1928; repr. New York: Harper, 1963), p. 422.

55. William Ainger, *Christ's Title, the Son of Man, Elucidated From its Application in the Gospel according to St John* (Cambridge: Smit, 1822), pp. 18-19.

modified traditional view. In the process he connected the Son of Man with the heavenly messiah. Ainger argued that the Son of Man in John is Jesus of Nazareth, the uniquely begotten human person, into whom the *Logos* became incarnated. In this assessment, Ainger averred that the Son of Man is the human Jesus, and it is this person from Nazareth who is the unique Son of God and Christ, that is, Messiah. Ainger observed regarding Jesus that the title, Son of Man

> is remarkable, as being one by which, throughout the gospels, he is represented repeatedly to have spoken of himself... And it has been commonly explained to belong to him in reference to his human nature. Nor need we hesitate to acquiesce in the propriety of that explanation, as far as it goes. We shall surely, however, possess but a very inadequate notion of the full signification of that most singular title, if we refer it to his human nature exclusively... On the contrary, when we come to investigate its import... we shall...perceive the strongest reason to conclude, that it both conveys, and *was intended* to convey, an intimation also of his essential and proper divinity...[56] [emphasis original].

The title page of Ainger's published lecture has a quote from Bishop Horsley's Sermons (Vol. I, p. 176), which is aligned with Ainger's conclusions. ' "Son of Man" is a title which belongs to the Eternal Word [Logos], describing that person of the Godhead who was made man by uniting himself to the man, Jesus'. Ainger's view had its root in the Patristic and Medieval usage, but he attempted to reach beyond that and see a more profound significance in the way the title Son of Man is employed by the author of the Fourth Gospel. For Ainger, Son of Man was in John a title for the divine *Logos* who took up residence in Jesus of Nazareth.

Ainger's scholarship constitutes a discernible bridge between pre-Reformation Son of Man scholarship and the critical work which lay ahead in the twentieth century. He avoided rejection of the ancient tradition of the Patristics, while asking new questions regarding the Son of Man. His emphasis is informed by the distinctive theological perspective of the Gospel of John.

Throughout the nineteenth century, many interpretations were offered in attempts to align the *Logos* of the Fourth Gospel with the designation, Son of Man. The line of scholarship proceeded mainly, however, upon the theme of the Son of Man as the humanity of the *Logos*. In spite of the fact that the early nineteenth century was the time of the rediscovery of the *Parables of Enoch* (*1 Enoch* 37–71), with its Son of Man as Eschatological Judge, that important addition to the literary resources from Second Temple Judaism did not effect any significant change in Son of Man studies prior to the twentieth century. The essential perspective of the Church Fathers continued to prevail.

56. Ainger, *Christ's Title*, pp. 4-5.

The nineteenth-century Son of Man scholarship was brought to a conclusion with the appearance in 1896 of Heinrich Appel's[57] comprehensive
survey of Son of Man studies, up to his time. It solidly reaffirmed the perspective of the Patristics and the pre-Reformation posture, along with the
advanced notion Ainger had articulated regarding the Gospel of John. Summarizing the history of research in the eighteenth and nineteenth centuries,
Burkett observes: 'Typical interpretations of this period included "Son of
Man" as the lowly human, the ideal human, the Messiah, the lowly human
Messiah, and the ideal human Messiah'.[58]

b. *Part II: 1900–1950*

At the turn of the twentieth century Samuel Driver published an article
on the Son of Man and set the course for The Modern Critical Part II.[59]
He believed the term Son of Man had a limited but significant titular cur-
rency in Second Temple Judaism traditions. His view countered that of such
late nineteenth and early twentieth-century scholars as James Drummond,
George Stevens, Maurice Goguel, William Sanday, and Edwin Abbott,[60] all
of whom doubted that Son of Man was a Second Temple Jewish title.

Alfred Loisy emphasized that the Johannine title was heavily dependent
upon Dan. 7.13 and bore significant messianic import. He was not certain whether this implied that it was apocalyptic.[61] Paul Billerbeck's concern related to whether the Danielic Son of Man, and hence the Johannine
figure that depended upon it, was to be considered preexistent.[62] He concluded that the Danielic Son of Man is not preexistent, the Enochic Son of
Man is preexistent only as an idea in God's mind, and hence the preexistence of the *Logos* Son of Man is a unique Johannine construct. Frederick

---

57. Heinrich Appel, *Die Selbstbezeichnung Jesu: Der Sohn des Menschen* (Stavenhagen: Beholtz, 1896).

58. Burkett, *Son of Man Debate*, p. 4.

59. Samuel R. Driver, 'Son of Man', in *A Dictionary of the Bible* (ed. James Hastings; Edinburgh: T. & T. Clark, 1902), IV.

60. James Drummond, *The Jewish Messiah* (London: Longmans, 1877); Drummond, 'The Use and Meaning of the Phrase "The Son of Man" in the Synoptic Gospels', *JTS* 11 (1901), pp. 350-58, 539-71; George Barker Stevens, *The Theology of
the New Testament* (New York: Scribner's, 1899); Maurice Goguel, *L'Apôtre Paul
et Jésus-Christ* (Paris: Fischbacher, 1904); Ernst Kühl, *Das Selbstbewusstsein Jesu*
(Berlin: Runge, 1907); William Sanday, 'On the Title, "Son of Man"', *Expositor* 4/3
(1891), pp. 18-32; Edwin A. Abbott, *The Message of the Son of Man* (London: Black,
1909); and Abbott, *'The Son of Man' or Contributions to the Study of the Thought of
Jesus* (Diatessarica, 8; Cambridge: Cambridge University Press, 1910).

61. Alfred Loisy, *La quatrième Evangile* (Paris: Picard, 1903); see also Loisy, *Les
Evangiles synoptiques* (2 vols.; Paris: Ceffonds, 1907).

62. Paul Billerbeck, 'Hat der Synagoge einen praexistenten Menschensohn gekannt?', *Nathanel* 21 (1905), pp. 89-150.

Foakes-Jackson and Kirsopp Lake wrestled with the question of a distinction between Jesus and the Son of Man in the Synoptics but concluded that in John from the outset Jesus *is* the Son of Man as bearer of the *Logos*.[63]

At the end of the first quarter of the twentieth century Walter Bauer published an influential work, *Das Johannesevangelium*, in which he described the Johannine apocalyptic Son of Man as dependent upon Hermetic, Mandaean, and Manichaean sources beyond the bounds of Second Temple Judaism.[64] Rudolph Bultmann seemed to give some support to this notion in his early work, arguing that John's Christology depended upon Gnostic Redeemer Myths. He did not agree with Bauer that the Johannine Son of Man is apocalyptic, but thought such apocalypticism in John (5.27) was a late gloss. Siegfried Schulz countered this in 1957, as we shall see, by asserting that the apocalypticism in John is early and is overlaid with a latter non-apocalyptic gloss.

In 1927 Shirley Case was agreeing, with Bauer, and Bultmann's early work, that the Johannine apocalypticism is a late addition. Case argued that in Second Temple Jewish traditions the Son of Man was not to appear on earth until the judgment day. The Johannine Son of Man does not fit into that but is a new idea of the late first century.[65]

That same year, Hermann Dieckmann painted the picture in apocalyptic terms in his important article, which one century after Ainger marked the second major scholarly contribution specifically devoted to the Son of Man concept in John.[66] Already in 1921 Dieckmann had staked out his argument against the notion that Son of Man meant mere human or ideal human.[67] In 1927 he emphasized the point that Ainger had made, recognizing both the divinity and humanity implied in the Johannine use of the title. Indeed, Dieckmann thought that the weight of divinity implied was comparable to

---

63. Frederick J. Foakes-Jackson and Kirsopp Lake (eds.), *The Beginnings of Christianity* (5 vols.; London: Macmillan, 1920).

64. Walter Bauer, *Das Johannesevangelium* (2nd edn; HNT, 6; Tübingen: Mohr–Siebeck, 1924).

65. See Rudolf Bultmann, *Die Geschichte der synoptischen Tradition* (Göttingen: Vandenhoeck & Ruprecht, 1921); Bultmann, *Jesus and the Word* (trans. from 1929 German edition by L.P. Smith and E.H. Lantero; New York: Scribner's, 1934); Bultmann, *Theology of the New Testament* (trans. K. Grobel; 2 vols.; New York: Scribner's, 1951), I, p. 130; Shirley Jackson Case, *Jesus: A New Biography* (New York: Greenwood, 1927), pp. 366-67, 370-71; see also Case, 'The Alleged Messianic Consciousness of Jesus', *JBL* 46 (1927), pp. 1-19 (17-18). See also Siegfried Schulz, *Untersuchungen zur Menschensohn-Christologie im Johannesevangelium, zugleich ein Beitrag zur Methodengeschichte der Auslegung des 4. Evangeliums* (Göttingen: Vandenhoeck & Ruprecht, 1957).

66. Hermann Dieckmann, 'Der Sohn des Menschen im Johannesevangelium', *Scholastik* 2 (1927), pp. 229-47.

67. Hermann Dieckmann, 'ὁ υἱὸς τοῦ ἀνθρώπου', *Biblica* 2 (1927), pp. 69-71.

the Patristics' use of the term, Son of God. Thus he argued that the Son of Man is the *Logos* who descended to become incarnate in Jesus of Nazareth, taking upon himself a human nature, but not in the sense of becoming flesh and blood. He reasoned that the *Logos* remained the *Logos* Son of Man in John's gospel. Reynolds interprets this to mean: 'That the Son of Man has flesh and blood means that the Son of Man has become flesh, not that "the Son of Man" is a reference to Jesus' humanity'.[68]

Dieckman thought the divinity of the Son of Man in John is reinforced by the fact that the 'lifting up' in which he will draw all men unto himself (12.32), in crucifixion, resurrection, and ascension, implies preexistence, hence divinity. This line of thought leads Dieckmann to describe the Johannine Son of Man as characterized by a nature and function that identifies him with or even as God. Dieckmann sees this as evident in the manner in which the Son of Man speaks of judgment and glorification. In both actions he is enmeshed with God. He declares, 'Diese Verherrlichung [13.31; 14.13] ist untrennbar von der Verherrlichung Gottes'.[69] Dieckman emphasizes that this glorification sets the Johannine Son of Man apart from that figure in the Synoptic Gospel, in that in John the glorification does not await the *parousia* but is realized in his ascent to his original home as God. That exaltation is not just a reward for the ordeal of his suffering but, in Dieckmann's view, it is part of the total package of being the Son of Man. The glory achieved in this exaltation is the preexistent glory of the preexistent Son of Man, to which he returns from earth to heaven. For Dieckmann, that is, the Johannine Son of Man is a divine man, of whose humanness and divinity one can only speak in one breath, as it were. He sees John as dependent upon Daniel but perceives the Johannine Son of Man to express a unique Second Temple interpretation of Daniel 7–9.

Hugo Odeberg has the same emphasis upon the significance of the descent of the Johannine Son of Man from his preexistence in heaven. He comes as God's heavenly agent of salvation to give life to the world; and anticipates a glorious return to his divine status in heaven. That ascent draws all humanity to him and, in Odeberg's view, also with him to an ultimate heavenly status.[70] He compares the Johannine Son of Man with competing Second Temple Judaism traditions and concludes with Dieckmann that the Johannine characterization of the messianic human person from Nazareth who carries within him the Son of Man as divine *Logos* is a unique interpretation of the Danielic tradition.

---

68. Reynolds, *Apocalyptic Son of Man*, p. 158.

69. Dieckmann, 'Der Sohn des Menschen', p. 241.

70. Hugo Odeberg, *The Fourth Gospel Interpreted in its Relation to Contemporaneous Religious Currents in Palestine and the Hellenistic-Oriental World* (Uppsala: Argonaut, 1929).

Bultmann's publication of *Jesus and the Word* in 1934 proved to be a watershed event in that he contended unequivocally for a thoroughgoing eschatological and apocalyptic Johannine Son of Man.[71] He asserted that Jesus is depicted in the Fourth Gospel as declaring that the kingdom of God has begun in his descent from heaven. In his ministry and that of his disciples the reign of God has broken in upon the world. When the kingdom has fully come the Son of Man will be vindicated and justified in his claims. This apocalyptic divine intervention in history places humanity before an immediate existential decision to identify with the supra-historical nature of the divine reign: 'There can be no doubt that Jesus like his contemporaries expected a tremendous eschatological drama'. According to Bultmann, the apocalyptic character of life is not a consequence of God's world being evil but of people being evil. The Son of Man has come to seek and save the lost and to institute the divine order. Jesus' use of the Son of Man does not refer to himself. After his death the disciples rose from their despair through the Easter visions which, combined with their anxiety about the delayed *parousia*, prompted them to see Jesus as the figure in his own message. They identified him as the Son of Man. The author of John's gospel saw him as the divine Son of Man in whom the kingdom was present, the judgment was in process, and his exalted glorification inevitably followed.

Matthew Black effectively brought the Modern Critical Part II to a close with his brief article in the *Expository Times* entitled 'The Son of Man in the Teaching of Jesus'.[72] He addressed the report of Jesus' message in all four gospels, contending that they presented a Son of Man who was the herald of the advent of God's reign on earth. This involved an ordeal of rejection, betrayal, suffering, death, resurrection, and exaltation. He discerned the difference between the Synoptic Gospels and John regarding the nature of the Son of Man and of his exaltation, but was sure that the Son of Man ideas and language in the gospels depended upon Daniel 7–9. He wondered 'to what extent has the original teaching been overlaid by current Jewish apocalyptic ideas of the Son of Man?'[73]

Black acknowledges that there is apocalyptic language in the Son of Man logia, but each time there is he thinks Jesus is represented as speaking of someone else than himself. He found as many problems with an apocalyptic eschatological Son of Man as with an Ezekiel-like mere human; but in the end he concluded that the Son of Man is presented by the Johannine author, at least, as an apocalyptic figure. Black thought that the gospels all intend to present the Son of Man as an apocalyptic figure who is in himself the revelation of the heavenly mysteries.

71. Bultmann, *Jesus and the Word*, pp. 38-39, 49, 23-124.
72. Matthew Black, 'The Son of Man in the Teaching of Jesus', *Expository Times* 60 (1948), pp. 32-36.
73. Black, 'The Son of Man in the Teaching of Jesus', p. 32.

3. *The Contemporary Critical Phase (1950–present)*

The work of Thomas Manson,[74] Théo Preiss,[75] Charlse de Beus,[76] Schulz,[77] and Ernest Sidebottom[78] launched the contemporary critical phase in the 1950s. Contrary to the previous period (where Ainger and Dieck-mann remained isolated voices), this phase is now characterized by the publication of a conspicuous amount of articles specifically devoted to the Son of Man in John. Most studies continued to refer the term Son of Man to the humanity of the *Logos incarnatus*. Burkett observes that while 'the human Son of Man declined in popularity after the nineteenth century, in the twentieth century this interpretation still recurred…in the form of either the lowly human Son of Man or the superior Son of Man'.[79] However, he noted that some Son of Man scholars came to assume that the Johannine Son of Man is a product of Second Temple Judaisms' apocalyptic literature, particularly Dan. 7.13, *1 Enoch* 37–71, and *4 Ezra*.[80] The work of Sidebottom, on the one hand, and Schulz, on the other, set the tone of the debate regarding the Son of Man as a human, who carried the *Logos* within him; and the Son of Man as the Apocalyptic Heavenly Messiah, the Eschatological Judge.[81] These two alternative trajectories have dominated the dialogue on the Johannine Son of Man ever since.

a. *The Non-Apocalyptic Son of Man*
The leading scholars who contended that the Johannine use of the Son of Man title refers to his humanity and is not remarkably different from that in the Synoptic Gospels, included Manson, Preiss, de Beus, Sidebot-

---

74. Thomas W. Manson, 'The Son of Man in Daniel, Enoch, and the Gospels', *Bulletin of the John Rylands Library* 32 (1950), pp. 171-95.

75. Théo Preiss, 'Le fils de l'homme dans le IVᵉ Evangile', *ETR* 28 (1953), pp. 7-61.

76. Charlse de Beus, 'Het gebruik en de betekenis van de uitdrukking "De Zoon des Mensen" in het Evangelie van Johannes', *Nederlands theologisch tijdschrift* 10 (1955–56), pp. 237-51.

77. Siegfried Schulz, *Untersuchungen zur Menschensohn-Christologie im Johannesevangelium, zugleich ein Beitrag zur Methodengeschichte der Auslegung des 4. Evangeliums* (Göttingen: Vandenhoeck & Ruprecht, 1957).

78. Ernest M. Sidebottom, 'The Son of Man as Man in the Fourth Gospel', *Expository Times* 68 (1957), pp. 231-35, 280-83; Sidebottom, 'The Ascent and Descent of the Son of Man in the Gospel of St. John', *ATR* 39 (1957), pp. 115-22.

79. Burkett, *Son of Man Debate*, p. 19.

80. Burkett, *The Son of Man in the Gospel of John*, p. 17.

81. Schulz, *Untersuchungen*; Maddox, 'The Function of the Son of Man'.

tom, Rudolph Schnackenburg,[82] Edwin Freed,[83] Elizabeth Kinniburgh,[84] Meeks,[85] Stephen Smalley,[86] Eugen Ruckstuhl,[87] Coppens,[88] Barnabas Lindars,[89] Burkett, Moloney, and Casey. This perspective has been characteristic of most scholars on this trajectory of the non-apocalyptic Son of Man. Burkett, for example, in his summary of Johannine Son of Man studies at the end of the twentieth century saw, in retrospect, an essential uniformity in the meaning of the title throughout the four gospels.[90]

Manson was primarily interested in the Synoptic Gospels' Son of Man. However, his inquiry focused on two crucial issues. First, can we make a reasonable connection between those logia and other Second Temple Jewish documents? Second, do these Synoptic logia explain the unique Christologies of John and Paul? He concluded that all four gospels are essentially shaped by the Danielic Son of Man tradition that is neither messianic nor apocalyptic, but rather expresses an implied hope of a Davidic kingdom. Moreover, they employ the Suffering Servant ideas of Deutero-Isaiah. However, he believed that the concept of the Eschatological Judge derived from *1 Enoch* and that this produced a tension evident in the gospels between a hope for a mundane socio-political messiah and a heavenly spiritual messiah. John's gospel definitively enunciates the latter expectation. In the Son of Man's descent into the mundane world the eschatological reign of God is already present.

Preiss assumed a position somewhat closer to the perspective established by Ainger and Dieckmann. He suggested that, while the Johannine Son of Man is human, there is a more primitive meaning to the title, which may be taken to imply divinity.[91] Reynolds interprets Preiss to mean that it is the

---

82. Rudolph Schnackenburg, 'Der Menschensohn im Johannesevangelium', *NTS* 11 (1964–65), pp. 123.

83. Edwin D. Freed, 'The Son of Man in the Fourth Gospel', *JBL* 86 (1967), pp. 402-409.

84. Elizabeth Kinniburgh, 'The Johannine "Son of Man"', *SE* 4 (1965), pp. 64-71.

85. Wayne Meeks, 'The Man from Heaven in Johannine Sectarianism', *JBL* 91 (1963), pp. 44-72.

86. Stephen S. Smalley, 'The Johannine Son of Man Sayings', *NTS* 15 (1968–69), pp. 278-301.

87. Eugen Ruckstuhl, 'Die johannische Menschensohnforschung, 1957–69', in *Theologischer Berichte I* (ed. J. Pfammatter and F. Furger; Eindsiedeln: Benziger, 1972), pp. 171-284.

88. Coppens, 'Le fils de l'homme'.

89. Barnabas Lindars, 'The Son of Man in the Johannine Christology', in *Christ and Spirit in the New Testament: Studies in Honour of Charles Francis Digby Moule* (ed. B. Lindars and S.S. Smalley; Cambridge: Cambridge University Press, 1973), pp. 43-60.

90. Burkett, *Son of Man Debate*.

91. Preiss, 'Le fils de l'homme', pp. 5, 222.

presence of the Son of Man as man in heaven before God, in John's gospel, which implies that his humanity has a divine overlay.[92] Preiss noted the heavenly nature of the Johannine Son of Man, and discerns this as the influence of Second Temple Judaism traditions. He sees Jn 5.27-29 as an indication of some type of eschatological *parousia* that will initiate a general resurrection at the sound of 'the voice of the Son of Man'. Nonetheless, for Preiss the Johannine Son of Man is the human Jesus who carries the *Logos* within him, and has his calling in the mundane sphere.

The perspectives of de Beus, Sidebottom , Meeks,[93] and Schnackenburg,[94] are strikingly similar. Each acknowledges the heavenly orientation of the Johannine Son of Man but insists, nonetheless, that it is the human Son of Man who ascends in the exaltation of the crucified and resurrected man, but not as an apocalyptic figure. Sidebottom expresses the sentiment of all of them in his comment that while Jn 5.27 may seem to reflect Second Temple apocalyptic influence, it is the human Jesus that has the authority and power to announce divine judgment that is already in process on earth (5.27-47). He thinks that possibly the *Testament of Abraham* influenced the author at this point. In that Second Temple tradition a human is the divinely appointed judge. The human Adam is enthroned in heaven, while his son Abel is assigned the judicial role on earth.[95] All four scholars emphasize that if we study deeply the background matrix in which the providential drama in Jesus' life unfolds in the gospel narrative, we see only a human person acting and not a supernatural presence depicted. The drama has a divine dimension; but the Son of Man who is acting in that divine vocation is the human Jesus.

Freed,[96] in some degree similar to de Beus, Meeks, Sidebottom, and Schnackenburg, did not distinguish between the three Johannine messianic titles: Son, Son of Man, and Son of God. However, it is unclear what is meant by the term Son of God, whether a divine being or a righteous man. We are compelled to conclude that they mean the latter, since Freed, *et alii*, urge that all three names are references to the human Jesus in his salvific vocation of proclaiming the reign of God and the eschatological judgment. Freed insists that there is no Son of Man Christology in John because there is no transcendental theology expressed in that Johannine title.

Kinniburgh[97] reads the Johannine use of the Son of Man title as a reference to the human nature of Jesus as a man called by God to carry out

---

92. Reynolds, *Apocalyptic Son of Man*, p. 5.

93. Meeks, 'Man from Heaven'.

94. De Beus, 'Het gebruik'; Sidebottom, 'Ascent', 'Son of Man'; and Schnacken-burg, 'Menschensohn'.

95.   Phillip B. Munoa, III, *Four Powers in Heaven: The Interpretation of Daniel 7 in the Testament of Abraham* (JSPSup. 28; Sheffield: Sheffield Academic Press, 1998).

96.   Freed, 'Son of Man'.

97.   Kinniburgh, 'Johannine'.

a human ministry on earth. She does not see the Johannine Son of Man as apocalyptic, in view of the 'realized eschatology' perspective of that gospel. The Johannine notion of the glorification of the Son of Man refers, according to Kinniburgh, to the crucifixion when all humanity will be compelled to notice him and realize who he is. Reynolds remarks in this regard, 'Most scholars see two moments of glorification, but there are various explanations as to what make up these two moments. Kinniburgh thinks that the past glorification comprises Jesus' ministry and that the future glorification comprises the cross'.[98] As in the case of Freed *et alii*, Kinniburgh tends to conflate Son, Son of Man, and Son of God, as slightly differently nuanced titles for the human Jesus, but not conveying a marked distinction between them. Kinniburgh holds that none of them has apocalyptic meaning or overtones.

Smalley, like John Ross,[99] a quarter century later, tended to revert to the nineteenth-century notions of Son of Man, referring to Jesus as representing the ideal human. Like Kinniburgh, *et alii*, Smalley and Ruckstuhl insist that Son, Son of Man, and Son of God all refer, with little significant difference, to the human Jesus in his earthly ministry.[100] Moreover, they see nothing apocalyptic in Jn 5.27, considering it a very ordinary reference to the human Son of Man, in the light of Second Temple Jewish traditions like Ezekiel, Daniel 7–9, and *1 Enoch*. For the same reason, they see nothing apocalyptic about the conjunction in John of other references to the Son of Man and judgment. As judge, Jesus, the human Son of Man, is accorded authority by God the father, precisely because he is a human among humans. He is in the requisite *locus* to have a right to judge. His subsequent glorification on the cross is both judgment and salvation, depending upon personal human responses.

Among those who reverted to the nineteenth-century picture of the *Logos*-bearing humanness of the Son of Man were Schalom Ben-Chorin, Wilfrid Stott, and John Bowker. They emphasized that Jesus' use of Son of Man as his self-designation was to point out the trivial insignificance of mere humanness, as in Ezekiel's Son of Man.[101] They saw this as Jesus' identification with human weakness, mortality, and death; while he described himself, nonetheless, as one who would be exalted by God as in Psalms 2, 8, 80, 110, Prov. 30.1-4, and Daniel 7–9. Ross claimed, that in Jesus' usage Son of Man meant 'the Man *par excellence*, the focal point of the human race in its relation to God'.[102]

---

98. Reynolds, *Apocalyptic Son of Man*, p. 208.

99. John M. Ross, 'The Son of Man', *JBS* 13 (1991), pp. 186-98.

100. Smalley, 'Johannine', pp. 298ff.

101. Schalom Ben-Chorin, *Bruder Jesus: Der Nazarener in judischer Sicht* (Munich: List, 1967); Wilfrid Stott, ' "Son of Man"—A Title of Abasement', *Expository Times* 83 (1972), pp. 278-81; John Bowker, 'The Son of Man', *JTS* 28 (1977), pp. 19-48.

102. T. Stephenson, 'The Title "Son of Man" ', *Expository Times* 29 (1917–18), pp. 377-78; Lily Dougall and Cyril W. Emmet, *The Lord of Thought* (London: SCM Press,

Coppens[103] and Lindars[104] also thought that Son of Man in John's Gospel was a title referring to the human person from Nazareth, but expressed specifically that he was the carrier of the incarnated divine *Logos*. The title depended completely upon that incarnation for its proper reference to Jesus. They argue that even if the Johannine Son of Man is described as preexistent, that does not change the import of the title, since they see the human figure in *4 Ezra* as also preexistent, in that competing Second Temple Judaism document that is approximately contemporaneous with the Fourth Gospel. Coppens and Lindars believe that the Johannine use of the title for a human Son of Man is consistent with Second Temple traditions, particularly those dependent upon Daniel 7–9. As for the scholars discussed above, the exaltation of the Son of Man is seen by Lindars and Coppens to refer to the crucifixion of the human Jesus as Son of Man. They see no reason to perceive this in an apocalyptic sense.

Moloney held a regressive position essentially like that which prevailed prior to Ainger, focusing upon the man, Jesus, as the Son of Man, while acknowledging that he was the carrier of the *Logos*. Ainger had emphasized the divinity of the Son of Man, despite his manifesting in human form. For Moloney, Son of Man refers to Jesus' humanity and Son of God to his divine nature.[105] This represented the Patristic and Medieval perspective carried forward into the modern era. Few twentieth-century scholars agreed completely with Moloney's approach, though he republished it repeatedly in essentially the same form. The original dissertation was written in 1975, digested as a journal article in 1976, published as a trade book in 1976, republished with a new cover and publisher in 1978, and then again with another new cover and publisher, but with no significant modification, in 2005. The lack of serious interest in his thesis lay in the fact that the scholarly world had moved beyond the ancient view of the Church Fathers. Interest was increasingly focused upon discerning how to understand the Johannine Son of Man in terms of Jewish apocalypticism.

Müller attempted to summarize the state of the question by a series of publications in the final quarter of the twentieth century,[106] which era was

1922); H. Francis Davis, 'The Son of Man. I. The Image of the Father', *The Furrow* 12 (1961), pp. 39-48; Margaret Pamment, 'The Son of Man in the First Gospel', *NTS* 29 (1983), pp. 116-29; Ross, 'Son of Man', p. 197.

103. Coppens, 'Le fils de l'homme'.

104. Lindars, 'Son of Man'.

105. Moloney, 'The Johannine'. See also Douglas R.A. Hare, *The Son of Man Tradition* (Minneapolis: Fortress Press, 1990).

106. Mogens Müller, 'Über den Ausdruck "Menschensohn" in den Evangelien', *ST* 31 (1977), pp. 65-82; Müller, *Der Ausdruck 'Menschensohn' in den Evangelien: Voraussetzungen und Bedeutung* (Leiden: E.J. Brill, 1984); Müller, 'The Expression "the Son of Man" as Used by Jesus', *ST* 38 (1984), pp. 47-64; Müller, 'Have You Faith

then closed with Burkett's critique in *The Son of Man Debate*.[107] Burkett's evaluation of the apocalyptic and messianic Son of Man in John noted that *1 Enoch, 4 Ezra*, Jewish tradition at the time of Jesus, Tertullian in *Adversus Marcion*, and Chemnitz in the Reformation era, all considered Dan. 7.13 as messianic. Thus, it is not surprising that Christian tradition associated Jesus' messianic claims with that passage from the Hebrew Bible.[108] Burkett observed, with Schleiermacher,[109] Robert Charles,[110] Willhelm Bousset,[111] Johannes Weiss[112] and others, that there was a reason this did not lead to the perspective that Jesus' use of the title Son of Man in John, had an apocalyptic meaning. That reason was simply, as Charles contended, that the apocalyptic messiah of *1 Enoch* stands in contrast to the Davidic Messiah of the prophets.

In marking out his position on the Son of Man, Burkett notes that the Synoptic Gospels' depiction of the Son of Man presents him as associated with the prophetic rather than an apocalyptic perspective. This was also seen to be the perspective of Daniel, and so a Danielic influence upon the meaning of the Son of Man in the gospels did not make that figure apocalyptic. Burkett, however, emphasized the probable influence of Daniel upon *1 Enoch* 37–71 and the high likelihood of the latter shaping the traditions of the first century in Judaism and Christianity. Surprisingly, this did not lead Burkett to see the Son of Man in any of the gospels as apocalyptic.

Burkett observed that an amazing spate of 'nuances' were imported into the interpretation of the designation Son of Man; most of which were merely their authors' personal concepts of humanity and divinity as, for example, the orthodox theological perspective of Moloney. This realization reinforced the urgency to move the focus of Johannine Son of Man studies toward a debate over the apocalyptic Son of Man as messianic Eschatological Judge. This gave rise to a minority tradition of scholars who focused upon the literary character of Jesus as the bearer of the divine *Logos*, as the apocalyptic Son of Man.

in the Son of Man? (John 9.35)', *NTS* 37 (1991), pp. 291-94. See also Ulrich B. Müller, *Messias und Menschensohn in judischen Apokalypsen und in der Offenbarung des Johannes* (SNT, 6; Gütersloh: Mohn, 1972).

107. Burkett, *Son of Man Debate*.

108. Burkett, *Son of Man Debate*, pp. 22-31.

109. Schleiermacher, *Christliche Glaube*.

110. Robert H. Charles, 'The Son of Man', *Expository Times* 4 (1892–93), p. 504.

111. Wilhelm Bousset, *Die jüdische Apokalyptic: Ihre religiongeschichtliche Herkunft und ihre Bedeutung für das Neue Testament* (Berlin: Reuther & Reichard, 1903).

112. Johannes Weiss, *Die Predigt Jesu vom Reiche Gottes* (Göttingen: Vandenhoeck & Ruprecht, 1982).

Maurice Casey enters the dialogue with a massive work exploring the original meaning of Son of Man.[113] His title suggests that he is responding to Higgins' question of four decades earlier.[114] Moreover, he follows the line of thought initiated as early as 1965 in a lecture on the Aramaic, *barnash/bar nasha*, delivered at Oxford by Geza Vermes. Vermes continued to develop this line of inquiry until 1973, and then revisited it with major publications in 1993 and 2003.[115] Casey's argument may be summarized as follows. First, he contends that since the phrase ὁ υἱὸς τοῦ ἀνθρώπου is a clumsy non-Greek construction in the gospels, it is obviously a translation of a Hebrew (בֶּן־אָדָם) or Aramaic (בַּר־אֱנָשׁ) expression. In those languages the expression is a normal construction. Second, Casey argues that in Aramaic Son of Man can only mean mere human, as in Ezekiel (e.g. 29.2). Vermes contests this point with 'ten examples of direct speech—monologue and dialogue—in which the speaker appears to refer to himself, not as "I", but as "the Son of Man" in the third person, in contexts implying awe, reserve, or modesty'.[116] Third, contrary to Vermes Casey insists that his claim in points one and two imply that any usage in the gospels must be read against the background of that original meaning of 'mere human'. Fourth, if some other more exotic meaning for the term is developed in the gospels, it must be concluded that the author did this intentionally, using the primitive term as a vehicle to make a larger point. Fifth, each of the gospels used the term as a tool to promote, in Greek transliteration, the ideological thrust that the gospel author wished to give to his gospel. Each evangelist used the term Son of Man as a vehicle to convey his own theological burden to his audience. Casey's sixth point is that the Son of Man logia in the gospels are theologically laden, and manufactured for the rhetorical and theological needs of the author, and perhaps the needs of his community. Seventh, the Synoptic Gospels tend to load the term with the notion that a human Son of Man is exalted through suffering to heavenly status. Eighth, John's gospel is a special case, for Casey.[117] He asserts that all of the Son of Man logia in the Fourth Gospel fit the overall theological thrust and trajectory of that gospel so well that

113. Maurice Casey, *The Solution to the 'Son of Man' Problem* (LNTS, 343; New York: T. & T. Clark, 2007); Casey brings all of his previous work together in this volume.

114. Angus J.B. Higgins, 'Is the Son of Man Problem Soluble?', in *Neotestamentica et semitica: Studies in Honour of Matthew Black* (ed. M. Wilcox; Edinburgh: T. & T. Clark, 1969), pp. 70-87.

115. Geza Vermes, *Jesus the Jew, A Historian's Reading of the Gospel* (Philadelphia: Fortress Press, 1973). See also Vermes, *Jesus in his Jewish Context* (Minneapolis: Fortress Press, 2003), pp. 81-90; and Vermes, *The Religion of Jesus the Jew* (Minneapolis: Fortress Press, 1993).

116. Vermes, *Jesus in his Jewish Context*, p. 82.

117. Casey, 'The Johannine Sayings'.

it must be concluded that each was created specifically for advancing the theological claims of that gospel. Ninth, the special claims of the Gospel of John are that the Son of Man descends from God and returns to God after proclaiming the advent of the kingdom of God on earth.

Paul Owen addressed Casey's thesis in an extended review, summarizing the book, affirming some of its rather standard insights about the humanness of the Son of Man in much of the Synoptic ideology, and the heavenly qualities of that figure in John.[118]

b. *The Apocalyptic Son of Man*

Julius Wellhausen had seen, already in the nineteenth century, the import of Schleiermacher's assertion that had Jesus not meant by Son of Man to distinguish himself from the general run of humanity, he would not have needed to use or emphasize the use of the term.[119] Thus by the rise of the twentieth century the seeds had been sown to call into question the interpretation of the Son of Man that merely emphasized his lowly or exalted humanness.

The apocalyptic trajectory saw in the gospels a Son of Man who became or always had been heavenly or divine or both. The new initiative regarding the nature and function of the Son of Man in John as shaped by the apocalyptic Son of Man traditions in Second Temple Judaism, was brought to front and center of the scholarly quest by the watershed work of Schulz and Maddox. They drew major and unavoidable attention to the central importance in the discussion of the Johannine Son of Man, of the nineteenth-century discovery of the *Parables of Enoch*. In their analytical scholarship Schulz, Maddox, Painter, Sasse, Ashton, and Reynolds have developed this apocalyptic theme as the appropriate description of the Johannine Son of Man.[120] The most recent work on this apocalyptic trajectory is that of Reynolds. He not only assumes that the Son of Man in John is a heavenly, even divine, apocalyptic figure, but argues it comprehensively.[121]

---

118. Paul L. Owen, 'Review: Maurice Casey, *The Solution of the 'Son of Man' Problem*', *RBL* (2009).

119. Julius Wellhausen, 'Des Menschen Sohn', in *Skizze und Vorarbeiten* (Berlin: Reimer, 1899), VI, pp. 187-215.

120. Schulz, *Untersuchungen*; Maddox, 'The Function of the Son of Man', pp. 203-204; Painter, *Quest*; Sasse, *Der Menschensohn*; John Ashton, *Understanding the Fourth Gospel* (Oxford: Oxford University Press, 1991); and Reynolds, *Apocalyptic Son of Man*. See also Burkett, *The Son of Man in the Gospel of John*, pp. 16-20 and Burkett, *Son of Man Debate*, pp. 22-23; and Sabino Chialà, 'The Son of Man: The Evolution of an Expression', in *Enoch and the Messiah Son of Man* (ed. Gabriele Boccaccini; Grand Rapids: Eerdmans, 2007), pp. 153-78.

121. Reynolds, *Apocalyptic Son of Man*. See particularly the cryptic summaries of his investigation on pp. 1-23, 214-28.

Apocalypticism is a dynamic world view which, as Ashton helpfully points out, 'is much more than a literary convention'. It is 'the urgent conviction of God's active intervention in human history. In this worldview the heavenly blueprint of his plan for the world will eventually, in his own good time, be revealed, but not communicated in any ordinary way. The seer or prophet who carries it down from the world above is an active agent and his revelation of what he is the first to know helps to accomplish this great design'.[122]

Schulz commented that the sources of the heavenly Son of Man in John's gospel, are the various competing traditions in Jewish Second Temple apocalyptic literature. The narratives of the Son of Man in the Synoptic Gospels and in the Fourth Gospel developed as additional first-century competing Son of Man traditions. Contrary to Reynolds, Schulz does not see all of the Johannine Son of Man logia as apocalyptic, nor does he believe that an apocalyptic worldview is always at the forefront of that gospel's narrative. However, he emphasizes that the Son of Man of Jn 1.51, as well as the other Johannine logia that emphasize a transcendental connection, is obviously apocalyptic. In those logia the Son of Man opens heaven as in other Second Temple apocalypses such as *1 Enoch* 37–71 and the Apocalypse of John.[123] Schulz sees the exaltation of the Johannine Son of Man in 3.14; 8.28 and corollary logia as reflective of and comparable to the exaltation of the Danielic Son of Man (Dan. 7.13). Moreover, he sees the logia about the glorification of the Johannine Son of Man to be dependent upon the obviously apocalyptic *Parables of Enoch*.

Maddox addresses mainly the question of what the Johannine designation Son of Man connotes and denotes in the context of Daniel 7–9 and the *Parables of Enoch*. He seems aware of the interesting similarity of ideas in *4 Ezra* and John's gospel; contemporaneous products of Second Temple Judaism Son of Man traditions.

Maddox wished to know whether those apparently apocalyptic connotations and denotations are uniform in all the Johannine logia or only present in such esoteric logia as 1.51 (Son of Man seen exalted in the open heaven), 3.13 (lifting up of the Son of Man), and 5.27 (Son of Man as Eschatological Judge). He inquired as to what they tell us about Johannine Christology in the context of competing Second Temple apocalypticism traditions. His conclusion was ambivalent. On the one hand he insisted that Son of Man was not Christological (messianic) in John and its fundamental significance was not different from that in the Synoptic Gospels. On the other hand, he pointed out specific differences between John and the Synoptics, particularly the *inherently* apocalyptic and heavenly nature of the Johannine Son

122. Ashton, *Understanding*, p. 329.
123. Schulz, *Untersuchungen*, pp. 99-103, 112-13, 118.

of Man compared with the human Son of Man who *becomes* heavenly in the Synoptic Gospels.

Maddox informs us that in the Synoptics, as 'In the Similitudes of *1 Enoch*, the Son of Man is the eschatological judge who stands in intimate relationship to those who look to him for vindication and salvation and... will save them at the end' when the judgment of the world will take place. However, 'in the case of John it is the general resurrection rather than the "parousia" of the Son of Man which is emphasized'.[124] In all the gospels, says Maddox, the judgment has already begun with the ministry of Jesus, but in John that fact is emphasized 'almost to the exclusion of the future aspect... Eschatological salvation and its negative counterpart of condemnation and punishment are in all essential features...assumed by the Fourth Gospel to be already accomplished' and hence absent from John's Gospel.[125]

John Painter took up the debate in keeping with the rubrics Maddox had set for it.[126] Painter opened his argument with the observation that the Johannine Son of Man is an enigma, though the designative phrase is certainly titular, messianic, and apocalyptic. This is in contrast to Moloney and Pamment. Moloney focused upon the *Logos*-bearing human Jesus and Pamment upon the Son of Man as ideal human. Maddox had built his essay around a brief but careful exegesis of each of the thirteen Johannine Son of Man logia. Painter followed a similar pattern while choosing essentially a thematic approach.

Of course, the theme he addressed that is most relevant to our interests is that of the apocalyptic dimension of the logia. Painter delineated that in a cryptic thesis: 'The use of Son of Man [in John] draws attention to Jesus as a heavenly being first descending and then ascending to heaven again. Ascent also carries something of the meaning of enthronement. This does not mean that John denies the humanity of Jesus. The humanity of Jesus is not questioned in the Gospel. What is questioned is the validity of a *man* claiming divine status (5.18; 10.33)' (emphasis added).[127] Painter emphasized that in the descent and ascent of the Son of Man in John, the gospel intended to emphasize the nature of divine intervention in history. It comes in the form of revelations of the mysteries of God to humans, and thus of the revelation of the salvation and judgment that is determined by each person's response to the Son of Man (Jn 3.18, 5.45-46 and related logia).

124. Maddox, 'The Function of the Son of Man', pp. 203-204.
125. Maddox, 'The Function of the Son of Man', p. 204.
126. Painter, *Quest*.
127. Painter, *Quest*, p. 321.

In agreement with John Ashton[128] and in contrast to James Louis Martyn,[129] Painter took Jn 5.27-29 as specifically indicating an apocalyptic tone for all the Son of Man logia in John. The logion in 5.27-29 is cryptic and clear, καὶ ἐξουσίαν ἔδωκεν αὐτῷ κρίσιν ποιεῖν, ὅτι υἱὸς ἀνθρώπου ἐστίν ('[God] has given [the Son of God] authority and power [*exousia*] to execute judgment, *because* he is the Son of Man'). Painter argued that this role of the Son of Man, and his implied exaltation as the Eschatological Judge, depends upon the apocalyptic tradition of Daniel 7–9. He pointed out that even those scholars who claimed that the original author of John had no apocalyptic view and that such logia as 5.27 belonged to a later redactor, nonetheless, acknowledged thereby that the Johannine Son of Man was apocalyptic in nature:

> The connection with the Danielic Son of Man is not…universally recognized. It has been challenged by scholars who take the second century understanding of the Son of Man as the point of departure for understanding the New Testament. For these scholars all 'Son of Man' sayings refer to the human, incarnate one. D.R.A. Hare notes that 'Higgins and Borsch have quite properly attacked this proposal (concerning dependence on Dan. 7.13-14) pointing out how very weak is the evidence for conscious allusion in this case'. He goes on to say, 'The non-apocalyptic nature of John's vision of truth suggests that he would not have found the Danielic apocalypse particularly congenial'. Hare's view is based on his rejection of the anarthrous *uios anthropon* as evidence of the influence of Dan. 7.13 and his judgement that Jn 'would not have found the Danielic apocalypse particularly congenial'. This latter judgement is superficial, taking no account of apocalyptic dimensions in John.[130]

Painter continued by pointing out that he believed that even Burkett, arguing for a non-apocalyptic Son of Man in John, gave up the apocalyptic association of Jn 5.27 with Dan. 7.13. He noted, moreover, that when Borsch critiqued Siegfried Schulz[131] for arguing that 5.27 was traditional Jewish apocalyptic, Borsch asserted that one verse is not enough evidence to make a claim for an apocalyptic Johannine Son of Man.[132] Painter responded that Borsch had not noted the agreement in wording between the LXX clause of Dan. 7.14 (καὶ ἐδόθη αὐτῷ ἐξουσία) and that of Jn 5.27 (καὶ ἐξουσίαν ἔδωκεν αὐτῷ). Moreover, he pointed out that even Borsch acknowledged

128. Ashton, *Understanding*, pp. 241, 361. See also Ashton (ed.), *The Interpretation of John* (IRT, 9; Philadelphia: Fortress Press, 1986).

129. James Louis Martyn, *History and Theology in the Fourth Gospel* (New York: Harper & Row, 1968), p. 139.

130. Painter, *Quest*, pp. 322, 323.

131. Frederick H. Borsch, *The Son of Man in Myth and History* (Philadelphia: Westminster, 1967), p. 294.

132. Borsch, *The Son of Man*, p. 332.

that whether the judicial function of the Son of Man was inherent in Daniel 7, that association was standard assumption in the first-century interpretations of the Danielic Son of Man tradition (*1 Enoch* 37–71).

Painter believed that the author of John was reading Daniel 7–12 into the interpretation illustrated by the Gospels, *1 Enoch*, and *4 Ezra*, as he crafted the Son of Man logia in the Fourth Gospel. Painter was quite certain that this accounts· for the fact that Jn 5.27-29 follows the trajectory from the description of the divinely accorded ἐξουσία of the Son of Man to the resurrection of the dead, exactly as does Daniel 7–12.

Painter rounded out his argument for an apocalyptic Johannine Son of Man by noting that the apocalyptic character was not just dependent upon the specific naming of his judicial role in 5.27. It was the only way of properly understanding the Johannine description of this extraordinary figure, from his first appearance in 1.51 as a heavenly figure surrounded by, and the focus of, the attention of other heavenly figures; to the final Johannine references to his ultimate glorification by being raised up to heaven, his true home. His ascent to heaven, whence he descended, is his definitive revelation of being the Son of Man: ὅταν ὑψώσητε τὸν υἱὸν τοῦ ἀνθρώπου, τότε γνώσεσθε ὅτι ἐγώ εἰμι ('When the Son of Man shall be lifted up then you shall know that I am he', Jn 8.28), κἀγὼ ἐὰν ὑψωθῶ ἐκ τῆς γῆς, πάντας ἑλκύσω πρὸς ἐμαυτόν ('And if I am lifted up from the earth, I will draw all unto me', 12.32).

Moreover, that ascent is not only *his* exaltation but the glorification of God himself, namely, the ultimate revelation of who *God* really is: πάτερ, ἐλήλυθεν ἡ ὥρα· δόξασόν σου τὸν υἱόν, ἵνα ὁ υἱὸς δοξάσῃ σέ, καθὼς ἔδωκας αὐτῷ ἐξουσίαν πάσης σαρκός, ἵνα πᾶν ὃ δέδωκας αὐτῷ δώσῃ αὐτοῖς ζωὴν αἰώνιον [...] ἐγώ σε ἐδόξασα ἐπὶ τῆς γῆς τὸ ἔργον τελειώσας ὃ δέδωκάς μοι ἵνα ποιήσω· καὶ νῦν δόξασόν με σύ, πάτερ, παρὰ σεαυτῷ τῇ δόξῃ ᾗ εἶχον πρὸ· τοῦ τὸν κόσμον εἶναι παρὰ σοί, Jn 17.1b-2, 4-5 ('Father, the hour has come; glorify your Son that the Son my glorify you, since you have given him power over all flesh, to give eternal life to all whom you have given him... I glorified you on earth, having accomplished the work which you gave me to do; and now, Father, glorify me in your own presence with the glory that I had with you before the world was made').

This conjoining of the heavenly and the earthly, as the former breaks in upon and definitively modifies the latter, is the essence of the apocalyptic perspective and the pervasive character of the Fourth Gospel, particularly of the Son of Man theme that shapes it throughout. It is, thus, obvious why Painter began his study, as noted above, with the pungent observation, 'The use of Son of Man [in John] draws attention to Jesus as a heavenly being first descending and then ascending to heaven again ... meaning...enthronement'.

John Ashton reasoned that the Son of Man in the Fourth Gospel is apocalyptic and eschatological in that Jesus, as Son of Man though delivering the substance of his message orally ('the words of eternal life'), also speaks of his 'works'—what the evangelist calls 'signs'—and, most significantly, in two key passages, of accomplishing (τελειόω) his 'work' (ἔργον), a comprehensive term that covers the whole task of revelation entrusted to him by his Father. In the first passage he speaks of his work as 'doing the will of him who sent me' (4.34); in the second this is seen as equivalent to glorifying God on earth (17.4). Jesus' task then, is not just to talk about God but to establish his glory. The concept of God's glory (כָּבוֹד) comes from the Old Testament theophanies, which were manifestations of God's power and authority to individual human beings and followed in every case by an event of exceptional significance... The *Logos* with whom Jesus is identified on the first page of the Gospel is more than just a Word. Jesus, as the fourth evangelist sees him, is the plan of God, his grand project for humanity (the world) made flesh and his glory made manifest. This is the very essence of apocalyptic.[133]

Ashton's emphasis throughout his volume is upon the revelatory and salvific perspective of the apocalyptic Son of Man in the Gospel of John. The Son of Man comes to earth as a divine intervention on behalf of humanity and the world of God's creation. He accomplishes this as revealer of the heavenly mysteries regarding the salvation of the world and the heavenly destiny of the Son of Man and all those identified in faith with him.

Sasse established his position on the Johannine Son of Man solidly in support of the apocalyptic trajectory of scholarship, relating that Son of Man with competing Second Temple apocalyptic traditions. He argued, as Reynolds notes, that John's Son of Man is inherently and unquestionably a heavenly figure, and by nature a divine figure. Johannine Christology is based upon the Johannine community's own ordeal at the end of the first century. This situation made it crucial, for the community's sense of itself, to answer the question of the identity of Jesus as the Son of Man in a way that avoided the accusations of ditheism and yet explained the death of the Son of Man and his transcendent exaltation. For Sasse the Johannine Son of Man descends for the purposes of affording salvific life to the human community, to excercise his function as eschatological judge, and to ascend to his heavenly home. He is sure that John's particular description of the Son of Man is influenced mainly by Dan. 7.13 and the theophanies and suffering servant passages of the Hebrew Bible.[134]

Reynolds feels that Sasse's assessment is deficient:

Sasse does not argue for a thorough-going apocalyptic Son of Man in John's Gospel. His argument that the Johannine Son of Man is a heavenly figure depends almost solely upon the Son of Man sayings in 3.13 and 6.25-59. Sasse relegates the 'lifting-up' and glorification sayings to one chapter and

---

133. Ashton, *Understanding*, p. 329.
134. Sasse, *Der Menschensohn*, pp. 173-74, 241, 247, 258-62.

gives little discussion to 8.28 and 13.31-32... The apocalyptic background
of the Johannine Son of Man is more evident in each of the Johannine Son
of Man sayings than Sasse's discussion indicates.[135]

Moreover, Reynolds feels that Sasse bases his notions about the Son of
Man being lifted up, that Reynolds names Sasse's martyr-theme, on Second
Temple traditions that have an altogether different 'center of gravity' than
the Danielic perspective of Sasse's main argument. These traditions with
a different focus and content, that Sasse introduces, are the Wisdom traditions, Moses ascent to Mt. Sinai, and the like.

In his recent monograph, Reynolds picks up Ashton's theme. In clearing
the ground for his discussion of it he describes succinctly the Son of Man
problem as the Christological question regarding what the title meant to the
four evangelists and their early audiences. Where did they get the phrase?
Did they use it as a title? Was there really a tradition of such apocalyptic
usage? Did it refer to the 'one like a son of man' in Dan. 7.13? Did it mean
simply human being, or 'one like me?' Reynolds suggests that these questions, while highly debated by scholars for a century, will continue to be
debated *ad infinitum*, but have no clear trajectory toward a solution.

Thus he focuses his work, instead, upon the question of whether the Son
of Man in John is wholly 'apocalyptic'.[136] Reynolds is clear and forthright
in his assessment of the apocalyptic issues regarding the Johannine Son of
Man. He sees his position as significantly different from the scholars who
argue for a human or non-apocalyptic Johannine Son of Man, of course.
However, he also believes that most scholars on the apocalyptic trajectory
also, like Sasse, fall short of a proper understanding of the Johannine logia.
He references scholars

> who locate the origin of the heavenly Son of Man mainly in apocalyp-
> tic literature, but they make this argument on the basis of a relatively few
> Johannine Son of Man sayings, namely 1.51, 3.13 and/or 5.27. Although
> the heavenly nature of the Johannine Son of Man has been correctly rec-
> ognized by these scholars, they fail to see 'son of Man' as either originat-
> ing principally in apocalyptic literature or that the apocalyptic depiction of
> the Johannine Son of Man is apparent in each of the Johannine Son of Man
> sayings and not only in a few of them.[137]

Reynolds argues that not only are there distinctive evidences in John of
the apocalyptic nature of the Son of Man, but this is John's central definition and description of the Son of Man. Moreover, he contends that this is
evident in all of the Johannine Son of Man logia. Reynolds declares that
what he demonstrates in his 'study is that the Johannine Son of Man is

135. Reynolds, *Apocalyptic Son of Man*, p. 8.
136. Reynolds, *Apocalyptic Son of Man*, pp. 1-2.
137. Reynolds, *Apocalyptic Son of Man*, pp. 8-9.

apocalyptic and that the evidence of this can be found throughout the Son of Man sayings, not merely in 1.51, 3.13, and/or 5.27'. Moreover, the Son of Man in John is connected with many apocalyptic texts from Second Temple Jewish Israelite literature, all of which form a relatively unified tradition, in his view.[138]

Reynolds affords clarity to the issue by declaring that 'the Son of Man in Jn 1.51 has three characteristics that have ... common features of the interpretations of the Danielic son of man in Jewish apocalyptic and early Christian literature'. These common features are: (1) the recognition of the Son of Man through seeing, (2) the recognition that he is the Messiah, and (3) the acknowledgement that he is a heavenly figure.[139] He continues by observing that these common apocalyptic features are given a special interpretation in the Gospel of John, as is evident particularly in 3.13-14 (lifted up), 1.51 (in opened heaven), 8.28 (lifted up), 12.23 (lifted up), 13.31 (glorified). In these logia we have the motifs of descent and ascent, of the 'lifting up', and of the glorification of the Son of Man. While these expressions are distinctively Johannine, Reynolds believes that does not negate their connection with the Jewish apocalypticism in the Danielic figure. Indeed, the entire burden of Reynolds' whole volume is to demonstrate that every Son of Man logion in John is directly connected with and dependent upon Dan. 7.13. He concludes that 'the Son of Man sayings in 3.13-14 highlight the apocalyptic characteristics of the Johannine Son of Man' throughout the gospel. Indeed, these logia confirm the Son of Man 'as a revealer of heavenly mysteries and as a heavenly, preexistent being'.[140]

Thus the state of the question reflects an ideological vacuum or scholarly *lacuna* that raises to prominence the significance of our three issues regarding what the Son of Man is in the Gospel of John. The questions are: the *identity* of the Son of Man, the *relationship* between the Son of Man in John and in other Second Temple traditions, including that in the Synoptic Gospels, and the *nature* of the Son of Man as Judge. Upon these three questions, as indicated from the outset, this work is focused.

C. *Methodology*

Central to the methodology of this work is its recognition that Second Temple Judaism was a varied fabric of multiple and competing Judaisms, rather than a monolithic ideology or literary tradition. Interest in Second Temple Judaism and in the relevance of its history and literature for the understanding of Christian origins has grown steadily since the

---

138. Reynolds, *Apocalyptic Son of Man*, p. 10.
139. Reynolds, *Apocalyptic Son of Man*, pp. 89ff.
140. Reynolds, *Apocalyptic Son of Man*, pp. 104ff.

Renaissance.[141] Scholars differed about the value of Judaism at the time of Jesus, and its influence upon the rise of the Jesus Movement and of Christianity. Scholars' religious biases and antisemitic prejudicees concurred in prompting them to treat 'Pharisaic-Rabbinic legalism' as a sort of inferior form of religion, in contrast with the Christian spirituality of grace. Regardless of their assessment of Judaism, however, the common scholarly assumption was that Pharisaic-Rabbinic Judaism was the normative form of Judaism at the time of Jesus, with the only exception being small marginal sects. This is the picture that emerges in the major and most influential introductions to the period, published by Emil Schürer in Germany, R.H. Charles in England, and George Foot Moore in America.[142]

The Holocaust and the discovery of the Dead Sea Scrolls changed dramatically the scholarly approach to the period, which became more sensitive to the richness, dynamism, and diversity of Jewish groups. Otto Eissfeldt was one of the earliest scholars to acknowledge in a positive perspective the rich contribution of Second Temple Judaisms to the study of the Jesus Movement, detailing his insights in his work on the Hebrew Bible, the Apocrypha, and the Pseudepigrapha.[143]

In the 1970s and 1980s Jacob Neusner began emphasizing that both Rabbinic Judaism and the Jesus Movement drank deeply from the well of the Hebrew Bible but followed distinctly different trajectories.[144] This perspective was specifically confirmed and elaborated in Segal's work which described Judaism and Christianity as twins born from the same womb.[145] Neusner and Segal emphasize that this pattern of religious and ideological

---

141. For a comprehensive analysis of the history of research in Second Temple Judaism, see Gabriele Boccaccini, *Portraits of Middle Judaism in Scholarship and Arts* (Turin: Zamorani, 1992) and the website of the Enoch Seminar, www.enochseminar. org.

142. Emil Schürer, *Lehrbuch der neutestamentlichen Zeitgeschichte* (Leipzig, 1874), 2nd edn, entitled *Geschichte des judischen Volkes im Zeitalter Jesu Christi* (3 vols.; 1886–90); rev. English edn by Geza Vermes, Fergus Millar, Matthew Black, Pamela Vermes and Martin Goodman (eds.), *A History of the Jewish People in the Time of Jesus Christ* (3 vols.; Edinburgh: T. & T. Clark, 1973–1987); R.H. Charles, *The Apocrypha and Pseudepigrapha of the Old Testament in English* (2 vols.; Oxford: Clarendon Press, 1913); George Foot Moore, *Judaism in the First Centuries of the Christian Era* (3 vols.; Cambridge, MA: Harvard University Press, 1927–30); see also Robert H. Charles, *The Book of Enoch* (Oxford: Clarendon Press, 1893).

143. Otto Eissfeldt, *Einleitung in das Alte Testament* (Tübingen: Mohr–Siebeck, 1943), English translation by Peter R. Ackroyd, *The Old Testament: An Introduction* (New York: Oxford, 1965).

144. Jacob Neusner, *Judaism and Scripture: The Evidence of Leviticus Rabbah* (Chicago: University of Chicago Press, 1986).

145. Alan F. Segal, *Rebecca's Children: Judaism and Christianity in the Roman World* (Cambridge, MA: Harvard University Press, 1986).

variety in the streams of tradition, drawn from the same sources, characterized the entire history of Second Temple Judaism. They emphasized correctly that formative Christianity demands to be studied in the context of formative Judaism and formative Judaism in the context of formative Christianity.[146]

Safrai and Stern, in the last quarter of the twentieth century, elaborated this variety, less in terms of grand ideologies and more in terms of the multiform patterns of political, social, cultural, and religious practices and institutions that were represented in the wide spread Jewish communities of the diaspora already in the first century BCE.[147] Sacchi addressed the matter of the variegated Judaisms in Jesus' day by means of a thematic approach.[148] His synthetic analysis emphasized the theological and philosophical streams of thought which can be identified in the unfolding Judaisms that influenced Philo and Jesus. In accomplishing this he treated with equal weight biblical documents and those that had formerly been referred to as intertestamental or apocryphal literary works.

A small clutch of other works, exploring in various distinctive ways the same theme of the multiplicity of Jewish religious ideologies before and during Jesus' time, appeared as the twentieth century drew to a close. Morna Hooker;[149] Kraft and Nickelsburg,[150] Neusner, Green, Frerichs,[151] and Flusser,[152] all put their hands imaginatively to this task but their work merely touched up the main points of what had already been set forth, and polished the highlights. By the end of the millennium a strong consensus had been reached by the scholarly community that Christianity was merely one form,

146. See Boccaccini's comment on Neusner's *Judaism at the Beginning of Christianity* in which the multiple Judaisms of the era from the exile to Jesus and Josephus are explicated in Gabriele Boccaccini, *Middle Judaism: Jewish Thought 300 BCE to 200 CE* (Minneapolis: Fortress Press, 1991), p. 70.

147. Shmuel Safrai and Moritz Stern (eds.), *The Jewish People in the First Century: Historical Geography, Political History, Social, Cultural and Religious Life and Institutions* (2 vols.; Philadelphia: Fortress Press, 1977).

148. Paolo Sacchi, *Storia del mondo giudaico* (Turin: SEI, 1976). See also Sacchi, *Storia del Secondo Tempio: Israele tra VI secolo a C. e I secolo d. C.* (Turin: SEI, 1994) = *The History of the Second Temple Period* (JSOTSup, 285; Sheffield: Sheffield Academic Press, 2000).

149. Morna D. Hooker, *Continuity and Discontinuity: Early Christianity in its Jewish Setting* (London: Epworth Press, 1986).

150. Robert A. Kraft and George W.E. Nickelsburg (eds.), *Early Judaism and its Modern Interpreters* (Philadelphia: Fortress Press, 1986).

151. Jacob Neusner, W.S. Green and E.S. Frerichs (eds.), *Judaisms and their Messiahs at the Turn of the Christian Era* (Cambridge: Cambridge University Press, 1987).

152. David Flusser, *Judaism and the Origins of Christianity* (Jerusalem: Magnes Press, 1988).

though a significant form, of Judaism.[153] It was seen as one ideology among many such competing movements that shaped the world of Judaism after the exile. It was one creative phenomenon among many that continued to appear until the rise in the fourth century CE of normative Rabbinic Judaism and normative Christianity.

In this work it is assumed, therefore, that all these various ideological, cultural, and religious forces at play in the first century BCE and in the first century CE, including the Jesus Movement, and embracing second-century Christianity as well, are to be understood and treated as forms of Second Temple Judaism.

From those variegated and competing traditions, I have chosen one document to analyze, the Gospel of John. I take that gospel as an expression of late first-century Judaism. The document is studied here in the form of its final redaction, so I make no attempt to critique the layers of the developing text nor the interpolations or additions which may have brought it to its final form. The subject of this dissertation is the gospel as it stands today, and within that document, specifically the thirteen Son of Man logia.

Moreover, this study, does not deal with the question or quest of the historical Jesus, nor the matter of Jesus' self image—the 'Son of Man problem' of New Testament Studies as described by Reynolds. Nor is this present work interested in how John's Son of Man theology relates to the historical Jesus.

This work is not a study of John's Christology. It is an inquiry into the meaning of the term, Son of Man, as it is applied by the Gospel of John to the literary character, Jesus of Nazareth. Thus it is a history-of-ideas assessment of the Son of Man sayings in the Gospel of John, based upon hermeneutical analysis. This distinguishes it specifically from Reynolds' address to *The Apocalyptic Son of Man in the Gospel of John*, in which he studied the Johannine Christology implied in the title, Son of Man, with a view to establishing whether it was apocalyptic.

So, this study is only interested in the literary figure of Jesus as a character in the story narrated by the author of John's gospel and specifically in the Son of Man sayings ascribed to him. As already noted, John's gospel expresses one form that Judaism took in the Jesus Movement and hence in early Christianity. Furthermore, whether the author of the Fourth Gospel knew of the Synoptic Gospels is not the main issue at stake here. The Son of

153. Boccaccini, *Middle Judaism*; Boccaccini, *Beyond the Essene Hypothesis: The Parting of the Ways between Qumran and Enochic Judaism* (Grand Rapids: Eerdmans, 1998); and Boccaccini, *Roots of Rabbinic Judaism: An Intellectual History, From Ezekiel to Daniel* (Grand Rapids: Eerdmans, 2002); Sacchi, *History*; James H. Charlesworth, *Jesus within Judaism: New Light from Exciting Archaeological Discoveries* (New York: Doubleday, 1988); Geza Vermes, *Jesus in his Jewish Context* (Minneapolis: Fortress Press, 2003).

Man in John seems to differ markedly from the Son of Man in the Synoptic Gospels, as well as from that titled figure in the other competing traditions of Judaism. Nonetheless, as indicated from the outset of this work, it will be important to compare the nature and meaning of the Son of Man in John with Mark, Matthew, and Luke–Acts, as well as the other Son of Man traditions of the Second Temple Period, particularly Ezekiel, Daniel, *1 Enoch*, and *4 Ezra*.

Using the criteria of historical methodology, including structural analysis of texts, and literary or narrative criticism, this study seeks to understand the ideology of the author of the Fourth Gospel, as presented in the Son of Man sayings. What is the Son of Man in John? That question has the three subunits already indicated in the survey of the history of research, namely, (1) the identity of the Son of Man in John, in comparison with the Son of Man in the Synoptic Gospels, (2) the relationship between the Son of Man in John and in other Second Temple Son of Man traditions, and (3) the nature of the Son of Man in John compared with other traditions of the Son of Man as Judge. Therefore, I will mine the literature of Second Temple Judaism, such as Daniel, *1 Enoch*, and the Synoptic Gospels, for traditions that may have impacted John's concept of the Son of Man.

In this process, for example, I shall address Maddox's proposal that the Son of Man in the Synoptic Gospels is no different than the Son of Man in John, since all four gospels have a Son of Man who is the Eschatological Judge, as in *1 Enoch* 37–71 and, some claim, in Daniel 7–9. Similarly, I shall explore whether and in what sense Painter and Burkett may be correct in emphasizing the difference between the Son of Man in the Fourth Gospel and the Son of Man in the other Second Temple Literature, including the Synoptic Gospels. It is my purpose to detail what the consequences of these kinds of similarities and differences will be for our main question.

This methodological approach will lead to a more comprehensive understanding of what the Son of Man is in the Fourth Gospel. That will make possible the conclusion as to whether the title, Son of Man, in John refers, for example, to the human Jesus in his humanity, or as the carrier of the *Logos*, or to the descended *Logos* itself, to the Apocalyptic Heavenly Messiah, to the Eschatological Judge, or to some other entity best described in some other way.

Chapter 2

THE SON OF MAN IN JOHN

A. *The Son of Man Logia in the Fourth Gospel*

There are thirteen Son of Man logia in the Gospel of John, all placed upon the lips of Jesus, as his most recurring self-identifying title. There are virtually no significant variants to any of the logia in the dependable manuscript sources. Thus, for the most part, the received text is trustworthy.[1] Minor exceptions will be noted when of interest.

1. *The First Logion: A Heavenly Son of Man*

In Jn 1.51, the first Johannine Son of Man logion, Jesus declares to the crowd gathered around Nathanael,

> καὶ λέγει αὐτῷ· Ἀμὴν ἀμὴν λέγω ὑμῖν ὄψεσθε τὸν οὐρανὸν ἀνεῳγότα καὶ τοὺς ἀγγέλους τοῦ θεοῦ ἀναβαίνοντας καὶ καταβαίνοντας ἐπὶ τὸν υἱὸν τοῦ ἀνθρώπου ('Truly, truly, I say unto you, you will see heaven opened, and the angels of God ascending and descending upon the Son of Man').

There are no variants indicated for this logion in the critical edition of the Greek New Testament.

1.1. *The Context: Placement in the Gospel*

The context of this logion is a conversation between Jesus and Nathanael and this pericope is followed immediately by the episode of the miracle of the wine at Cana. Following the prologue in Jn 1.1-18, John the Baptist is presented in dialogue with the priests and Levites (1.19-28). In that setting Jesus appears on the scene and John introduces him to his disciples and to the crowd gathered to John's ministry at the Jordon. Two of John's disciples promptly leave John to follow Jesus. One of them, Andrew, found his brother Peter and both followed Jesus. Jesus then left Judea for Galilee and there found Philip, whom he called to discipleship; and Philip brought Nathanael to Jesus.

---

1.   Eberhard Nestle, Erwin Nestle, Barbara Aland, Kurt Aland, Johannes Karavido-poulos, Carlo M. Martini and Bruce M. Metzger (eds.), *Novum Testamentum graece* (27th edn; Stuttgart: Deutsche Bibelgesellschaft, 1996), pp. 250-51.

Jesus opened his conversation with Nathanael by commending him on the quality of his character and integrity. Nathanael expressed surprise that Jesus could discern his guilelessness without getting to know him well. Jesus' response is that Nathanael will see greater things than this from Jesus.

This Son of Man logion disturbs the grammar and the narrative at this point in the gospel and may have been interpolated into this spot. It appears that the original text immediately followed this exchange with the miracle of the wine at Cana (2.1-10), for that miracle is followed with the relevant conclusion (2.11) to the conversation with Nathanael:

> Ταύτεν ἐποίησεν ἀρχὴν τῶν σημείων ὁ Ἰησοῦς ἐν Κανὰ τῆς Γαλιλαίας καὶ ἐφανέρωσεν τὴν δόξαν αὐτοῦ, καὶ ἐπίστευσαν εἰς αὐτὸν οἱ μαθηταὶ αὐτοῦ ('This, the first of his signs [wonders—great things], Jesus did at Cana in Galilee, and manifested his glory; and *his disciples believed in him*').

The Son of Man logion at 1.51 disturbs the syntax in that there is an inappropriate shift in the number of the verb:

> ἀπεκρίθη Ἰησοῦς καὶ εἶπεν αὐτῷ· ὅτι εἶπόν σοι ὅτι εἶδόν σε ὑποκάτω τῆς συκῆς, πιστεύεις μείζω τούτων ὄψῃ ('Jesus answered him, "Because I said to you, I saw you under the fig tree, do you believe? You shall see greater things than these"', 1.50).

Thus far the verbs in Jesus' discourse are appropriately in the second-person singular (πιστεύεις, ὄψῃ) for they are addressed to Nathanael, personally. However, when the Son of Man logion is introduced, while the pronoun of the indirect object (αὐτῷ) is masculine dative singular, the verb shifts to second-person plural (ὄψεσθε), a form inappropriate to Jesus' personal dialogue with Nathanael.

> καὶ λέγει αὐτῷ· ἀμὴν ἀμὴν λέγω ὑμῖν, ὄψεσθε τὸν οὐρανὸν ἀνεῳγότα καὶ τοὺς ἀγγέλους τοῦ θεοῦ ἀναβαίνοντας καὶ καταβαίνοντας ἐπὶ τὸν υἱὸν τοῦ ἀνθρώπου ('And he said to him, "Truly, truly, I say to you (plural), you (plural) will see heaven opened, and the angels of God ascending and descending upon the Son of Man"', 1.51).

Ernst Haenchen[2] and Craig Keener[3] both note the shift in the number of the verb and suggest that the pericope originally ended at 1.49 with Nathanael's expostulation,

> ῥαββί, σὺ εἶ ὁ υἱὸς τοῦ θεοῦ, σὺ βασιλεὺς εἶ τοῦ Ἰσραήλ ('Rabbi, you are the son of God, the king of Israel').

---

2. Ernst Haenchen, *John 1: A Commentary on the Gospel of John, Chapters 1–6* (trans. Robert Funk; Hermeneia; Philadelphia: Fortress Press, 1998), pp. 166, 167.
3. Craig S. Keener, *The Gospel of John: A Commentary* (Peabody, MA: Hendrickson, 2003), pp. 488-91.

It seems more likely that Jesus' response in 1.50 is part of the Nathanael pericope and that the story line then continues directly from 1.50 to the wedding scene in 2.1ff.

1.50 ἀπεκρίθη Ἰησοῦς καὶ εἶπεν αὐτῷ· ὅτι εἶπόν σοι ὅτι εἶδόν σε ὑποκάτω τῆς συκῆς, πιστεύεις μείζω τούτων ὄψη 2.1 γάμος ἐγένετο ἐν Κανὰ τῆς Γαλιλαίας, καὶ ἦν ἡ μήτηρ τοῦ Ἰησοῦ ἐκεῖ· 2.2 ἐκλήθη δὲ καὶ ὁ Ἰησοῦς καὶ οἱ μαθηταὶ αὐτοῦ εἰς τὸν γάμον ('Jesus answered and said to him, "Because I said to you that I saw you under the fig tree you believe? Greater things than these you shall see" …There was a wedding at Cana in Galilee, and Jesus' mother was there, and Jesus and his disciples were also invited to the wedding…').

Then Jesus changed the water into excellent wine, and the disciples 'believed on him'. Nathanael believes because of Jesus' perspicacity. The disciples believe because this promised greater thing (1.50) has now come to pass at Cana (2.1ff.).

Raymond Brown found the semantic difficulty in this Son of Man logion to be more problematic even than does Haenchen.[4] He noted that the clumsiness of the narrative flow from 1.43 to 2.11 is atypical of the author of John. Brown developed the idea at length, making the following points. First, as Jn 11.11 indicates, John usually manages to indicate more smoothly a continuation of a conversation. Brown posits the possibility that the 1.51 was originally addressed to a group in connection with Jesus' trial before Caiaphas (Mt. 26.64), as the early commentators saw, and was displaced to this location. There is similar wording after all in the narratives just before his death and resurrection (Mt. 16.21-28); as well as just before Peter's confession at Caesarea Philippi (Mt. 16.13-20). Third, the Cana story seems a natural follow-on narrative to 1.50, depicting the promised 'greater things'. Fourth, nowhere in the gospel is the promise of 1.51 fulfilled.[5]

Another reason to think that this logion was interpolated at the end of the first chapter, and before the miracle at Cana, arises from the confusion in chapters 1 and 2 regarding the sequence of numbered days, suggesting that the original flow of the narrative has been disturbed. On a certain day in 1.19ff. John encounters the priests and Levites, in 1.29 we have 'the next day', in 1.35 again 'the next day', in 1.39 'that day', in 1.43 'the next day', in 2.1 'on the third day there was a wedding at Cana'. So we have here five days referred to, plus whatever time it took to get from the Jordan near Jericho to Cana in Galilee. Obviously the text has been corrupted by foreign material.

---

4. Raymond E. Brown, *The Gospel according to John I–XII. Translation with an Introduction and Notes* (Anchor Bible, 1–2; Garden City, NY: Doubleday, 1966), pp. 88ff.

5. Brown, *Gospel according to John I–XII*, pp. 88-89.

1.2. *The Meaning of Logion One*

Brown was also certain that the original meaning of this logion, set in its original and correct context, referred to the resurrection or second coming of the Son of Man, 'where the presence of the angels about the glorified Son of Man would be appropriate. There are no angelophanies in the Johannine account of the public ministry; but angels are associated in all the Gospel accounts with the empty tomb and often with the final judgment'.[6] This would urge us to conclude that the final redactor of the Gospel of John borrowed this Son of Man logion from some source like Mt. 16.27-28, as urged by Brown and Keener, and injected it into the fourth gospel at 1.51 because his gospel needed Son of Man sayings to make it believable; and this was a place it could be injected because of Jesus' reference to seeing great things to come, namely, the redactor must have thought, a heavenly vision of the exalted Son of Man.

Leon Morris, Gerard Sloyan, Merrill Tenney, Wilbert Howard and Arthur Gossip, George Beasley-Murray, William Barclay, and Francis Moloney take no note of the infelicity of this logion in this location at 1.51, but all emphasize, with Haenchen, Keener, and Brown, that the presence of this statement regarding the Son of Man is intended to reinforce the divine identity of the incarnate *Logos* of the prologue, as the Son of Man and the apocalyptic messiah.[7]

Archibald Hunter explains the scene of the angels ascending and descending upon the Son of Man functioning as Jacob's ladder between the earthly and heavenly spheres. He notes that Jesus promises Nathanael a revelation of God's glory through the man, Jesus, in whom that revelation is present. Hunter thinks Jesus is promising that when the heavens really open to humanity they will see the historical Jesus to be the one true mediator between heaven and earth, between God and humankind. Moreover, Hunter emphasizes the importance of the series of signs that follow this moment in the gospel and make human history. Jacob's vision at Bethel is a kind of apocalyptic precursor of such an unveiling of the glory of God. 'In the story about to be unfolded the disciples are promised "a realized apocalypse"—an

---

6. Brown, *Gospel according to John I–XII*, p. 89.

7. See Leon L. Morris, *The Gospel of John* (Grand Rapids: Eerdmans, rev. edn, 1995), pp. 150-52; Gerard S. Sloyan, *John* (Interpretation, A Biblical Commentary for Teaching and Preaching; Atlanta: Knox, 1988), pp. 22-29; Merrill C. Tenney, *The Gospel of John* (The Expositor's Bible Commentary, 9; Grand Rapids: Zondervan, 1981), pp. 39-41; Wilbert F. Howard and Arthur J. Gossip, *The Gospel according to St John* (The Interpreter's Bible, 8; Nashville: Abingdon Press, 1952), pp. 488-90; George R. Beasley-Murray, *John* (Word Biblical Commentary, 36; Waco, TX: Word, 1987), pp. 18-30; William Barclay, *The Gospel of John* (Philadelphia: Westminster, rev. edn, 1975), I, pp. 91-95; Francis J. Moloney, *The Gospel of John* (Sacra Pagina Series, 4; Collegeville, MN: Liturgical Press, 1998), pp. 48-63.

unveiling in history, i.e. in the life, death and resurrection of Jesus, of the glory of the eternal God'.[8]

The opinion is virtually uniform among scholars that the image of the Son of Man in this logion is reminiscent of Jacob's dream of the ladder between heaven and earth (Gen. 28.10-17). In both passages heaven is open to earthly viewing, God provides an avenue of access between the earth and heaven, and angels ascend and descend upon the ladder in Jacob's dream and upon the Son of Man in this Johannine logion. The Son of Man constitutes the access for humans to the heavenly sphere. James McGrath[9] notes that numerous scholars, such as Charles Dodd,[10] Angus Higgins,[11] Jerome Neyrey,[12] and John Ashton[13] urge that the redactor is here influenced by rabbinic exegesis of the Genesis passages.

For instance, Rudolph Bultmann noted that in interpreting Gen. 28.12 the rabbis sometimes correctly understood the angels to ascend and descend upon the ladder and sometimes incorrectly understood the access to the heavenly world to be upon Jacob. 'The latter interpretation, which appears to be assumed...here, is connected with a mystical interpretation of the passage as a whole in *Gen. Rab.* 68.18, which interprets the ascending and descending of the angels as the communication between the earthly Jacob... and his heavenly archetype (εικων)'. Bultmann thought that this latter interpretation lay behind Jesus' statement in Jn 1.51, and that behind that interpretation lay the Gnostic notion of the relation of an earthly person with his or her heavenly archetype. Bultmann observed that Rabbinic tradition sometimes indicated that this relationship between 'the messenger on earth and his heavenly home' was facilitated by helping spirits. This would imply,

8. Archibald M. Hunter, *The Gospel according to John* (The Cambridge Bible Commentary on The New English Bible; Cambridge: Cambridge University Press, rev. edn, 1986), p. 28.

9. James F. McGrath, *John's Apologetic Christology: Legitimation and Development in Johannine Christology* (Cambridge: Cambridge University Press, 2001), pp. 206-207. See also Pierre Letourneau, *Jesus, fils de l'homme et fils de Dieu: Jean 2.23– 3.36 et la double christologie johannique* (Recherches. nouvelle série, 27; Montreal and Paris: Bellarmin & Cerf. 1993), p. 312; Jeyaseelan J. Kanagaraj, *'Mysticism' in the Gospel of John: An Inquiry into its Background* (JSNTSup, 158, Sheffield: Sheffield Academic Press. 1998), pp. 188-89; and Maurice Casey, *Is John's Gospel True?* (London: Routledge. 1996), pp. 60, 106.

10. Charles H. Dodd, *The Interpretation of the Fourth Gospel* (Cambridge: Cambridge University. 1953), p. 246.

11. Angus J. B. Higgins, *Jesus and the Son of Man* (London: Lutterworth, 1964), pp. 158-61.

12. Jerome Neyrey, 'The Jacob Allusions in John 1.51', *CBQ* 44 (1982), pp. 586-605 (589).

13. John Ashton, *Understanding the Fourth Gospel*, p. 342.

according to Bultmann, that the earthly man is distinct from his archetype who dwells in heavenly glory (δόξα).[14] Moreover,

> In the Gnostic and in the Johannine view the 'Son of Man' must be 'glori-fied' (i.e. in Gnostic terms: be united with its heavenly archetype) ... but it is not correct to suggest that the title 'Son of Man' has here an 'inclu-sive' meaning, which would mean that the believers themselves received here the promise of the communication with their heavenly archetypes. For even though John has taken over the Gnostic idea of the original commu-nity [communion] between the believers and the Revealer...he has reserved the title of the 'Son of Man' for Jesus; the believers are not here promised communion with the divine world, but the vision of the communion which is enjoyed by Jesus.[15]

McGrath[16] cites Jarl Fossum[17] in arguing that 'In the Johannine Chris-tological reading and exegesis of the Genesis passage... Jesus does not appear to be identified with Jacob-Israel, or we should say with the earthly figure of Jacob-Israel. It may be suggested, however, that John was aware of the idea of a heavenly counterpart to the earthly Israel, which could then be identified with the messianic Son of Man who embodies the iden-tity of Israel'.

This line of interpretation, which was once commonplace in scholarship, has lost ground in recent times, because of the difficulty in proving that such later speculations were already developed at the time of the composition of John. Brown asserted that the rabbinic texts do not establish the date of this kind of exegesis of Gen. 28.12, in terms of the earthly and heavenly Israel, earlier than the 3rd century CE. This raises the question whether there was an earlier Second Temple tradition of which the author of John could have been aware.[18] Contemporary scholars are struggling to locate the passage within a more likely Second Temple Jewish context. James Charlesworth sees here a Johannine apocalyptic dualism of heavenly and earthly realms, influenced by Qumranic ideology now evident to scholars in the Dead Sea Scrolls (1QS III, 13ff.).[19]

---

14. Rudolf Bultmann, *The Gospel of John: A Commentary* (trans. G.R. Beasley-Murray; Oxford: Blackwell, 1971), p. 105. Originally published as *Das Evangelium des Johannes* (KEK, 1; Göttingen: Vandenhoeck & Ruprecht, 1968).

15. Bultmann, *The Gospel of John*, p. 105.

16. McGrath, *John's Apologetic Christology*, p. 210.

17. Jarl E. Fossum, *The Image of the Invisible God: Essays on the Influence of Jewish Mysticism on Early Christology* (Novum Testamentum et orbis antiquus, 3; Freiburg: Universitätsverlag Freiburg, 1995), pp. 135-51.

18. Brown, *The Gospel according to John*, p. 90.

19. James H. Charlesworth (ed.), *John and the Dead Sea Scrolls* (New York: Crossroad, 1991), pp. 89-90, 98, 172.

1.3. *Theological Import of Logion One: Identity and Function of the Son of Man*

Reynolds asserts that the Son of Man in Jn 1.51 is depicted in an obvious manner as the Messiah. He argues this on the basis of the context in which Andrew informs Peter that he has found the Messiah, Philip's claim to Nathanael without using the title, and finally Nathanael's expostulation, 'You are the Son of God, the King of Israel'. He may be correct that these references tie Jn 1.51 to Dan. 7.13, an issue we will address in Chapter 4.[20]

On the contrary, however, even if this logion is related to Dan. 7.13 that does not determine that it is messianic, or more particularly that it describes the Son of Man as the Messiah. Whether the Son of Man in Daniel is messianic is still an open question in scholarly opinion and Reynolds does not martial the evidence to resolve that dilemma. Instead he imports meaning from elsewhere in the gospel (11.26-27; 12.13; 14.25-26; 20.30-31) to give 1.51 a messianic ring. While there may be reasons to note that the Son of Man in John is messianic, particularly in these other contexts, there is nothing inherent to this logion in 1.51 that declares or implies anything about his being either the Messiah, or messianic in some characteristics. The fact that this is quite obviously out of place at this juncture of the gospel narrative should make us very careful to let the logion say only as much as it actually says.

Moreover, throughout his work Reynolds employs a similar methodology in tying the titles Son of Man and Son of God into intimate connection, to the point that he frequently suggests that the latter implies deity. The problem is that, as in the Hebrew Bible and Second Temple Judaism, the title refers to a righteous man, such as the messianic ruler from David's line (Psalms 8, 80, 110); so Son of God in the gospels has the same import as in other Second Temple literature, and does not imply deity.[21] In Second Temple Tradition Son of God was a title significantly inferior to the title Son of Man, of revered tradition, as is especially evident in the Gospel of John.

The theological import of this logion is that the Son of Man is a *heavenly figure*, associated naturally with, and the focus of the attention of, the heavenly realm. Heaven will be open to human access by means of Jesus as Son of Man, as Keener, Brown, Heanchen, and others emphasized. In this manner the heavenly mysteries associated with Jesus will be revealed. Jesus is seen as prospectively *exalted* to a status directly associated with God and things heavenly, and as a *revealer* of the things of God, as well as the instrument for commerce between heaven and earth by both angels and humans.[22]

---

20. Reynolds, *Apocalyptic Son of Man*, pp. 91, 101-103.

21. Reynolds, *Apocalyptic Son of Man*, p. 91.

22. See Anthony T. Hanson, *The Prophetic Gospel: A Study of John and the Old Testament* (Edinburgh: T. & T. Clark, 1991), p. 38.

2. *The Second Logion: The Descending and Ascending Son of Man*

The title, Son of Man, appears next in 3.12-13 where Jesus declares in his conversation with Nicodemus,

εἰ τὰ ἐπίγεια εἶπον ὑμῖν καὶ οὐ πιστεύετε πῶς ἐὰν εἴπω ὑμῖν τὰ ἐπουράνια πιστεύσετε καὶ οὐδεὶς ἀναβέβηκεν εἰς τὸν οὐρανὸν εἰ μὴ ὁ ἐκ τοῦ οὐρανοῦ καταβάς ὁ υἱὸς τοῦ ἀνθρώπου ('If I tell you earthly things and you do not believe, how will you believe if I tell you heavenly things? No one ascends into heaven but he who descended from heaven, the Son of Man').

The future form of the verb, πιστεύσετε, in πῶς ἐὰν εἴπω ὑμῖν τὰ ἐπουράνια πιστεύσετε, is witnessed by the earliest and most trustworthy sources, though a rare variant prefers the present tense, πιστεύετε, here as well as in the previous clause.[23] This does not significantly alter the meaning or thrust of the logion that follows in v. 13. However, a variant adds to the end of v. 13, 'the one being (he who is) in the heavens'.[24] While the accepted reading is strongly attested,[25] the variant has raised scholarly debate regarding whether Jesus is here referring to himself as the Son of Man, or to a third person, a heavenly Son of Man who remains in heaven.

Douglas Hare asserts that if we considered such logia as 1.51 and 3.13 in isolation from the rest of the gospel narrative and argument, we might argue that Jesus refers to a figure other than himself.[26] Bultmann raised that argument regarding comparable logia in Lk. 12.8 and Mk 8.38. In that case, this pericope about the Son of Man gives Nathanael no information about Jesus, himself. However, when we consider the theological argument of the entire gospel, it is clear that the author of John intends in these logia to identify Jesus as the Son of Man. In this passage it is established that the Son of Man is intimately associated with the heavenly world. Thereafter, throughout the rest of the gospel that Son of Man is increasingly and unambiguously identified with Jesus of Nazareth as the incarnated *Logos* (1.14).

2.1. *Context: From Greater Things to Heavenly Mysteries*

The context that forms the transition between the first and second logia in John contains the narratives of the wedding at Cana, the assault upon the temple, the observation that the disciples discerned the meaning of that act

23. P[75], 050, 083, 579, 2211, and is reflected in both some Vulgate manuscripts and in the Bohairic[pt].

24. A, Θ, 050, the majority of Latin, some Syriac, and Bohairic[pt] sources.

25. P[66] and P[75], as well as the uncials ℵ B L T W[s]; such other Greek codices as 083, 086, 33, 1241; and Eusebius and Epiphanius.

26. Douglas R.A. Hare, *The Son of Man Tradition* (Minneapolis: Fortress Press, 1990), pp. 82-83.

only in their post-Easter reflections, and Jesus' movement from the celebra-
tion of the Passover Feast to the conversation with Nicodemus. The geo-
graphical setting for that conversation is Jerusalem. Jesus remarks at the
cleansing of the temple and in engaging Nicodemus emphasize the importance of personal spirituality shaped by divine revelation from heaven.
Thus, it is not a surprise that in 3.12, 13, as Jesus launches into a didac-
tic monologue, he should refer to his revealing heavenly things and earthly
things, and then observe that only the Son of Man can do this because he is
the only one who descended from heaven. This passage is reminiscent of
the evangelist's earlier observation in 1.18:

> Θεὸν οὐδεὶς ἑώρακεν πώποτε· μονογενὴς θεὸς ὁ ὢν εἰς τὸν κόλπον τοῦ πατρὸς
> ἐκεῖνος ἐξηγήσατο ('No one has ever seen God; the unique Son, who is in
> the bosom of the Father, he has made him known').

Bultmann was confident that the context of 3.13 indicated that Jesus was
referring to himself in this instance, and not to a third person in heaven. 'John
took over the Gnostic view of the Redeemer and applied it to the person of
Jesus in an interpretation determined by his idea of revelation', i.e., that in
the world's ignorance of its own transcendental origin, nature, and destiny,
it finds all things mysterious and creates mythologies to explain them; while
the Son of Man has appeared to reveal the true divine mysteries by his teaching.[27] This perplexity is evidenced in the context of this logion, in which
Jesus despairs of teaching Nicodemus any of the heavenly mysteries because
he seems unable even to comprehend the truth about earthly things.[28]

Keener cites *4 Ezra* 4.5-9, 21 with regard to the Second Temple Judaism traditions about earthly and heavenly wisdom, rather than envision-
ing Gnostic traditions as the influence shaping John's gospel. Moreover, he
thinks *4 Ezra* is citing Wis. 9.15-16 and thence dependent upon Job 38–41
and the *Testament of Job*.

> Thus when in the *Testament of Job* Baldad challenges Job's knowledge of
> the heavens, Job stumps Baldad with a question and concludes, 'If you do
> not understand the functions of the body, how can you understand heavenly
> matters (ἐπουράνια)?' Similarly, Ezra could not answer the angel's ques-
> tion about wind, fire, or a past day; how could he answer questions about
> heaven or hell?

The theodicy in *4 Ezra* explains that earthly people cannot understand
heavenly things, which are only grasped by celestial beings. Keener observes

27. Bultmann, *The Gospel of John*, pp. 143 n. 1, 296.
28. See also Keener, *The Gospel of John*, p. 559; Robert H. Strachan, *The Fourth
Gospel: Its Significance and Environment* (London: SCM Press, 1917), p. 96; and Raymond F. Collins, *These Things Have Been Written: Studies on the Fourth Gospel* (Louvain Theological and Pastoral Monographs, 2; Louvain: Peeters, 1990), p. 66.

that we have here reflections of the *Wisdom of Solomon* that declares, 'the corruptible body weighs down the soul, and the earthly tabernacle weighs down the mind which has many considerations. And we barely figure out the things on earth [τὰ ἐπί γῆσ], and find the things at hand only with toil; but who has discovered the things in heaven [τὰ ἐν οὐρανοῖς]?'[29]

2.2. *Meaning: Son of Man, the Apocalyptic Heavenly Messenger, is the Savior*

Hare sees 3.13 as a polemic against all Jewish apocalyptic and *Merkabah* mysticism traditions that describe a human ascent into heaven and descent from heaven, to reveal heavenly information. Such a tradition is described, for example, in *1 Enoch* 37–71 regarding the patriarchal figure, Enoch, turned into an apocalyptic mythic patronym in Second Temple Enochic literature. Hare declares that this logion means 'No one can claim to have returned from heaven with supernatural knowledge except the one who came from heaven in the first place'. Moreover, he is confident that we must take the statement of 3.13 and the implications of 1.51 as reinforcing the claim in the prologue that the Son of Man as incarnate *Logos* is preexistent, and that it is this divine phenomenon that is encountered in history in Jesus of Nazareth.[30]

Contrary to Hare's position, Reynolds argues that this logion is specifically apocalyptic, and once again bases his discussion on the relationship he discerns between 3.13-14 and Dan. 7.13, asserting that the latter is unquestionably apocalyptic.

> In 3.13, the motif of the Son of Man's ascent and descent appears for the first time, and likewise the 'lifting up' of the Son of Man in 3.14. These themes are particularly characteristic of the Johannine Son of Man, but they do not negate the Johannine Son of Man's connection to the Jewish apocalyptic… In fact, the Son of Man sayings in 3.13 and 14 highlight the apocalyptic characteristics of the Johannine Son of Man. Specifically, 3.13 draws attention to the Son of Man as a revealer of heavenly mysteries and as a heavenly, preexistent being. John 3.14 points to the Son of Man's role in salvation and judgment…and worthy of exaltation.[31]

Reynolds' insights here are accurate and particularly helpful in understanding the content of 3.13-14, except for his unfortunate claim that we have here indication of the preexistence, of the Son of Man, and that he is connected to judgment. There is nothing in this logion *per se* to lead us to the conclusion that he is preexistent. Such an interpretation of 3.13-14 can only be made if one imports into it the meaning of 1.1-3, and the like, from

29. Keener, *The Gospel of John*, pp. 559-60.
30. Hare, *Son of Man Tradition*, pp. 86-87.
31. Reynolds, *Apocalyptic Son of Man*, pp. 104ff.

elsewhere in this gospel. Moreover, this logion does not speak of judgment; its nearest context speaks of salvation (vv. 16-17); and it has only an indirect connection to the fact that humans judge themselves if they do not believe on the name of the Son of God (3.18), who more importantly happens to be the Son of Man (3.16-17).

Hare continues his discussion: 'The contrast John wishes to develop opposes not angels and humans but the one unique human being and all other members of the species. John has already alluded to his belief in angels who descend from heaven at 1.51, but their descent is not at all comparable to that of the Word, who descends into flesh; it is incarnation that distinguishes the Son of man from Gabriel, Michael, and other angels whose itinerary is superficially the same as his'. Hare believes this interpretation of 3.13 is confirmed by the way the titular phrase, Son of Man, continues to be employed throughout the Fourth Gospel.[32]

Contrary to Rudolf Schnackenburg[33] and Eugen Ruckstuhl,[34] Hare holds that 3.12 and 13 belong together and continue the conversation with Nicodemus as opposed to 3.13 initiating an independent monologue. Hare argues for this unity on the basis of the present tense of the verb in 3.14, which, like the synoptic passion prophecies, looks forward to the crucifixion and 'therefore, belongs in direct discourse attributed to the earthly Jesus and not in a post-Easter kerygmatic discourse of the evangelist... The one who speaks of his capacity to reveal *ta epourania* in v. 12 reveals the basis of this capacity in v. 13, referring to himself as the Son of man'.[35]

Keener sees Jesus' reference to the earthly and heavenly things as key to understanding the Son of Man logia in 3.11-18, indeed, in the entire gospel. He notes that philosophers in the Greco-Roman context of Jesus' teaching often claimed that, since the soul is of heavenly substance, they lived by the heavenly values revealed in nature and not by the earthly values of the society around them. They declared that philosophy progressively freed them from earthly corruption and degradation. Heavenly matters had to do with the divine, as in Jn 3.3. In Second Temple apocalyptic texts heavenly revelations could include meteorology and such material world aspects, but mainly had to do with mystical *Merkabah* visions of God enthroned.

In John's gospel, Keener is sure, heavenly revelations refer consistently to the things of God which Jesus, as Son of Man, shares with his disciples. These include the allusion to Jacob's ladder and the implication that Jesus, as Son of Man, is the unique bridge between earth and heaven. He is thus

32. Hare, *Son of Man Tradition*, p. 87.

33. Rudolf Schnackenburg, *Das Johannesevangelium* (4 vols; Freiburg: Herder, 1965).

34. Eugen Ruckstuhl, *Die johanneische Menschensohnforschung, 1957–69* (Theologischer Berichte, 1; Zürich: Benziger, 1972), pp. 171-284 (35ff.).

35. Hare, *Son of Man Tradition*, p. 88.

the avenue of access to the heavenly and eternal world.[36] Alfred Leaney concludes that this logion implies the author's belief that Jesus, as Son of Man, could have made known a large *corpus* of divine doctrine about heavenly things, if he could only have found hearers capable of accepting it.

> Neither Nicodemus, representing the ancient wisdom, nor disciples (whether contemporary with Jesus or with the author), representing the new revelation, could understand and therefore 'bear' or 'tolerate' some of the more advanced doctrine which the author evidently himself already entertained and at which he hints more than once in the course of the Gospel. See for example 3.12, 32; 5.41-44; 14.17; and note that 13.20 authorizes such development in the Church.[37]

The capacity of the Son of Man to reveal heavenly things is inherent to his being the *Logos*, the very object and highest expression of that revelation. In his crucifixion, which is to be the climax of his earthly sojourn, his true nature as the Son of Man is to be revealed and in that the true nature of God himself.[38]

In discounting the variant to this text, Bultmann also took vv. 12 and 13 as belonging together, and insisted that Jesus' reference to τὰ ἐπίγεια, 'earthly things' in v. 12 must be taken in a Gnostic sense. He thought this observation by Jesus in 3.12 implied a direct connection to the descent (καταβάς) and ascent (ἀναβέβηκεν) in 3.13, in that the Son of Man descended into the evil Gnostic world of materiality to rescue it by providing a new opening for the heavenly journey back to the heavenly world. This concept of the descending and ascending Son of Man is borrowed from the Gnostic notion of the heavenly preexistence of souls, who find salvation in deliverance

---

36. McGrath addresses this discussion of Jesus with Nicodemus regarding the closing of the door to heavenly things if he cannot even understand earthly things. He thinks it is an apologetic for the Johannine Community withdrawing fellowship from the rest of the Jewish community, probably especially the Jewish community which had initially been a part of the Johannine Community. If the heavenly mysteries revealed by the Son of Man are unbelievable or spiritually inaccessible to those others, no concession will be made to their spiritual blindness. 'If they will not accept what the community claims about earthly things, no attempt will be made to convince them by telling them of heavenly things (John 3.11-12)'. McGrath alludes to Jn 14.18-22 and the Synoptic Gospel narrative about Jesus' trial when Jesus declares that his opponents will see him enthroned in heaven. Since this never happened, John may be spiritualizing that assertion, referring to a spiritual seeing which only believers can experience. However, in Jn 8.28 there seems to be an expectation that the adversaries will really be confronted by the Son of Man sometime after his crucifixion and exaltation (p. 212).

37. Alfred R.C. Leaney, 'The Johannine Paraclete and the Qumran Scrolls', in *John and the Dead Sea Scrolls* (ed. James H. Charlesworth; New York: Crossroad, 1991), p. 61.

38. Leaney, 'The Johannine Paraclete', p. 41.

from earthly materiality and return to their true home in the heaven of their origin by identifying with the Son of Man.

The gospel does not teach this Gnostic doctrine of preexistence of all souls, but is referring specifically and only to Jesus as *Logos* and Messiah. However, Bultmann argued that the Gnostic line of thought flows smoothly through the salvific lifting up of the Son of Man of vv. 14-15, and into the watershed idea of the salvation of the world in Jn 3.16-17. For Bultmann, the descended Son of Man, in Jn 3.13 and following, is Jesus, and by revealing the heavenly mysteries he saves the world from Gnostic despair, providing human access to those heavenly mysteries and thereby to heaven itself, i.e., eternal life.[39]

Fossum[40] and Bruce Chilton[41] agree with Bultmann that John is heavily influenced by Gnosticism, and see in 3.13 references to a Gnostic or *Merkabah* ascent to heaven by Jesus in his lifetime and prior to his post-crucifixion ascension. They hold that the author here weaves such an event into Jesus' conversation with Nicodemus. Both scholars allude to the transfiguration pericope as some clue to this ascent. McGrath definitively argues, however, that this is not the case.[42] He notes that John's gospel has no transfiguration narrative, probably because John wishes to portray Jesus' entire ministry as an expression of glorious divine revelation for the whole human community and does not value such special revelations to a small group of elite followers. Moreover, John holds that the Son of Man is superior to Moses and does not reveal the divine mysteries as a result of heavenly visits but by reason of his descent from heaven as the Son of Man. He knows heavenly things because of his preexistence in heaven (1.1-3, 14).[43]

Talbert[44] and Keener also disagree with Bultmann on the notion that behind Jn 3.12-14 stands a Gnostic influence. Keener thinks the Gnostic Redeemer myth is far too late to have shaped the Fourth Gospel and joins Talbert in discerning the real source of the imagery to be the descent and ascent of Wisdom. In Second Temple Jewish literature Wisdom descends to reveal God and the divine mysteries. To that end she descends to take up residence with human kind. In Sirach Wisdom is poured out upon all aspects of God's creation (1.1–4.10), she especially fills the spirits of humans (16.24–18.14), and she takes up her dwelling in the Jerusalem temple of Israel (24.1-12), specifically in the 'Book of the Covenant', the Torah (24.13-34).

39. Bultmann, *The Gospel of John*, pp. 105, 144-51.

40. Fossum, *Image of the Invisible God*, pp. 71-94.

41. Bruce D. Chilton, 'The Transfiguration: Dominical Assurance and Apostolic Vision', *NTS* 27 (1981), p. 121.

42. McGrath, *John's Apologetic Christology*, pp. 157-71, 194.

43. McGrath, *John's Apologetic Christology*, p. 169.

44. Charles H. Talbert, *What Is a Gospel? The Genre of the Canonical Gospels* (Philadelphia: Fortress Press, 1977), p. 56.

In Baruch, as well, she dwells in Israel, taking up residence upon earth in 'the book of God's commandments, the Torah' (3.27–4.4).

However, in *1 Enoch* Wisdom's descent to earth, searching for a dwelling place, was not successful; Wisdom could not find a resting place in the earthly sphere, which is corrupted by evil, and so returned permanently to heaven until the eschaton (*1 En.* 42.1-2).[45] John's incarnated *Logos*, the Son of Man, descended from heaven and took up residence with humankind, with the expectation that, having revealed the mysteries of God, he would return to his heavenly home. Reynolds summarizes this messianic aspect of the ministry of the Son of Man in John simply and articulately: 'The Johannine Son of Man accomplishes the benefits of [his]…coming during Jesus' life on earth, yet not all recognize him in the present…there is still some expectation of future consummation (cf. 5.28-29; 8.28; 12.32), but the Son of Man is present and can be recognized now (1.51), life and judgment take place now (3.18; 5.24), and the heavenly things are presently being revealed (3.13-21)'.[46]

2.3. *Theological Import: Heavenly Man, Revealer of Divine Mysteries, and Savior*

Hare summarizes the import of 3.12-14 by noting that 3.13 informs Nicodemus that Jesus can answer his question about the meaning of being born from above because Jesus is from above and knows τὰ ἐπουράνια, including God's plan of salvation. Precisely because the Son of Man is not a Gnostic redeemer 3.14 must add that salvation is provided through the death of a unique human being, not as a propitiary event performed by a human on behalf of humans, but as a divine event enacted by the divine man. Wayne Meeks, Charles K. Barrett, Brown, and Nils Dahl debate, in terms of the *Akedah* of Isaac and Rom. 8.32, the existential and propitiatory theology that has been associated with the death of the Son of Man.[47] Hare observes that it is the theological point of Johannine incarnational Christology that the gospel has the Son of Man making here. He is grounding the inadequate pre-Pauline formula, 'Christ died for our sins in accordance with the Scriptures' (1 Cor. 15.3), specifically in the relationship of Jesus, as Son of Man, with God.

---

45. Keener, *The Gospel of John*, p. 562. See also Wis. 6.18-20; 7.27; 8.10, 13, 17; 9.10.

46. Reynolds, *Apocalyptic Son of Man*, p. 128.

47. Wayne A. Meeks, 'The Man from Heaven in Johannine Sectarianism', *JBL* 91 (1963), pp. 44-72 (63); Charles Kingsley Barrett, *The Gospel according to St John* (New York: Macmillan, 1955), p. 180; Brown, *The Gospel according to John*, p. 147; and Nils A. Dahl, 'The Atonement—An Adequate Reward for the Akedah? (Rom 8.32)', in *Neotestamentica et semitica: Studies in Honour of Matthew Black* (ed. E. Earle Ellis and Max Wilcox; Edinburgh: T. & T. Clark, 1969), pp. 15-29 (28).

The Son of Man is not simply a man acting for humanity. Jesus' impending death is not to be just a saving human act of obedience to God, but rather it is God acting. God gives and sends (3.16-17). Consequently those who really understand the Son of Man discern God, because Jesus, as Son of Man, is God acting. He 'has his origins outside the realm of humanity'.[48] John uses the themes of descent (3.13) and sending (3.17) to communicate the crucial Christological truth of preexistence in order to express clearly this divine heavenly reality.

Hermann Strathmann notes that even if the variant ending were adequately attested, as Black argues,[49] it could not be taken to refer to someone other than Jesus. He insists that the dialogue between Jesus and Nicodemus is only a rhetorical form and the focus throughout is on Jesus, not his auditor; 'the latter tacitly disappears in the course of the conversation'. He is only 'the occasion of Jesus' discourse on the topic'. The topic here is God's intervention to save the world by means of the Son of Man.

So Strathmann is certain that we must conclude that Jesus refers to himself in 3.12-13; and that the accepted reading of the text is correct. The variant interrupts the flow. The transition moves smoothly from the reference to the descending and ascending Son of Man to Jesus' specific talk about himself in 3.14-18. Moreover, Strathmann notes, 'the entire Gospel…is an evangelistic witness on behalf of Jesus'.[50] Hunter agrees and declares simply that even if the variant is original, it means nothing more or less than that 'Christ does not cease to be with the Father—and so in heaven—even while he walks the ways of earth'.[51] In keeping with the Prologue of the Fourth Gospel, 3.13 may imply but does not overtly declare, or even require, the claim of the preexistence of the Son of Man.[52] This may reflect the tradition

48. Hare, *Son of Man Tradition*, p. 89. See also Bultman, *The Gospel of John*, p. 249.

49. David A. Black, 'The Text of John 3.13', *GThJ* 6 (1985), pp. 49-66.

50. Hermann Strathmann, *Das Evangelium nach Johannes* (NTD, 4; Göttingen: Vandenhoeck & Ruprecht, 1968), pp. 66-67.

51. Hunter, *The Gospel according to John*, p. 38.

52. McGrath, *John's Apologetic Christology*, pp. 56, 100 n. 75, 137 n. 28. See *1 En.* 48.2-3, 6; *4 Ezra* 12.32; 13.52; James D.G. Dunn, 'Christology (NT)', in *The Anchor Bible Dictionary* (ed. David N. Freedman; New York: Doubleday, 1992), I, pp. 978-79. Dunn thinks John 3.13 is an apologetic against *1 Enoch*. In the latter Enoch only ascends into heaven to view it and report on it; rather than being from heaven, knowing it inherently, and revealing its nature and essence, as does the true Son of Man in John 3.13. Dunn also notes the connection between John 5.27 regarding the function of the Son of Man as Eschatological Judge; and *1 En.* 69.27 in which Enoch is appointed as Eschatological Judge. Geza Vermes, Hare, and others confirm that the Son of Man was given a Danielic Son of Man-type of messianic interpretation during the first century CE in Second Temple Judaism traditions. See Geza Vermes, *Jesus the Jew: A Historian's Reading of the Gospels* (London: Collins, 1973), p. 175; and Hare, *Son of Man Tradition*, pp. 11-12.

of the Son of Man from Dan. 7.13. McGrath notes that the 'Fourth Evangelist appears to be the first to draw out from this tradition the implication that
the Son of man, because he pre-existed in heaven, can reveal the heavenly
things he saw there'.[53]

Haenchen emphasizes the fact that the Fourth Gospel is the testimony of
the post-Easter church regarding events that have already transpired. This
explains the perfect tense of the verb, ἀναβέβηκεν. The descent and ascent
are history, as is the ministry of the Son of Man proclaiming the heavenly
mysteries regarding his role in God's salvific reign on earth and in heaven.
The perspective of the community is clear: 'there is really only one who
came down from heaven and will return there, viz., the Son of Man. That
implies that he alone has brought the true message, the correct gospel from
God and has thereby opened up access to God'.[54] There is no other mysterious third figure called the Son of Man who was in heaven while Jesus, the
Son of Man, spoke to Nicodemus on earth. Nor does anyone else in Judaic
tradition have any rightful claim to the title, Son of Man.[55]

Brown,[56] Morris,[57] Tenny,[58] Howard and Gossip,[59] Beasley-Murray,[60] and
Moloney,[61] generally agree with this line of thought, and with Haenchen
they counter Thüsing's claim that τὰ ἐπίγεια refers to Jesus' entire ministry
on earth and τὰ ἐπουράνια refers to what transpires in heaven.[62] They make

53. McGrath, *The Gospel according to John*, p. 168. See also McGrath, 'Change in
Christology: New Testament Models and the Contemporary Task', *ITQ* 63/1 (1998),
pp. 39-50 (45-46).

54. Haenchen, *John 1*, p. 204.

55. 'Since Odeberg's work on this passage, it has become more and more widely
accepted that John 3.13 reflects a polemic against claims made for other figures to
have ascended into heaven, whether figures like Moses and Elijah, or Merkabah mys-
tics' (McGrath, *The Gospel according to John*, p. 157). See Hugo Odeberg, *The Fourth
Gospel Interpreted in its Relation to Contemporaneous Religious Currents in Palestine and the Hellenistic-Oriental World* (Uppsala: Argonaut, 1929), p. 72; Wayne A.
Meeks, *The Prophet-King, Moses Traditions and the Johannine Christology* (NovT-
Sup, 14; Leiden: E.J. Brill, 1967), pp. 297-299, 301; Meeks, 'The Man from Heaven
in Johannine Sectarianism', in *The Interpretation of John* (ed. John Ashton; IRT, 9;
Philadelphia: Fortress and London: SPCK, 1986), pp. 141-73 (147); and Alan F. Segal,
'Ruler of This World: Attitudes about Mediator Figures and the Importance of Sociol-
ogy for Self-Definition', in *Jewish and Christian Self-Definition* (ed. Albert I. Baumgarten and Alan Mendelson; London: SCM Press, 1981), II, pp. 255-56.

56. Brown, *The Gospel according to John*, I, pp. 128-49.

57. Morris, *The Gospel of John*, pp. 196-97.

58. Tenney, *The Gospel of John*, p. 48.

59. Howard and Gossip, *The Gospel according to St John*, pp. 507-508.

60. Beasley-Murray *John*, pp. 49-50.

61. Moloney, *The Gospel of John*, pp. 94-95.

62. W. Thüsing, *Die Erhöhung und Verherrlichung Jesu im Johannesevangelium*
(Münster: Aschendorff. 1960), pp. 225, 255.

the point that the reference to the earthly and heavenly is a description of two kinds of divine action by Jesus, as the Son of Man, here and now. The earthly action is in process as Jesus speaks to Nicodemus and the heavenly operations include the heavenly mysteries which the Son of Man is just then revealing, as well as those eschatological things that will take place when the Son of Man ascends.

Brown thought that the perfect form, ἀναβέβηκεν, was troublesome. It may have been the motive for the addition of the variant phrase to the end of 3.13: 'who is in heaven'. However, Brown took the perfect tense to express the timelessness with which the post-Easter church saw the earthly and heavenly ministry of the Son of Man. This is similar to Haenchen's observation. It is as though the evangelist is saying, 'The Son of Man, Jesus, is the one who descended and who ascended, as we now know in retrospect'.[63] Thus, 'The textual evidence is not strong' for the variant, in Brown's view; moreover, 'The whole purpose of v. 13 in John is to stress the heavenly origin of the Son of Man ... The Son of Man remains close to the Father even when he is on earth'.[64]

We may conclude that in 3.12-13 the Son of Man is a *heavenly figure* who has previously descended from heaven and anticipates the ascent that will return him to his true home. As such, he is the *revealer* of the heavenly mysteries (εἴπω ὑμῖν τὰ ἐπουράνια—'I tell you the heavenly things'). Both of these functions are stated or implied already in the prologue of the Gospel of John, even before Jesus' first identification of himself as the Son of Man. Moreover, the Son of Man described here is *unique*, and in the light of the Prologue, he is not merely heavenly, but divine, the incarnate *Logos*. No one else in Second Temple Judaism tradition has descended from heaven to reveal the heavenly mysteries and to do the work of bringing in the divine reign, so no one else has a claim to the title, Son of Man.[65]

63. Brown, *The Gospel according to John*, p. 132.
64. Brown, *The Gospel according to John*, p. 133.
65. It is of some oblique interest regarding this point of descent and ascent of a significant messianic figure that in *The Prayer of Joseph* Jacob is apparently depicted as an angel who descended for a redemptive role. The association is with Jacob's wrestling at the brook Jabok in Gen. 32.24-31. Origen seems to have used this text in suggesting that John the Baptist was an angel who became a man and witness to Jesus. According to the *Stichometry* of Nicephorus this document originally had 1100 lines, unfortunately, however, we have only fragments providing 164 words. Moreover, it is impossible to discern whether *The Prayer of Joseph* is a document contemporary with John's gospel or later, Jewish or Christian; nor can we determine whether it was Palestinian or Alexandrian in origin, whether originally Aramaic or Greek. Consequently, this ancient reference is intriguing for its descent narrative, but it is difficult to establish a direct link with the Gospel of John. In any case, the idea of an angel's embodiment differs substantially with John's concept of incarnation, which made the divine Logos become flesh. See L.Z. Smith, *The Prayer of Joseph, A New Translation with*

3. *The Third Logion: 'Lifted up' = Killed*

As indicated above, the logion of descent and ascent is followed immediately by the one in 3.14-15:

καὶ καθὼς Μωϋσῆς ὕψωσεν τὸν ὄφιν ἐν τῇ ἐρήμῳ οὕτως ὑψωθῆναι δεῖ τὸν
υἱὸν τοῦ ἀνθρώπου ἵνα πᾶς ὁ πιστεύων ἐν αὐτῷ ἔχῃ ζωὴν αἰώνιον ('As
Moses lifted up the serpent in the wilderness, so must the Son of Man be
lifted up, that whosoever believes in him may have eternal life').

Reynolds cites Godfrey Nicholson's[66] five categories of meaning for
ὑψόω—ὕψωσεν: crucifixion, crucifixion and something more such as exaltation, crucifixion in conjunction with ascension and heavenly exaltation, a lifting up toward heaven by means of a cross, or the same without reference to a cross. He notes that a scholarly debate has arisen between the second, third, and fourth proposed meanings, however, most agree that the reference is to the combined crucifixion and anticipated exaltation of the Son of Man.

3.1. *Context: Lifted up as Redemptive Crucifixion*[67]
John 3.16-18 constitutes a brief explication of the meaning of 3.14-15, particularly of the last line in 3.15 regarding the gift of salvation or eternal life. The immediate context of this Son of Man logion is the discussion with Nicodemus about spiritual rebirth. Nicodemus expresses difficulty in comprehending Jesus' metaphor about being born again. This leads Jesus' into a monologue in which he sets forth the essential principles of the divine mystery unveiled by the heavenly messenger sent to reveal God to humankind and so save the world. The larger context is that of Jesus' presence at the feast of the Passover in Jerusalem and the accumulation of crowds of people who 'believed in his name, when they saw the signs which he did'. Nicodemus seems to have been one of these seekers. He apparently falters in his quest, finding it difficult to comprehend the psychospiritual import of a rebirth and the radically innovative suggestion that the divine messenger must suffer and die (ὕψωσεν—be lifted up) for the salvation of humankind, as was Moses serpent in the wilderness.

There is no variant to this Son of Man logion. Apparently the audience for whom this monologue by Jesus was written, would have understood that being lifted up referred to death. The kerygma of the early church

---

Introduction, in James H. Charlesworth (ed.), *The Old Testament Pseudepigrapha*, II (Garden City, NY: Doubleday, 1985), pp. 699-723 (699).

66. Godfrey C. Nicholson, *Death as Departure: The Johannine Descent–Ascent Schema* (SBLDS, 63; Chico, CA: Scholars Press, 1983), p. 141.

67. Reynolds, *Apocalyptic Son of Man*, p. 122.

emphasized that in his crucifixion and resurrection Jesus was exalted as savior. Beasley-Murray, Morris, and Brown emphasize that this conjoining of these two symbolic events is clearly the intended kerygmatic proclamation of this text.[68] 'The redemptive event is the crucifixion-resurrection of the Son of Man. Accordingly it is in the risen, crucified Lord that the believer has eternal life'.[69]

Beasley-Murray elaborates by noting that the brief kerygmatic formula in vv. 14-15 presupposes v. 13 and echoes the Synoptic passion predictions, illuminating their meaning. The elevated snake in the Moses' story saves God's people, and the elevated Christ saves in his crucifixion. Salvation depends upon the cross, i.e. the lifting up. 'The term ὑψωθῆναι is associated with δοξασθῆαι, 'be glorified' (cf. 12.23; 13.31f.). The opening sentence of the last Servant Song in Isa. 52.13 is clearly in mind: ἰδοὺ συνήσει ὁ παῖς μου καὶ ὑψωθήσεται καὶ δοξασθήσεται σφόδρα (LXX), "My servant will be wise and exalted and greatly glorified" '.[70]

This Hebrew Bible backdrop to the evangelist's proclamation indicates the vindication and exaltation of the Son of Man as a result of his suffering, therefore the author of John *repeatedly* speaks of his being lifted up. 'Curiously several Semitic terms encourage this language and its repitition'. In Aramaic *'ezdᵉqeph* literally means 'lift up' as well as 'lift up one bowed down, and lift up on a cross, crucify', to exalt or to execute on a gibbet.[71] Similarly *'istᵉlaq* means to be lifted up, depart, or die; while *'arim* means lift up or remove.[72] In prison Joseph informed one royal servant that in three days Pharaoh would lift up his head in exaltation; and he informed the other royal servant that in that same time Pharaoh would lift up his head in decapitation (Gen. 40). The association of this terminology with crucifixion and death had a deep and long Judaic tradition.

3.2. *Meaning: Crucifixion as Exaltation: Son of Man as Object of Saving Faith*

Sloyan links the references to descent and ascent in 3.13 to the heavenly and earthly status of the Son of Man in 1.51, and sees these logia as post-Easter *kerygma*. Sloyan discerns it to be of related theological significance that in both 3.13 and 3.14 what comes down must go up. The salvific effect of the descended Son of Man depends upon his being lifted up. Moloney, Barclay, Haenchen, and Keener agree, and with Sloyan emphasize the fact that

---

68. Beasley-Murray, *John*, pp. 50-51, Morris, *The Gospel of John*, pp. 198-200, Brown, *The Gospel according to John*, p. 133.

69. Beasley-Murray, *John*, pp. 50-51.

70. Beasley-Murray, *John*, pp. 50-51.

71. Tenney, *The Gospel of John*, p. 49.

72. Beasley-Murray, *John*, pp. 50-51.

the *crucified* and *exalted* Son of Man is the object of salvific faith through-out the Fourth Gospel.[73] Sloyan declares: 'The Son of Man descends from heaven. He must be raised aloft if anyone is to believe in him. This is the Johannine double 'upraising' in crucifixion and resurrection that will occur more than once in the text of this gospel (cf. 8.28; 12.32, 34)'. G. Bertram comments that 'In Jn. ὑψόω has intentionally a double sense in all the pas-sages in which it occurs... It means both exaltation on the cross and also exaltation to heaven'.[74] Howard and Gossip essentially agree but focus the double upraising on his crucifixion and ascension (Acts 1.6-11; Lk. 24.50-51), rather than on crucifixion and resurrection.[75]

Moses' serpent of bronze, if looked upon with trust in God, preserved the Israelites from death (cf. Num. 21.4-9). The exalted Jesus, looked upon believingly, gives the life of the final and perpetual eon ('eternal life') to those who believe (v. 15; cf. Dan. 12.2).[76] It is likely that the author of John's gospel is here, as well as in 12.32, reflecting his awareness of Wis. 16.6-7, which recalls poetically the salvific import for the Israelites, of Moses' bra-zen serpent, and sees in it the analogue of the analogous crucified Son of Man.

> But for admonition
> They were troubled for a short space,
> Having a token of salvation,
> To put them in remembrance
> Of the commandment of thy law;
> For he that turned towards it
> *Was not saved by that which was beheld,*
> *But because of thee, the Savior of all.*[77]

Brown notes that in Jn 3.14-15 Jesus may be citing an old exegesis preserved in the Targumim, since their interpretation of the brazen ser-pent story emphasizes turning in faith toward the *memra* of God. Targum Pseudo Jonathan mentions the importance of the use of the name of the

---

73. Moloney, *The Gospel of John*, pp. 95, 101; William Barclay, *The Gospel of John* (Philadelphia: Westminster, 1975), I, pp. 134-35; and Haenchen, *John 1*, pp. 204-205, 207; Keener, *The Gospel of John*, pp. 564-65. It is interesting that Bultmann is unchar-acteristically unhelpful here, observing only that Jn 3.14, unusual for this gospel, does not depend on Gnostic sources or ideology (see Bultmann, *The Gospel of John*, pp. 151-53).

74. G. Bertram, 'ὑψόω', in Gerhard Kittel (ed.), *Theological Dictionary of the New Testament* (trans. Geoffrey W. Bromiley; Grand Rapids: Eerdmans, 1964), VIII, p. 610.

75. Howard and Gossip, *The Gospel according to St John*, p. 508.

76. Sloyan, *John*, p. 46.

77. This quote is cited by Howard and Gossip, *The Gospel according to St John*, p. 508 (English Revised Version).

memra, just as Jn 3.18 mentions the crucial role in salvation of believing on the name of the Son of Man.[78]

Hunter declares that Jesus is here depicted as the one who at the cross 'stood alone as the true incarnation of the Son of Man. He was rejected and crucified. But His death proved the birth pangs of the Son of Man, and after the Resurrection the Son of Man found new and glorious embodiment in the Church...', in which role Stephen envisions him in Acts 7.56.[79]

In 3.15 we have a completion of the sentence and sense of 3.14. There ἐν αὐτῷ is strongly attested but alternatives of minor grammatical variation are also indicated, probably as scribal errors or emendations.[80] The differences are between ἐν, ἐπί, and εἰς. Morris acknowledges these variants in a note, indicating that they are probably scribal emendations prompted by difficulty with πιστεύω ἐν and 'this is rendered all the more probable since some MSS have imported μὴ ἀπόληται ἀλλ' ("not perish but...") from v. 16 and have placed it between ἐν αὐτῷ and ἔχῃ'. Scholars do not generally consider the difference between believing in the Son of Man and believing on or upon him to be significant enough for comment. Brown insists that, though the reference to Moses' snake (Num. 21.8) urges the Israelites to look *on it* for salvation, the received text for Jn 3.15 is by far better because the entire theme of John's Gospel, as much of the *Corpus paulinum*, emphasizes the importance of 'being in Christ' for salvation.[81]

3.3. *Theological Import: Suffering Savior*

The theological burden of the logion in 3.14-15, especially emphasized by Lightfoot,[82] is the depiction of the Son of Man as the *suffering servant* and the *savior*. This import of John's third Son of Man logion is elaborated throughout the subsequent context in 3.16-18, particularly in the assertion that God *gave* his unique son, the Son of Man, to save the world (v. 16), and specifically not to condemn it (v. 17), such salvation being effectuated by belief in the name of the Son of Man. That is to say, humans should believe on the name of the righteous man, Son of God (3.18). The name of that righteous man on whose name all should believe is Son of Man.

---

78. Brown, *The Gospel according to John*, p. 133.

79. Archibald M. Hunter, *Interpreting the New Testament, 1900–1950* (London: SCM Press, 1951), pp. 56, 117.

80. The text is strongly attested by P[75] B T W[s] 083; P[66] and pc L have ἐπ' αὐτῷ, in 086 א A Θ we have εἰς αὐτόν, and ἐπ' αὐτόν also in some MSS of A.

81. Morris, *The Gospel of John*, p. 200 n. 68. Cf. also Brown, *The Gospel according to John*, p. 133.

82. Robert H. Lightfoot, *St John's Gospel. A Commentary* (Oxford: Oxford University Press, 1957), p. 117.

4. *The Fourth Logion: Son of Man, Eschatological Judge*

One of the most interesting references to the Son of Man in the Fourth Gospel is in 5.25-27. There we read

ἀμὴν ἀμὴν λέγω ὑμῖν ὅτι ἔρχεται ὥρα καὶ νῦν ἐστιν ὅτε οἱ νεκροὶ ἀκούσουσιν τῆς φωνῆς τοῦ υἱοῦ τοῦ θεοῦ καὶ οἱ ἀκούσαντες ζήσουσιν ὥσπερ γὰρ ὁ πατὴρ ἔχει ζωὴν ἐν ἑαυτῷ οὕτως καὶ τῷ υἱῷ ἔδωκεν ζωὴν ἔχειν ἐν ἑαυτῷ καὶ ἐξουσίαν ἔδωκεν αὐτῷ κρίσιν ποιεῖν ὅτι υἱὸς ἀνθρώπου ἐστίν ('Truly, truly, I say to you, the hour is coming, and now is, when the dead will hear the voice of the Son of God, and those who hear will live. For as the Father has life in himself, so he has granted the Son also to have life in himself, and *has given him authority* (ἐξουσίαν) *to execute judgment, because he is the Son of Man*', 5.25-27).

John 5.27 declares plainly that John's concept of the Son of Man recognizes that the Son of Man of Judaic tradition is invested with the *function* of eschatological *judge*.

There are no significant variants to this text. The received text is strongly attested in all the earliest sources. D and Θ together with most of the late latin and syriac manuscripts place a καὶ between αὐτω and κρίσιν but the commentators see no significance in this, since A B L N W 070 33 579 and Origen favor the received text.

4.1. *Context: Messianic Son of Man*

The context of this pericope and its Son of Man logion is Jesus' discussion of the fact that he is the one from heaven (3.31-36) and that in him divine light is come into the world but people generally prefer the darkness (vv. 19-21). A side discussion of John's and Jesus' baptism seems inserted at 3.22-32 and 4.1-6. There follows Jesus' discourse with the woman at Jacob's well in Sychar, to whom he declares that he is the Messiah for whom she is looking (4.7-42), and the healing of the son of an official at Capernaum (4.43-54). John 5 finds Jesus back in Jerusalem where, on the Sabbath, he healed the paralyzed man at the Bethzatha pool and debated the Sabbath law with the religious authorities in a similar manner as in John 9, on the occasion of his healing of the blind man on the Sabbath.

In 5.18 the authorities accused Jesus of making himself equal with God by calling God his father. This launched Jesus into a monologue about his being able to do only what the father wishes him to do, what he sees the father do, and what the father instructs him to do. In this speech, as in 1.51, Jesus declares that his auditors will see greater things than the healing of the blind man. Perhaps he meant the healing of another blind man that followed in 9.1-41. In any case, this discourse creates the setting for 5.27-47 in which Jesus declares that the father is the source of life and conveys it to him, together with the authority and power (ἐξουσία), as the Son of Man, to function as the Eschatological Judge.

Nonetheless, contrary to Moloney,[83] it is significant that Jesus' monologue, from 5.27 to 5.47, refers repeatedly to the fact that the Son of Man will not exercise his power and authority as prosecutor. That pericope draws to a close with Jesus' declaration in 5.45,

> Μὴ δοκεῖτε ὅτι ἐγὼ κατηγορήσω ὑμῶν πρὸς τὸν πατέρα ('Do not think that I shall accuse you to the Father').

This sentiment is reinforced throughout the Fourth Gospel, but particularly in 3.17,

> οὐ γὰρ ἀπέστειλεν ὁ θεὸς τὸν υἱὸν εἰς τὸν κόσμον ἵνα κρίνῃ τὸν κόσμον ἀλλ ἵνα σωθῇ ὁ κόσμος δι' αὐτοῦ ('God sent not his son into the world to [judge or] condemn the world but that the world might be saved through him');

and in 12.47,

> καὶ ἐάν τίς μου ἀκούσῃ τῶν ῥημάτων καὶ μὴ φυλάξῃ ἐγὼ οὐ κρίνω αὐτόν· οὐ γὰρ ἦλθον ἵνα κρίνω τὸν κόσμον ἀλλ ἵνα σώσω τὸν κόσμον ('If any one hears my sayings and does not keep them, I do not judge him; for I did not come to judge the world but to save the world').

4.2. *Meaning: The Authority and Power of the Son of Man as Judge*

Morris and Brown note the absence of the articles in this logion but insist that the title should, nonetheless, be taken to have the same weight and meaning as all those instances when it appears with an article placed before υἱὸς and/ or before ἀνθρώπου.[84] That is, there is no possibility of taking the logion here to intend a reference to Jesus as a mere human, since, as Beasley-Murray also affirms, it is precisely the Son of Man in the Danielic and Enochic traditions that has the authority and power to function as Eschatological Judge; as we shall see in more detail in Chapter 4. In Daniel the Son of Man is not a judge but functions as God's emissary to bring down evil and establish the divine kingdom. In Enoch he is the Eschatological Judge. Therefore, despite the objections of Hare, Borsch, and Higgins,[85] the preponderance of New

---

83. Moloney, *The Gospel of John*, p. 184. Moloney argues that 5.27 indicates that Jesus, as Son of Man, intends to and does exercise his *exousia* to judge the world. He seems not to notice the constant Johannine insistence that this is not so, and Jesus' repeated monologues disuading the audience from such an association of judgment with his ministry, instructing them instead to associate him with God's work of salvation.

84. Morris, *The Gospel of John*, p. 283. Cf. also Brown, *The Gospel according to John*, p. 215.

85. Hare, *Son of Man Tradition*, p. 92; Frederick H. Borsch, *The Son of Man in Myth and History* (Philadelphia: Westminster, 1967), p. 166; Angus J.B. Higgins, *Jesus and*

Testament scholars, including Morris, Brown, and Beasley-Murray, assert that the absence of the articles is merely an individual stylistic factor, just as in Dan. 7.13 where the definite articles are also missing.[86]

Even if he does not employ his prerogative or *function* of judging in the sense of prosecuting, Tenney, with Lightfoot[87] and Hunter,[88] thinks the lack of the article may be seen as a way of further affirming the Son of Man's *prerogative* to judge, since he is in any case human like us and has experienced our pilgrimage.[89] Moloney agrees with Morris, *et alii*, that the absence of the articles is likely to be an intentional attempt on the part of the author to indicate clearly that he has Dan. 7.13 in mind.[90]

Both of these emphases seem accurate. The Son of Man is one of us and has a right to judge the human predicament, and he is also the heavenly figure who brings to that judgment the transcendent perspective. This line of argument is reinforced by the fact that it seems to reflect awareness on the part of the Johannine author of the worldview, if not of the narrative, reflected in the *Testament of Abraham*. There Abel, *ben Adam* (*uios anthropou*), is depicted as the man who is enthroned to judge the world of both righteous and sinful persons. His role is justified on the basis of God's declaration, 'I do not judge you, but every man is judged by man'.[91] This emphasis in the *Testament of Abraham* is echoed in Jesus' monologue (5.27-47) in

the Son of Man (Philadelphia: Fortress Press, 1964), p. 166. See also Gunter Reim, *Studien zum alttestamentlichen Hintergrund des Johannesevangeliums* (SNTMS, 22; Cambridge: Cambridge University Press, 1974), p. 186, who denies that the Fourth Gospel alludes to Daniel at all.

86. Morris, *The Gospel of John*; Brown, *The Gospel according to John*; Beasley-Murray, *John*, p. 77.

87. Robert H. Lightfoot, *St. John's Gospel: A Commentary* (Oxford: Oxford University Press, rev. edn, 1966), p. 144, 'Possibly [...] St. John wishes his readers to remember that their Judge is not only One who in virtue of His office as the Son of man exercises this prerogative, but is also truly human, one of themselves; and on this interpretation the prerogative of judgement may be regarded as belonging to the Lord's humanity'.

88. Hunter, *The Gospel according to John*, p. 60.

89. Morris, *The Gospel of John*, p. 283; Brown, *The Gospel according to John*, pp. 215, 220; Tenney, *The Gospel of John*, p. 65; Beasely-Murray, *John*, p. 77.

90. Moloney, *The Gospel of John*, p. 183. See Ernst C. Colwell, 'A Definite Rule for the Use of the Article in the Greek New Testament', *JBL* 52 (1933), pp. 12-21, in which he argues that the article will typically be absent when a predicate nominative is definite and precedes its verb. Reynolds (Reynolds, *Apocalyptic Son of Man*, p. 134) discusses the intricacies of this rule and confirms its general applicability. He sees this to be important with regard to arguments which erroneously associate the Son of Man's ἐξουσία to judge with Jesus' humanity, rather than correctly relating it to his authority as the divine and incarnated *Logos*.

91. *T. Ab.* 13.2-3. See Phillip B. Munoa, III, *Four Powers in Heaven: The Interpretation of Daniel 7 and the Testament of Abraham* (Sheffield: Sheffield Academic Press, 1998), pp. 43-81.

connection with his certification as eschatological judge, and his refusal to carry out the role of prosecutor. McGrath, Ernest Sidebottom, Reynolds, and Rhea confirm the significance of this allusion to earlier Second Temple literature for our understanding of the Johannine Son of Man as judge.[92]

With this much Hare agrees. John does not repudiate the tradition that Jesus will function as the judge, but the emphasis is on a different point: God is not calling for ethical conduct, though that is not negligible (cf. 13.34f.), but belief and trust in God's salvific presence in the incarnate Son of Man. The judgment is the outcome of being confronted by God's intervention in the Son of Man and rejecting it: 'It is in this sense that all judgment has been committed to the Son: the incarnation is the locus of judgment. We might paraphrase v. 27: "...and he has given him authority to execute judgment, because he is the incarnation of the Word." Does John intend by this anarthrous phrase to recall the self-designation of Jesus, *ho huios tou anthropou*? Indubitably. The two are not identical; *huios anthropou* does not serve as a name but expresses a quality or status, yet its connotative force appears to be the same as that of the fuller appellative. Both forms of the phrase can refer to the humanity of the Word that became flesh for our salvation'.[93]

Bultmann agreed that this is an existential declaration by the evangelist, himself, likely dependent upon Second Temple Judaism sources, and not derived from Gnostic sources. However, he believed that the following verse was a redactor's addition attempting to draw the stark declaration of this Son of Man logion back toward the more conventional eschatology of a final divine judgment.[94] Strangely, Keener observes upon the appointment of the Son of Man as judge and suggests that in 5.27ff. Jesus 'explains why he will judge'. He appears to overlook the fact that in 5.27-47 it is exactly the opposite that Jesus explains, i.e., why he will not *function* as a judge in the sense of prosecuting unbelievers.[95]

4.3. *Theological Import: Non-judging Judge and Non-terminal Terminus*
Haenchen draws the import of this logion neatly into focus. He disagrees with Bultmann and Keener, emphasizing strongly the fact that vv. 27-28

---

92. McGrath, *The Gospel according to John*, pp. 96-99; Ernest M. Sidebottom, *The Christ of the Fourth Gospel* (London: SPCK, 1961), pp. 94-95; Reynolds, *Apocalyptic Son of Man*, pp. 131-36; Robert Rhea, *The Johannine Son of Man* (Zurich: Theologischer Verlag Zürich, 1990), p. 71. See also Munoa, *Four Powers*. Munoa agues for Adam as the Ancient of Days and Abel as the Son of Man in the *Testament of Abraham*. He perceives that Daniel's People of the Holy Ones of the Most High are the twelve disciples who in the gospels will sit on eschatological thrones to judge the twelve tribes of Israel.

93. Hare, *Son of Man Tradition*, p. 96.

94. Bultmann, *The Gospel of John*, pp. 260-62.

95. Keener, *The Gospel of John*, p. 654.

have been inserted here to establish the redactor's claim for a realized eschatology, which contrasted strongly with the expectation of a final history-ending judgment, held by the Christian community generally. This was a controversial message for the early church. Many preferred the tradition of a catastrophic *parousia* of judgment that terminated history, carried out by a Danielic Son of Man. The transformation of this anticipated eschatology into a realized eschatology of this present existential moment did not meet their expectations. So the author penned 5.27-29 to satisfy this expectation, v. 27 reassuring the reader that God has sent the Son of Man with the authority to execute judgment because that is what a Son of Man does (Daniel 7–9).

> The futuristic and mythological expectations connected with the end time are again introduced with this apocalyptic title. The Son of man is understood here as the judge of the world and identified with Jesus, as may be deduced from v. 28: 'Do not marvel at this; for the hour is coming' (the dialectic of the times, the 'now' and the 'then', is here deliberately corrected in that what had been said earlier is interpreted in a traditional sense) 'when all who are in the tombs will hear his voice and come forth', and indeed 'those who have done good, to the resurrection of life, and those who have done evil, to the resurrection of judgment'.[96]

So in this Son of Man logion the Son of Man is *judge, heavenly figure* (sent from God), *revealer, exalted one* (potentially testifying before God), and *savior*. However, he does not prosecute or judge and does not anticipate a history terminating *eschaton* and *parousia*.

5-6. *The Fifth and Sixth Logia: Son of Man as Bread of Heaven*

In 6.27-59 there is a set of two Son of Man logia. In the first of the two, the fifth Johannine Son of Man logion, Jesus declares

> ἐργάζεσθε μὴ τὴν βρῶσιν τὴν ἀπολλυμένην ἀλλὰ τὴν βρῶσιν τὴν μένουσαν εἰς ζωὴν αἰώνιον ἣν ὁ υἱὸς τοῦ ἀνθρώπου ὑμῖν δώσει· τοῦτον γὰρ ὁ πατὴρ ἐσφράγισεν ὁ θεός... ('Do not labor for the food which perishes, but for the food which endures to eternal life, which the Son of Man will give to you, for on him has God the father set his seal...', 6.27).

There are no variants to this text which in any significant way modify it.[97]

96. Haenchen, *John 1*, pp. 253-54. See Bultmann, *The Gospel of John*, pp. 260f.

97. In ℵ and D we have ὑμῖν δώσει replaced by δίδοσιν ὑμῖν but this change to the future tense does not change the sense of the text. Brown (*The Gospel according to John*, p. 261) and Moloney (*The Gospel of John*, p. 210) prefer the future tense for theological reasons, despite their acknowledgment that the present tense is much more well attested in the early sources (ℵ B *al* L, and Curetorian Syriac), with the exception of P[75]. Their emphasis is upon the allusions to the Eucharist in vv. 35, 50-51, and

In the pericope containing the sixth Johannine logion (6.35-59 [53]) Jesus continues his discussion of the food of eternal life that he gives believers:

> εἶπεν αὐτοῖς ὁ Ἰησοῦς· Ἐγώ εἰμι ὁ ἄρτος τῆς ζωῆς· ὁ ἐρχόμενος πρός ἐμὲ οὐ μὴ πεινάσῃ καὶ ὁ πιστεύων εἰς ἐμὲ οὐ μὴ διψήσει πώποτε... (35) ἐγώ εἰμι ὁ ἄρτος ὁ ζῶν ὁ ἐκ τοῦ οὐρανοῦ καταβάς· ἐάν τις φάγῃ ἐκ τούτου τοῦ ἄρτου ζήσει εἰς τὸν αἰῶνα καὶ ὁ ἄρτος δὲ ὃν ἐγὼ δώσω ἡ σάρξ μού ἐστιν ὑπὲρ τῆς τοῦ κόσμου ζωῆς... (51), εἶπεν οὖν αὐτοῖς ὁ Ἰησοῦς· Ἀμὴν ἀμὴν λέγω ὑμῖν ἐὰν μὴ φάγητε τὴν σάρκα τοῦ υἱοῦ τοῦ ἀνθρώπου καὶ πίητε αὐτοῦ τὸ αἷμα οὐκ ἔχετε ζωὴν ἐν ἑαυτοῖς ὁ τρώγων μου τὴν σάρκα καὶ πίνων μου τὸ αἷμα ἔχει ζωὴν αἰώνιον κἀγὼ ἀναστήσω αὐτὸν τῇ ἐσχάτῃ ἡμέρᾳ (53) ('Jesus said to them, "I am the bread of life, he who comes to me shall not hunger, and he who believes in me shall never thirst..." [35]. "I am the living bread, that which came down from heaven; if any one eats of this bread, he will live forever; and the bread which I shall give for the life of the world is my flesh..." [51]. Then Jesus said to them, *"Truly, truly, I say to you, if you do not eat the flesh of the Son of Man and drink his blood, you have no life in you*; he who eats my flesh and drinks my blood has eternal life, and I will raise him up at the last day"' [53-54]).

No significant variants appear in the sources regarding v. 53 in which this Son of Man logion appears.[98]

5-6.1. *Context: Son of Man as Source of God Given Nurture*

As noted in the foregoing, the discussion in John 5 regarding the Son of Man as judge, leads naturally to this pericope in Jn 6.27-59. The only intervening narrative is the feeding of the multitude near Capernaum and the calming of the Sea of Galilee that night. It is the story of Jesus being sought intensely by the crowd which has acknowledged him as a prophet. They wish to see his miracles and hear his teaching. John 6 is the unfolding of that teaching. This pericope with its two Son of Man logia is followed by another such logion (vv. 60-65), as well as by the disaffection of many of

---

53-59, which they point out as still forthcoming at the point of v. 27. Their argument is unpersuasive and basically irrelevant, even regarding the theological issue they raise.

98. D has λάβητε instead of φάγητε; thus, 'unless you take my flesh...'. replaces 'unless you eat my flesh...'. Clearly the sense of the metaphor is the same in either case, particularly since it is followed immediately with the clause, 'and drink my blood...'. Brown (*The Gospel according to John*, p. 282) cites Joseph J. O'Rourke, 'Two Notes on St. John's Gospel', *CBQ* 25 (1963), pp. 126-28, as making a significant issue of the fact that in the various references in John 6 to eating and drinking, in verses 26, 50, and 51, 'the verb "to eat" (*esthiein* [sic], *phagein*) takes *ek* and the genitive before its object; it is used with direct accusative in vi 23, 31, 49, 53'. O'Rourke makes the same issue of the fact that *pinein* ('drink') is 'used with *ek* and the genitive in ch. iv, and with the accusative here'. Brown's criticism of this unnecessary attenuation of what is essentially a non-issue, is gentle. He declares, almost humorously that O'Rouke's 'differentiation seems oversubtle'.

his disciples (vv. 66-71), and Jesus' fearful refusal to go to Jerusalem for the feast (7.1-9). Thereafter the tragic drama of the final days of Jesus' life are set in motion (7:10–19.42). This context heightens the psychological urgency implied in these three Son of Man logia in this intriguing and complicated sixth chapter of the gospel.

5-6.2. *Meaning: Theology of Incarnation, Eucharist, or Son of Man as Savior*

Haenchen, with Bultmann, thinks a redactor is at work in this pericope (vv. 27-59) endeavoring to establish theological claims regarding the Eucharist and associating them directly with the teaching of Jesus. He is confident that these two Son of Man logia (vv. 27 and 53), set in this eucharistic context, form an intentional anti-gnostic statement. While the Christian Eucharist, as described here, 'is a mystery that is not to be made rationally accessible to those outside…, "to have life in oneself" means the prospect of being raised up at the last judgment', and has inherently to do with being 'in Christ' by virtue of one's faith, not by reason of an esoteric knowledge and exalted role or station in the gnostic psychology or cosmology.[99] Hare thinks this logion is only secondarily eucharistic and its main meaning refers to the theology of the incarnation, the Word becoming flesh (1.14).[100] Reynolds observes that 'As one who is able to give the food that does not perish but remains to eternal life, the Son of Man plays an important role as the giver of eternal life'. The important emphasis here, in Reynolds' view, is the 'Johannine Son of Man's role in salvation'. He sees this as a reinforcement of the theme in 3.12-18.[101]

Undoubtedly, Jn 6.27 and 53 are the most perplexing passages in the Fourth Gospel, but the narrative linking them assures us of their metaphoric meaning and setting. In 6.56 Jesus is reported as saying,

ὁ τρώγων μου τὴν σάρκα καὶ πίνων μου τὸ αἷμα ἐν ἐμοὶ μένει κἀγὼ ἐν αὐτῷ
('He who eats my flesh and drinks my blood abides in me, and I in him').

Apparently the simile of eating and drinking is intended to describe devoted identification with Jesus as the Son of Man: presumably belief in him as the revealer of the divine mysteries and the one who saves. Keener thinks the concluding clause in 6.27 regarding God setting his seal on Christ is indication of a special effort on the part of the gospel author to resolve the perplexity in 6.27 and 53 by citing Jewish tradition that if God seals something it can be taken as absolute truth (*Gen. Rab.* 81.2).[102]

---

99. Haenchen, *John 1*, pp. 290, 295, 300.
100. Hare, *Son of Man Tradition*, pp. 98-99.
101. Reynolds, *Apocalyptic Son of Man*, p. 148.
102. Keener, *The Gospel of John*, p. 678.

Moloney focuses his interpretation of this entire pericope, and its two Son of Man logia, upon the cross, asserting that the primary reference throughout is the crucifixion. Drawing out the mysterious symbolism of this narrative to that extent and in that direction, seems, at best, an imposition of Orthodox creedal theology upon a proto-eucharistic text.[103] Another incongruity in Moloney's perspective, as we noted in the Introduction to this work, and that is particularly important to mention at this juncture, is his tendency to divide the heavenly *Logos* in Jesus from the man, Jesus; consistently reading the title, Son of Man, as a reference to Jesus' humanity while asserting the separate divine and heavenly nature of the incarnate *Logos*. 'There is a concentration on the human figure of Jesus in the use of the "Son of Man"'.[104]

Ashton counters Moloney forthrightly, declaring that in all the Son of Man sayings in John we are constantly confronted with Jesus' central expression of his self-revelation as the divine *Logos*-infested person from heaven.

> The title embodies the theme of Jesus' heavinly origin and destiny, and does so often enough to be significant in terms of his descent and (more frequently) ascent. It therefore adds to Messiahship and Sonship...the notion of pre-existence. What it does *not* convey, paradoxically, is either humanity (which mostly rests upon the messianic titles) or any suggestion of sonship (differing in this respect from the title 'Son', which points directly to Jesus' relationship with God).[105]

Six times in this pericope of 32 verses, Jesus states or alludes to the fact that he is a heavenly figure and he has descended from heaven (6.33, 35, 38, 46, 50, 51). Four times he describes himself as the one who raises the dead to everlasting life (6.39, 40, 44, 54). Eleven times he declares that he gives life and eternal life to all believers (6.27, 33, 35, 40, 47, 48, 50, 51, 53-54, 57, 58). Six times Jesus emphasizes that he is unveiling the mysteries of God to the world of humans (6.29, 32-33, 37-40, 44-45, 46, 57). Moreover, he makes it plain that this form and level of vitality is intended to be given to the entire universe (6.51).

Keener observes that Jesus' expression, in 6.27-59 about eating his flesh and drinking his blood,

> invites disgust from his contemporaries. The ancient Mediterranean world shared nearly universally a disgust for cannibalism... Some claimed that their patron deities, such as Isis and Osiris, put an end to an earlier practice of cannibalism. This disgust probably rose to one of its greatest heights in

---

103. Moloney, *The Gospel of John*, pp. 210, 224.
104. Moloney, *The Johannine Son of Man* (Rome: Pontifical Institute Press, 1976), p. 213.
105. Ashton, *Understandig the Fourth Gospel*, p. 243.

Judaism. It is known that second-century Christians faced accusations of
cannibalism, based on a misinterpretation of the Lord's Supper; possibly
such accusations were already circulating when John was written.[106]

Bultmann found these logia in chap. 6 particularly revolting. He is
sure they were inserted into the gospel at a late moment in the post-Easter
church's life, and were included to ground its eucharistic practices.[107] Both
he and Lightfoot do not clarify what one is to do with the enigmatic Son of
Man logia in 6.35 and 53, as Jesus' own definitions of his identity and role.
Lightfoot spiritualized the entire chapter and focused only on the Gnostic-
like idea of a believer's esoteric experience of life derived from identification with Jesus as Son of Man: 'All these similtudes are to be understood as
descriptive of some aspect of the Lord's work as the Word become flesh...
The words, "I am the bread of life" reveal that the Lord Himself is the gift
which He brings...but the expression should be understood as including the
power to bring life into being; life proceeds from life'.[108]

Hunter, with Sloyan, Morris, Howard and Gossip, Tenney, Beasley-
Muray, and Haenchen mainly express interest, as did John Calvin, in the
proto-eucharistic character of the Son of Man monologues in John 6 and
in the fact that these focus constantly upon his conveyance of the life-giv-
ing spiritual nurture (bread from heaven) that lends a heavenly dimension
to earthly human existence. It affords the gift of salvation in the sense of
mundane spiritual satisfaction (an end to spiritual hungering and thirsting),
resurrection at the last day, and eternal life. They see this long, unique discourse on the *bread of life* as sacramental language, but meaningful in terms
of the fact that Jesus has just fed the multitude and is going shortly to the
Passover meal. The meaning of both of these 'bread events' is illumined
by this monologue on Jesus as the source of true spiritual nourishment.
The Son of Man is the one who refreshes the human spirit as he reveals the
divine mysteries about God's action in the world in bringing in the kingdom. This is a metaphor about faith in the Son of Man. The one who eats
the celestial bread and drinks the celestial wine is identified with the Son
of Man (ἐν Χριστῷ) and experiences the refreshing nurture of the spirit
that comes with the transcendental perspective on life and eternity. Moreover, there is an anti-Gnostic reference in the notion that such a believer
shall 'have life in himself' in time and in eternity, rather than merely being
absorbed in the *pleroma*.[109]

---

106. Keener, *The Gospel of John*, pp. 687-88.
107. Bultmann, *The Gospel of John*, pp. 222-37.
108. Lightfoot, *St. John's Gospel*, pp. 151-64, 167.
109. Hunter, *The Gospel according to John*, pp. 68-74. See also Sloyan, *John*, pp.
67-75; Morris, *The Gospel of John*, 317-37; Howard and Gossip, *The Gospel according to St. John*, pp. 566-74; Tenney, *The Gospel of John*, pp. 75-78; Beasley-Murray,

Jesus had already twice referred, in his conversation with Nicodemus, to the believer's experience of the reign of God as advent into *real life* (3.3, 6).[110] Sloyan adds that it is common for the leader in any religion to be figuratively identified as the source of nourishment.[111] Beasley-Murray discerns in the symbolism of eating and drinking allusions to eschatological salvation through the word of wisdom from God, as found in Isa. 55.1, Prov. 6.5, and Sir. 24.21. In contrast to the incarnated divine *Logos* in John, Sirach has personified divine Wisdom, declaring, 'Whoever feeds on me will be hungry for more, and whoever drinks from me will thirst for more'.[112] Morris and Tenney note that this figure of bread is a way of linking real life in the closest fashion with the Son of Man.[113]

Keener thinks that in this passage Jesus moves from the attention-getting provocation of disgust in his hearers to symbolic reference to Passover image and terminology. Eating flesh and drinking blood elicit memory of rabbinic debate about eating the Passover lamb and drinking the blood of grapes in the Passover cup. Keener thinks the manna image is evoked but the paschal lamb is a Johannine motif (1.19; 19.36), and surely lies here in the background, at least. In eating his flesh and drinking his blood we have a decisive reinterpretation of the Passover. 'Here Jesus probably refers not to a sacrament in the modern sense, but to embracing his death... One thinks also of the language of eating and drinking divine wisdom'.[114]

In 6.35, as in his conversation with the Samaritan woman in John 4, Jesus alludes directly to the sapiential tradition, employing the symbolism of water (4.7-15), bread (6.27, 35, 50, 53), and blood (6.53-56), for the spiritually satisfying gifts of divine wisdom which must be ingested. Undoubtedly, Jesus is speaking here of personified Wisdom herself: 'Wisdom invites hearers, "Come to me", addressing their hunger and thirst (Sir. 24.19-21)'.[115]

Moloney's perspective on Jn 6.35 and 53 is wholly post-Nicene sacramental theology, emphasizing the critical nature of renewed spiritual life related to mystical faith in the experience of the Eucharist.[116] Brown summarized modern theories regarding the Son of Man in Jn 6.27-59. This passage

---

John, pp. 92-95; Haenchen, *John 1*, pp. 291, 295. See also John Calvin, *The Gospel according to St John, Part One: A New Translation 1–10* (trans. T.H.L. Parker; *Calvin's New Testament Commentaries*; Grand Rapids: Eerdmans, 1961), pp. 153-72.

110. Hunter, *The Gospel according to John*, pp. 69, 73-74.

111. Sloyan, *John*, pp. 67-75 (70a).

112. Beasley-Murray, *John*, p. 92.

113. Morris, *The Gospel of John*, pp. 324-25, 334-35.

114. Keener, *The Gospel of John*, pp. 688-89.

115. Keener, *The Gospel of John*, p. 683.

116. Moloney, *The Gospel of John*, pp. 207-26.

(vv. 35-58) is about the revelation present in Jesus, a 'sapiential' interpretation of vv. 35-58, but in vv. 51-58 the bread refers to both revelation and the
eucharistic flesh of Jesus [as Son of Man]. Many regard vv. 51-59 as a later
addition. 'Leon-Dufour sees these themes running throughout the discourse
(35-58). Our view, which is also that of Feuillet, sees the two themes in the
first discourse (35-50) which refers primarily to revelation but secondarily to
the Eucharist; the second part (51-58) refers only to the Eucharist'.[117]

Reynolds sees the Son of Man as judge in John 6, reinforcing his claim
that he finds apocalyptic evidences here for a relationship to Dan. 7.13.
This Danielic connection is a claim made by Reynolds with regard to all the
Son of Man logia in John. In this case of John 6, and in many of the other
instances, it is difficult to discern grounds for this claim in the logia themselves or in their contexts.

5-6.3. *Theological Import: Revealer of Heavenly Mysteries and Savior*

Brown saw the bread in John 6 and the water in John 4 as parallel expressions depicting revelation. So he favored the sapiential dynamics of achieving the new life through being taught, that is, gaining the proper insight.
However, he avoided falling into a Gnostic interpretation by emphasizing
the growth in insight through the eucharistic identification with the Son of
Man. For Brown the entire passage was wholly metaphorical, and related
to the Hebrew tradition of Wisdom, as in Sir. 24.21 and more particularly
Sir. 15.3. There the pious person is informed that he or she will experience
the life giving ministry of Wisdom: 'She will nourish him with the bread of
understanding and give him the water of learning to drink'.[118] Specifically
regarding the Son of Man logia in 6.27 and 53, Brown observed that Jesus
spoke of God's bread descending from heaven as a source of life and spiritual vitality for the world. Since 3.13 asserts that Jesus has come down from
heaven he is obviously speaking of himself as the life giving bread from
God, meaning that he reveals the truth that nourishes and refreshes humanity. This moves his claim beyond the Wisdom literature to the personification of divine revelation.

> When Jesus says that those who believe in him shall never be hungry or
> thirsty, he is expressing the same idea that he will proclaim in xi 25-27:
> 'I am the life...he who believes in me shall never die at all'. Under all
> these metaphors of bread, water, and life, Jesus is symbolically referring to
> the same reality, ...which, when once possessed, makes a man see natural
> hunger, thirst, and death as insignificant.[119]

117. Brown, *The Gospel according to John*, p. 272.
118. Brown, *The Gospel according to John*, p. 273.
119. Brown, *The Gospel according to John*, p. 275.

In an effort to understand what these logia (6.27, 53) intend us to discern about the Son of Man, Keener observes that it is difficult to miss some eucharistic language shining through these expressions, but it is even more difficult to discern what one should make of that language. John actually fails to report the final paschal meal in the narrative of Jesus' final week. He thinks that, in view of the fact that some Christians had, according to Paul, begun to be preoccupied with the *agape* meal itself rather than with the event to which it pointed (1 Cor. 11.17-26) John seems here to be redirecting attention to the bread (and wine, 6.35) as a lens through which to understand identification with the Son of Man in his crucifixion. In this he would be trying to avoid a kind of proto-Docetism.[120]

McGrath sharpens the point, noting that the issue is not whether there is eucharistic imagery here but that the imagery is shaped to make the Christological declaration of the Son of Man, himself, being the bread of life from heaven.[121] John creatively employed Second Temple and Pharisaic traditions to link the Son of Man with the divine Wisdom that descended into the world, certifying the Son of Man as having the qualifications both to reveal God and to do so in a way superior to Moses. God gives the bread of heaven and the Son of Man is that bread of life. Both Wisdom and the Son of Man come down from heaven and reveal the mysteries of God, and both are identified in John with Jesus.[122]

This set of Son of Man logia in 6.27 and 6.53, in their extraordinary context (6.27-58), are indicating the theological understanding that the Son of Man is a *heavenly figure* who has descended to earth; that he is the *savior*, the source of spiritual nurture, vitality and life for time and eternity; and that for this reason he is also the resurrector of the dead. Thus he is the *revealer* of the divine mysteries of authentic spirituality, salvation, and eternal life.

7. *The Seventh Logion: The Ascending Son of Man*

The final Son of Man logion in chap. 6, and the seventh such logion in this gospel, is in v. 62. The audience of Jesus' monologue on the bread from heaven had found it enigmatic and had expressed real problems with understanding and tolerating it. Jesus' purported response was:

Τοῦτο ὑμᾶς σκανδαλίζει ἐὰν οὖν θεωρῆτε τὸν υἱὸν τοῦ ἀνθρώπου ἀναβαίνοντα ὅπου ἦν τὸ πρότερον ('Do you take offense at this [references to eating his flesh and drinking his blood]? Then what if you were to see the Son of Man ascending where he was before?' 6.61b-62.)

120. Keener, *The Gospel of John*, p. 690.
121. McGrath, *The Gospel according to John*, p. 174.
122. McGrath, *The Gospel according to John*, pp. 178, 222.

Some insignificant and poorly attested variants appear in a few late sources for 6.62, for example the replacement of the present tense, second-person plural subjunctive, θεωρῆτε, with the aorist, second-person plural subjunctive θεωρήσητε of θεωρέω, without substantially altering the meaning.[123]

While these variants are of little account, the complexity of the hypothetical implications of the subjunctive produces a stressed syntax which Brown described well in words similar to Morris' sentiments.[124] Brown stated that this sentence is elliptic and is not clear on the implied ending or consequence. Does it refer to the scandal mentioned in v. 61 (Bultmann and Bauer), or to what was said in 48-58 about understanding the meaning of the bread from heaven (Thüsing, 261), or 51-58 about definitive decision making regarding the Son of Man? 'Notice that Jesus does not say definitely that they will see this ascension; it is left hypothetical. ... There is an implication that the Son of Man has descended, a notion which we have seen... to be quite unusual. This ascension to the Father is through crucifixion and resurrection'.[125]

7.1. *Context: Heavenly Nurture from the Heavenly Son of Man*
The context of this logion is formed mainly by Jesus' preceding monologue regarding his being the bread of life which came down from heaven (6.25-59), his subsequent ambivalence about attending the feast in Jerusalem, and the consternation of the Jerusalem religious authorities regarding his interpretation of the Mosaic law. The troublesomeness of his interpretation is exacerbated by his breaking of that law through healing on the Sabbath. Since the crowd (6.41) and the disciples (6.60) cannot accept Jesus' claim to have descended from heaven, he asks (6.62) how they would handle it if they should see him ascending to where he was before. Chapter 7 ends with the chief priests and Pharisees designing to kill him because the crowd began to acclaim him as a prophet and as the Messiah. This led to Nicodemus' remarkable statement that the law does not judge any one until he has been given a judicial hearing.

7.2. *Meaning: Son of Man as the Watershed of the Divine Reign*
It is clear that Jesus intended his remark in 6.62 to stir up debate and quandary among the multitude regarding the watershed nature and role of the Son

---

123. This variant is attested only by P[66] and pc lat; W and pc have ἴδητε, and P[66] D and Θ have οὐ before the last clause in 6.62 so as to read: οὐ ὅπου ἦν τὸ πρότερον See Stanley E. Porter, *Idioms of the Greek New Testament* (Sheffield: Sheffield Academic Press, 1992), Chapters 1 and 2 on Tense and Aspect, and Mood and Attitude, particularly pp. 24-26, 28-39, 52-61.

124. Morris, *The Gospel of John*, p. 339.

125. Brown, *The Gospel according to John*, p. 296.

of Man in history, in God's reign in history, and in their personal salvation. Moreover, it is evident that his remark succeeded in doing just that. Haenchen sees it as theologically important that Jesus, as Son of Man, here sets himself against all biblical and Second Temple Judaism traditions, indeed, against the entire world, as the only person who knows the true mysteries of God and the heavenly world, and is the only source of eternal life.[126] Moloney understands this logion as linking Jesus to all the great revealers in Jewish history who were thought to have ascended to heaven, such as Enoch, Elijah, and especially Moses.[127] However, the point of John 6 is to depict the absolute distinctiveness of Jesus presence in the world. Moreover, it follows closely upon the declaration in 3.13 that no one ascends into heaven except the one who descended from heaven, i.e., the Son of Man.

Tenney agrees with Beasley-Murray, who catches the profundity of this passage in its context much more comprehensively than most of the scholarly community. He comments that Jesus' reply in v. 62 has a dual application. 'They who stumble at the doctrine of the descent of one who calls himself the Living Bread, who gives himself for the life of the world, are to be confronted with a terrible and awesome phenomenon: they will see the Son of Man ascend where he was before. […] The Son of Man is to be "lifted up" (3.14), and the world will be divided before him (12.31-32). They who deny the descent will look upon it as the final ground of rejection, whereas they who can see signs may see in this event the ultimate sign which illuminates all their problems'. Crucifixion will be the occasion of recognizing the Son of Man, making the new interpretation of the Passover meaningful. Members of the post-Easter church who found this teaching difficult, would find that 62-63 could lead to the falling of the scales from the eyes. 'The words of Jesus in the discourse are "Spirit and life"—for those who receive them in faith, since they who accept them and believe in the Son receive the Spirit and the life of which he speaks (5.39-40 and 7.37-39)'.[128]

Sloyan agrees, 'The life giving spirit that Jesus' spoken words constitute, if received in faith, make everything spirit not flesh, life not death (v. 63)'.[129] It is Sloyan's perception that this sentiment binds together the entire message from 6.25-71, epitomized in 6.62, i.e., that everything is believable to those who see the ascent of the Son of Man to the true heavenly home of the incarnate *Logos*. Hare and McGrath add that this passage focuses particularly on the preexistence of the Son of Man.[130] Hoskyns elaborates this

126. Haenchen, *John 1*, p. 305.
127. Moloney, *The Gospel of John*, p. 234.
128. Beasley-Murray, *John*, p. 96. See Tenney, *The Gospel of John*, p. 79.
129. Sloyan, *John*, p. 76.
130. Hare, *Son of Man Tradition*, p. 100; McGrath, *The Gospel according to John*, pp. 56, 100 n.75, 137 n. 28, 180, 218.

idea with the observation that the heavenly ascent of the Son of Man will 'provide the solution to the riddle of the Eucharistic terminology' that pervades the bread of life passages in John 6.[131]

7.3. *Theological Import: Heavenly Logos, Exalted Savior*
Keener notes the connection between this logion and the one that follows in 8.28. The ascent of the Son of Man is described in 6.62 as the proof of his identity. If the lifting up of the crucifixion is inadequate proof, the combination of lifting up on the cross and lifting up to heaven in the Son of Man's ascension will be persuasive for the whole world of humanity. All humankind will be drawn to him.[132] This is likely an echo of the frequently repeated Pauline *dictum* that in the end every eye shall see him, every knee shall bow, and every tongue confess that Jesus Christ is Lord, to the glory of God the Father.[133]

It is interesting that in this there is no perseveration, ambiguity, or ambivalence about the optimistic outcome of this event. It is to be universally salvific. Nonetheless, some commentators continue to pose the possibility that the logion implies, as so many have historically interpreted Paul's declaration, that some will be drawn to him for their judgment and some for their salvation. That might be discerned from 5.27 if it were isolated from the rest of the gospel, but the implications of 5.27-47, 6.62, and 8.28 can only mean a Johannine emphasis upon the universality of divine grace.

Theologically, this logion in 6.62 depicts the Son of Man as the descended and incarnate *Logos*, a *heavenly figure* who shall return to heaven. Moreover, implied in this logion, set as it is in its particular context, is the role of the Son of Man as divinely *exalted one* and universal *savior*.

8. *The Eighth Logion: The Cross as Divine Revelation*

We return in 8.28 to the figure of the Son of Man being lifted up, reminiscent of 3.14. Again we read,

---

131. Edwin C. Hoskyns, *The Fourth Gospel* (London: Faber & Faber, rev. edn, 1947), p. 301.

132. Keener, *The Gospel of John*, p. 694.

133. ζῶ ἐγώ, λέγει κύριος, ὅτι ἐμοὶ κάμψει πᾶν γόνυ καὶ πᾶσα γλῶσσα ἐξομολογήσεται τῷ θεῷ, 'As I live, says the Lord, every knee shall bow to me, and every tongue shall give praise to God' (Rom. 14.11); ἐν τῷ ὀνόματι Ἰησοῦ πᾶν γόνυ κάμψῃ ἐπουρανίων καὶ ἐπιγείων καὶ καταχθονίων, 'at the name of Jesus every knee should bow, of things in heaven, and things in earth, and things under the earth' (Phil. 2.9-11): both quoting Isa. 45.23b: ἐμοὶ κάμψει πᾶν γόνυ καὶ ἐξομολογήσεται πᾶσα γλῶσσα τῷ θεῷ, כִּי־לִי תִּכְרַע כָּל־בֶּרֶךְ תִּשָּׁבַע כָּל־לָשׁוֹן, 'To me every knee shall bow, every tongue shall swear'.

εἶπεν οὖν ὁ Ἰησοῦς· "Οταν ὑψώσητε τὸν υἱὸν τοῦ ἀνθρώπου τότε γνώσεσθε ὅτι ἐγώ εἰμι καὶ ἀπ᾽ ἐμαυτοῦ ποιῶ οὐδέν ἀλλὰ καθὼς ἐδίδαξέν με ὁ πατὴρ ταῦτα λαλῶ ('So Jesus said, "When you have lifted up the Son of Man, then you will know that I am he, and that I do nothing on my own authority but speak thus as the father taught me" ').

The wording of the text is strongly attested in the ancient sources: א D Θ P⁶⁶ᶜ·⁷⁵ lat sy and co. P⁶⁶ B L T W omit αὐτοῖς after εἶπεν οὖν, without changing the import of the passage. Similarly, א adds πάλιν after Ἰησοῦς without altering the meaning.

8.1. *Context: The Son of Man's Collision Course*

The context of this logion is the ferment among the Pharisees about doing away with Jesus and their fear of the crowd which increasingly celebrates him. Jesus is aware of this ferment and has retired to Galilee to avoid confrontation with the religious leaders in Jerusalem. Consequently, he resists going with his brothers to Jerusalem to the Passover, then changes his mind and quite obviously goes alone to aggressively challenge the crowds and the Jerusalem authorities. This precipitates a decision to arrest and kill him. Jesus predicts his death and resurrection and leads into the pronouncement of the Son of Man logion in 8.28. This is followed by an aggressive debate with the leaders and the crowd regarding their lineage from Abraham and their accusation that Jesus is a Samaritan in his messianic theology.

8.2. *Meaning: Apocalyptic Eschatological Son of Man?*

Ragnar Lievestad[134] and Markus Sasse[135] deny that this logion has apocalyptic implications, while Reynolds argues that it is particularly apocalyptic.[136] Bultmann, Lightfoot, and Morris, observed that Jesus is acknowledging that those in dialogue with him know that the Son of Man is the Messiah and savior, but they will not recognize that it is *he, Jesus of Nazareth*, until his crucifixion and ascension: 'Thus everything that he is, can be referred to by the mysterious title, "Son of Man". It is mysterious, not in so far as it is an eschatological title; for this was how his hearers understood it, as is shown by their question in 12.34; for them the Son of Man is the Messiah, the bringer of salvation. But it is mysterious in that they do not see that the eschaton which they await in the future is already present, that this man Jesus is the Son of Man'.[137]

---

134. Ragnar Leivestad, 'Exit the Apocalyptic Son of Man', *NTS* 18 (1972), pp. 243-67 (250).

135. Markus Sasse, *Der Menschensohn im Evangelium nach Johannes* (TANZ, 15; Tübingen: Francke, 2000), p. 158.

136. Reynolds, *Apocalyptic Son of Man*, pp. 162-74.

137. Bultmann, *The Gospel of John*, p. 349.

Jesus is declaring that the crowds will not understand his real identity until they have nailed him up on the cross. With regard to the identity and role of the Son of Man, 'There is a revelatory aspect to the cross and after the crucifixion those who reflect on it will be in a position to appreciate that Jesus is indeed more than a man... What he says to people is what God has spoken to him. His message is not of human origin, but divine'.[138] He is the revealer and judge, who will not act as prosecutor, but, rather is the one who saves.

Moreover, stated Bultmann, the greater mystery for the crowd is that they know the Son of Man also as the Eschatological Judge, but cannot imagine that by crucifying Jesus they make him *their* judge. They know the double meaning of 'lift up', but they do not catch on to the double meaning of 'judge', i.e., that to encounter the Son of Man is to be under judgment regarding how one will respond. When one encounters a person of high accomplishment, noble bearing, regal status, or great beauty, the manner in which one behaves produces a judgment regarding ones own character, nature, style and decorum. It does not reflect on or change the status of the regal personage.

When the crowds discern who the Son of Man really is, they will understand that he is the *Messiah,* a *savior,* the *judge* who refuses to prosecute them, and the one in whom God's heavenly kingdom mysteries are *revealed*: grace that works and love that heals. Whoever hears of the divine revealer and fails to believe him as Messiah and savior, identifies with the crowd that crucified him. 'The Cross was the Jews' last and definitive answer to Jesus' word of revelation, and whenever the world gives its final answer in the words of unbelief it "lifts up" the Revealer and makes him its judge'.[139]

Sloyan and Schnackenburg emphasize mainly that this logion presents the Son of Man as revealer of the divine mysteries, i.e., of God's purposes in history and in eternity and the impending reign of God on earth.[140] Tenney and Beasley-Murray notice a slightly different point of interest suggested by the term 'lifted up'. They are quite sure that in Jn 3.14 it is a specific reference to the crucifixion of the Son of Man. However, they note that Jesus there relates his being 'lifted up' to the healing effect of Moses' bronze serpent. Moreover, both scholars emphasize that the biblical term, 'lift up', usually means 'to set in a place of prominence, to exalt'. Thus, the lifting up of the Son of Man will give visible prominence to him, so that he will be hard to miss and hard to avoid. They conclude that Jesus intends to say that

---

138. Morris, *The Gospel of John*, p. 401. See Lightfoot, *St. John's Gospel*, pp. 191-93.

139. Bultmann, *The Gospel of John*, p. 350.

140. Sloyan, *John*, pp. 99-100. See also Rudolf Schnackenburg, *The Gospel according to John* (3 vols.; New York: Crossroad, 1968–1982).

in his impending crucifixion he will (1) be identified for who he really is as the Son of Man, (2) be known as the one who heals by his role as Suffering Servant, and (3) be exalted or glorified. All this he asserts later in 12.23: 'The hour has come for the Son of Man to be glorified;' and in 12.32: 'I, when I am lifted up from the earth, will draw all men to myself'.[141]

Beasley-Murray connects this logion with Isa. 52.13, ἰδοὺ συνήσει ὁ παῖς μου καὶ ὑψωθήσεται καὶ δοξασθήσεται σφόδρα ('My servant will be exalted and greatly glorified').[142]

The eschatological context and redemptive content depends upon Dan. 7.13, according to Beasley-Murray. There 'one like a son of man' appears as the representative of the kingdom of God and its lord (possibly agent too). 'In the synoptic predictions of the Passion (notably Mk 8.31; 9.31; 10.32), which are closely related to the Johannine lifting up sayings, the Son of Man suffers, dies, and rises as the instrument of the kingdom of God. This Christological, soteriological, and eschatological tradition is assumed in the Johannine counterparts'.[143] What is special about the Johannine content is the claim that those responsible for Jesus' death will finally understand his real identity, his heavenly nature, and the vocation of his ministry.

Hoskyns urgently makes the point that this is not a statement about judgment or punishment, as Rudolph Schnackenburg,[144] Bultmann,[145] Barrett,[146] Joseph Blank,[147] Haenchen,[148] Brown,[149] and Jürgen Becker[150] claimed; but about hope and the role and identity of the Son of Man in salvation.[151] In John's Gospel the Son of Man is the judge who refuses to judge or prosecute because he does not need to do so. He insists instead on the role of savior.

Bultmann claimed that the text means, as Hare phrases it in criticism of Bultmann, 'When you crucify me, then you will realize, too late, that I am your judge'. Hare says that Bultmann is in error here. However, there is some suggestion in Hare's argument that he might be erroneously proposing that the term Son of Man refers here to Jesus' human nature, rather than to the

---

141. Tenney, *The Gospel of John*, p. 94.

142. Beasley-Murray, *John*, p. 131.

143. Beasley-Murray, *John*, p. 131.

144. Rudolf Schnackenburg, *The Gospel according to St John* (3 vols.; HTCNT; London: Burns & Oates, 1982), pp. 202-203.

145. Bultmann, *The Gospel of John*, pp. 349-50.

146. Barrett, *Gospel*, p. 344.

147. Joseph Blank, *The Gospel according to St John* (NTSR, 8–9; New York: Crossroad, 1981), pp. 329-30.

148. Haenchen, *John 1*, II, p. 28.

149. Brown, *The Gospel according to John*, p. 351.

150. Jürgen Becker, *Das Evangelium des Johannes* (2 vols.; OTKNT, 4/1–2. Gütersloh: G. Mohn, 1981), p. 296.

151. Hoskyns, *The Fourth Gospel*, p. 337.

humanly incarnated *Logos*.[152] The title, Son of Man, throughout John's gospel, as we have demonstrated repeatedly so far, and as is evident in the remaining logia to be discussed, is the incarnated *Logos*; it is the identity of Jesus; and it is the messianic suffering servant who will be divinely glorified.

Hare asks: 'Is the prediction intended positively or negatively, as a promise of salvation or of judgment? The commentators divide on this issue, partly on the basis of whether, …since Jesus' relationship with God involves him in both salvation and judgment, it is possible that both are in mind here'.[153] He thinks that some will discern the truth about the Son of Man and be saved through their identification with him; while others will perceive who he really is and acknowledge that he is their judge because they do not embrace him as the savior. Hare thinks the Fourth Gospel here parallels the Synoptic Gospels. He overlooks, however, that the entire trajectory of this gospel is in opposition to the Synoptic Gospels specifically on this point. In Mark, Matthew, and Luke Jesus is the earthly Son of Man who will become the heavenly Eschatological Judge; whereas in John he is the divine and heavenly Son of Man as incarnated *Logos*, who has the ἐξουσία to judge (5.27), decides not to judge or prosecute (3.17; 5.22, 27-47; 8.15; 12.47), and so stands as the watershed factor in history that will draw all humanity to salvation (3.16; 8.28; 12.32), returning to his heavenly home as savior of the world (3.16-17).

Tenney and others note that in this passage, while clarifying his identity and role as the Son of Man, Jesus repeatedly employs the term, 'I am'. The term ἐγώ εἰμι appears three times in this pericope (8.24, 28, 58) and frequently throughout the Fourth Gospel. It means, 'I am who I claim to be, namely, the Son of Man'. There is reason to believe that the frequent ἐγώ εἰμι statements associated with the Son of Man in John are instances of the intentional employment of a Greek translation of the Hebrew tetragrammaton, the divine name, put into the mouth of Jesus and predicating self-existence and eternal being. In the context of this logion, the repetition of the ἐγώ εἰμι statement expresses Jesus' identity with God and the derivation from God of both his nature and message as Son of Man. Hare agrees: 'In his use of the *ego eimi* formula, the Johannine Jesus presents himself as the one uniquely related to God, the one who in some sense is the bearer or manifestation of the sacred Name'.[154] Daube takes *ego eimi* in this passage as meaning 'the Messiah is present', following an unpublished suggestion of Thomas Manson.[155]

152. Hare, *Son of Man Tradition*, p. 103.

153. Hare, *Son of Man Tradition*, p. 104.

154. Hare, *Son of Man Tradition*, p. 102.

155. David Daube, *The New Testament and Rabbinic Judaism* (London: Athlone Press, 1956), pp. 325-29.

Keener speaks poignantly on the matter. He suggests that we have here an atypical Johannine double *entendre*. The Evangelist refers to Jesus as the Word present at the beginning of creation (1.1-2; 8.16-30, 58; 9.32). Then he also sets up the equation in which the opponents of the Son of Man will lift him up on the cross without recognizing his real identity; but in this act his deity as the incarnate *Logos* will be revealed (8.24; 4.26), and that will inspire faith in them (12.32-33; 8.30). In this they will fulfill the divine mission on earth and exalt the Son of Man to glory. Therein they will glorify God.[156]

8.3. *Theological Import: Son of Man Who Embraces All Humanity*
The author of John's gospel has Jesus identifying himself in this logion as the Son of Man who is the *suffering servant*, the *revealer* of divine mysteries, and by implication, the universal *savior* of the world.

9. *The Ninth Logion: Son of Man as Illuminating Revealer of God's Purposes*

The entire narrative in John 9 is devoted to a profound and tragi-comic story of the healing of the blind man on the Sabbath day. The critical moment for our purposes arrives after the authorities have thrown the healed blind man out of the sanctuary and exiled him from the community. We read of this in 9.35, and its import is amplified by 9.39:

> ῞Ηκουσεν ᾿Ιησοῦς ὅτι ἐξέβαλον αὐτὸν ἔξω καὶ εὑρὼν αὐτὸν εἶπεν· Σὺ πιστεύεις εἰς τὸν υἱὸν τοῦ ἀνθρώπου ... καὶ εἶπεν ὁ ᾿Ιησοῦς· Εἰς κρίμα ἐγὼ εἰς τὸν κόσμον τοῦτον ἦλθον ἵνα οἱ μὴ βλέποντες βλέπωσιν καὶ οἱ βλέποντες τυφλοὶ γένωνται ('Jesus heard that they had cast him out, and having found him he said, "Do you believe in the Son of Man?"' ...Jesus said, "For judgment I came into this world, that those who do not see may see, and that those who see may become blind"').

The text containing this logion is adequately attested in the dependable ancient sources. There are no significant variants. The context in the last pericope in chap. 8 concerns the Jews' accusation that Jesus' perspective on God and things messianic reminds them of Samaritans. They accuse him of being crazy, that is, possessed of a demon (8.48). Jesus' response is enigmatic. He denies that he is crazy but claims he does the will of his father, God. This provokes the discussion about their father Abraham and Jesus' superiority to Abraham. They prepare to stone him. He is immediately distracted by the blind man and spends the entire narrative of chap. 9 dealing with him. Sloyan observes that 'This chapter is unique in its narrative power and delineation of the work of Jesus', as Son of Man.[157]

---

156. Keener, *The Gospel of John*, p. 745.
157. Sloyan, *John*, p. 121.

9.1. *Context: Son of Man versus the Religious Authorities*

Bultmann's reading of John 9 is of special interest. He discerned the dynamics of the narrative to be those of an encounter between an informed Second Temple Jew and the Son of Man as revealer of the heavenly mysteries. The blind man whom Jesus has healed knows the tradition of the Messiah and he associates the Son of Man with that messianic expectation. The man does not envision the messianic Son of Man, however, as appearing on the clouds of heaven in a future *parousia*. He responds to Jesus' question in a manner indicating that he expects that messianic figure to be around there somewhere, as a person he may encounter. He asks, 'Who is he, Sir, that I may believe in him. Which one of these persons around here is the Son of Man. I would like to meet him and know him'.[158] The blind man, now seeing, must encounter the Son of Man as *revealer* of the heavenly mysteries of salvation, said Bultmann, if he is to move the one step further in his Judaism, to believe in the name of the Son of Man (3.16-18) as *savior*.

9.2. *Meaning: Son of Man as Judge or Savior?*

Hunter, Lightfoot, Morris, Howard and Gossip, and Tenney all emphasize that this logion especially expresses the Second Temple Judaism tradition that the Son of Man is the Eschatological Judge. However, they note, this logion typifies, indeed, epitomizes the distinctive Johannine emphasis. The Son of Man who has the power and authority to be the Eschatological Judge consistently chooses instead to function as the savior. Beasley-Murray, Martyn, Barrett, Barclay, and Schnackenburg note that Jesus' question of the blind man, 'Do you believe in the Son of Man?', does not mean 'Do you believe in the existence of the Son of Man?' It means, rather, 'Do you put your trust in the Son of Man?' as in 3.14-18, 28, 36, and the like. This is in keeping with Bultmann's reading. The import of this question is to represent the Son of Man not simply as the expected Eschatological Judge, but 'as the one who mediates the salvation of the kingdom of God, which in this Gospel is chiefly represented as eternal life'.[159]

Hare explains that the belief that is required for receiving this salvation is the acceptance of the mystery of the incarnation, that is, to believe in Jesus means accepting him as the Word made flesh for our salvation. 'John's entire Christology and soteriology are thus implied in his use of *pisteuein*... When a prepositional phrase employing *eis* or *en* is used with *pisteuein*, the

---

158. Bultmann, *John*, pp. 338-39.
159. Beasley-Murray, *John*, p. 159. See also James Louis Martyn, *History and Theology in the Fourth Gospel* (Nashville: Abingdon Press, 1979), p. 134; Charles Kingsley Barrett, *The Gospel of John and Judaism* (trans. D.M. Smith; London: SPCK, 1975), p. 364; Barclay, *The Gospel of John*, II, pp. 46-55; and Schnackenburg, *The Gospel according to St John*, II, p. 253.

verb implies the Johannine doctrine of salvation through incarnation, and the prepositional phrase identifies the historical person to whom this faith is related'.[160] Hare rephrases Jesus' question, put to the healed man: 'Do you believe that the one who calls himself the Son of Man is the incarnate Son of God, the Savior of the world?' This does not ask for information about the man's beliefs but challenges him to be a 'believer in the Johannine sense'. Hare preserves the emphasis upon the unique Johannine perspective, though he seems to load the simple question in 9.35 with a great deal of technical theological terminology and definition that probably took the Christian community at least another century to formulate in this way.

Moloney emphasizes that the blind man's journey in this narrative from blindness to sight is intended as a symbolic expression of the spiritual journey from being under judgment for unbelief to the experience of salvation in Christ.[161] As usual with Moloney's interpretation, this seems to load the text with more post-Nicene theological orthodoxy than the text itself warrants. Moloney also wishes to emphasize the negative side of the presence of the Son of Man as judge, in line with the emphasis in the Synoptic Gospels. He seems not to take into account the unique Johannine emphasis upon the Son of Man who has set aside his *function* as judge and prosecutor, for which of course he has the divine sinecure and ἐξουσία (5.27), in favor of his role so obviously demonstrated here, namely, healing savior. This is solidly confirmed in Brown's opinion, not only by the entire thrust of the narrative in John 9 and its immediate context, but as the special theological burden of the entire Fourth Gospel.[162]

Conversely, Keener insists that in 9.35-38 Jesus not only defends the healed man who was expelled from the community of the *Ioudaioi*, but he also judges the Pharisees for their bad leadership of the people of God: 'Thus Jesus fulfills the role of an "advocate" (14.16) and prosecutor (16.8-11), just as the Spirit continues to do in John's own day'.[163] However, the narrative does not warrant the conclusion that the Son of Man here exercises judgment in the overt sense of condemnation of the unrighteous, in this case the Pharisees.

Reynolds fixes upon Jesus' ironic remark that follows this logion (9.35) four verses later (9.39),

> εἰς κρίμα ἐγὼ εἰς τὸν κόσμον τοῦτον ἦλθον, ἵνα οἱ μὴ βλέποντες βλέπωσιν καὶ οἱ βλέποντες τυφλοὶ γένωνται ('For judgment I came into this world, that those who do not see may see, and that those who see may become blind').

160. Hare, *Son of Man Tradition*, p. 105.
161. Moloney, *The Gospel of John*, pp. 295-96, 298.
162. Brown, *The Gospel according to John*, p. 375.
163. Keener, *The Gospel of John*, p. 794.

He makes much of the reference here to judgment. He is sure that it links this Son of Man logion to the Son of Man in Dan. 7.13 and, therefore, guarantees that this Johannine pericope about the Son of Man is apocalyptic.[164]

However, this argument fails on two counts. First, Daniel's Son of Man is not a judge, nor does he execute judgment. He is merely the commander of the field forces who implement the judgment that God has already executed, namely, that the evil empires of the world shall be destroyed and in their place The People of the Holy Ones of the Most High shall establish the kingdom of God on earth. Second, there is no textual reason to import into this pericope notions of eternal judgment, since Jesus makes it clear that as Son of Man he is playfully taunting the Pharisees about their blindness to their own proper calling of leadership of God's people. Their failure to see God's will and way is particularly evident in regard to their misinterpreting the Torah law of the Sabbath, and in their failure to embrace the healed blind man and the divine revealer who healed him. To import into this passage notions of apocalyptic and eschatological judgment is eisegesis.

Jesus' point in his remark about judgment is that he is making an evaluation of the Pharisees' ministry and finding it wanting. The remark is about being blind and being illuminated. In this regard his discernment is that they are their own judges in the sense that they have the opportunity to see the divine will but behave as if blind to it. There is no eschatological reference, nor an apocalyptic implication here. Nor can we discern a relationship between this logion and Dan. 7.13, except that in both, quite non-apocalyptically, the Son of Man is the agent implementing the revelation of the divine will and intentions.

As is the case throughout the Fourth Gospel, Jesus speaks in less than condemnatory tones and implies that the Pharisees are, in effect, their own judges if they have eyes to see and refuse to see. This emphasis conforms to the tone set in 3.12-18 (esp. 17); 5.22, 27-47; 8.15; and 12.47. Neither God, the Father, nor the Son of Man will judge anyone, however, if light has come into the world and people love darkness more than the light, their behavior is their own judge. If the Pharisees were blind they would have no guilt. However, the very fact that they see, but turn away from the light, namely, fail to believe in the Son of Man, indicates that their behavior is their own judgment. In John, the Son of Man has the right and authority to be the judge of the living and the dead, but is, instead the revealer of the heavenly mysteries of salvation and the God-sent savior, as McGrath confirms emphatically.[165]

---

164. Reynolds, *Apocalyptic Son of Man*, pp. 101-102, 121, 136, 140, 179, 186, 215.
165. McGrath, *The Gospel according to John*, pp. 186-92 (190).

9.3. *Theological Import: Son of Man Illuminates by Revealing Divine Salvation*

The gospel, thus, depicts Jesus here as *judge, revealer* of the heavenly mysteries, and in that sense the *savior*. The latter is evident in the fact that illumination by the divine mysteries and identification with the Son of Man is the watershed issue for authentic salvation, meaningful life, and eternal security. Reynolds remarks, 'No other saying speaks so explicitly of belief in the Son of Man as when Jesus asks the man who was blind from birth: "Do you believe in the Son of Man?" '.[166] Here is epitomized the general message of John's gospel (3.18; 6.53-56; 9.35) that the acquisition of eternal salvation exclusively requires identification with the Son of Man.

10-11-12. *The Tenth, Eleventh, and Twelfth Logia: Divine Glorification*

There are three references to the Son of Man in John 12, one in Jesus' part of a dialogue and two in the crowd's response. The context is the assembly of a crowd that is curious about the resurrection of Lazarus. This gathering of people soon becomes the crowd that hails his entry into Jerusalem at the outset of his last week. Amidst this large audience that the Pharisees anxiously describe as the 'whole world' that has gone out after him (Jn 12.19), Philip and Andrew bring to Jesus' attention some Greek proselytes or Jews from the diaspora, who had indicated their desire to meet him. Then the text informs us in 12.23:

> ὁ δὲ Ἰησοῦς ἀποκρίνεται αὐτοῖς λέγων Ἐλήλυθεν ἡ ὥρα ἵνα δοξασθῇ ὁ υἱὸς τοῦ ἀνθρώπου ('Jesus answered them, "The hour is come for the Son of Man to be glorified" ').

These words are followed by Jesus' discourse on a seed needing to die before it can bring forth new life and fruit. That discourse turns into a dialogue with the crowd in which Jesus declares for a third time in the Fourth Gospel (3.14; 8.28; 12.32) that he is to be lifted up,

> κἀγὼ ἐὰν ὑψωθῶ ἐκ τῆς γῆς πάντας ἑλκύσω πρὸς ἐμαυτόν ('And I, when I am lifted up from the earth, will draw all humankind to myself').

It is his declaration about the Son of Man in 12.23ff., and his comment in 12.32 about being lifted up from the earth, that the crowd correctly interprets as a declaration that the Son of Man is to suffer death. Neither 12.23, nor 12.32-35, have significant variants. The accepted Nestle–Aland text is well attested in the ancient sources.

---

166. Reynolds, *Apocalyptic Son of Man*, p. 175.

10-11-12.1. *Context: Second Temple Son of Man and Glorified Son of Man*

Surprisingly, the crowd is clear about the fact that the Son of Man is the Messiah (Christ, the Anointed One). There is no strong tradition of linkage in Second Temple Judaism between the Messiah and the Son of Man prior to this dialogue between Jesus and the crowd. Nonetheless, the crowd seems to make this connection spontaneously, and notes that Jesus' perspective links the two as well. However, in its reference to the Son of Man-Messiah, the crowd apparently means to be referring to the concept of messiah as the human scion of David's line who was to reestablish the Davidic political domain in Palestine, expelling foreign rulers. Therefore, the narrative declares:

> ἀπεκρίθη οὖν αὐτῷ ὁ ὄχλος· Ἡμεῖς ἠκούσαμεν ἐκ τοῦ νόμου ὅτι ὁ Χριστὸς μένει εἰς τὸν αἰῶνα καὶ πῶς λέγεις σὺ ὅτι δεῖ ὑψωθῆναι τὸν υἱὸν τοῦ ἀνθρώπου τίς ἐστιν οὗτος ὁ υἱὸς τοῦ ἀνθρώπου ('So the crowd answered him, "We have heard from the law (Torah) that the Christ remains for ever. How can you say that the Son of Man must be lifted up? Who is *this* Son of Man?"', 12.34).

10-11-12.2. *Meaning: The Hour of Ultimate Divine Revelation*

Bultmann made much of the fact that the Greeks' request to know Jesus comes just at the hour of the glorification of the Son of Man, that is, his promise that he will be raised up both on the cross and also in resurrection and ascension, thus returning to his heavenly home. Bultmann also thought it interesting that the request comes through the disciples, as a practical matter of convenience, but thinks this has no principial import or meaning for a preferential role for the Son of Man in the Jewish Christian, Hellenistic Jewish Christian, or Hellenistic Christian Churches. The issue at stake for the Johannine author, Bultmann thought, is the definition of the theological role of the Son of Man as exalted Lord, with whom all humans must and eventually will gain a spiritual relationship.[167]

Beasley-Murray emphasizes this same point in observing that Jesus' reply to Andrew and Philip about the arrival of the Greeks indicates that he sees their arrival as the climax of his ministry. The hour has finally arrived, contrary to Jn 2.4 at Cana, 7.30 in Jerusalem, and 8.20 in the temple; but as in 13.1 at the Passover, 16.32 in the apocalyptic prophecy, and 17.1 in the high-priestly prayer. This hour will witness his glorification and 'the Gentiles will come under the saving sovereignty of God' through his death and subsequent exaltation to his heavenly home. Thus he will draw all to him, not just to his cross but to himself as the crucified and exalted Redeemer.[168]

---

167. Bultmann, *The Gospel of John*, pp. 423-24, 427-33.
168. Beasley-Murray, *John*, pp. 211, 213-14.

Keener and Hunter, in keeping with Lightfoot's position,[169] agree and note that Jesus does not respond to the request of the Greeks, except to interpret it as indication of the glorification of the Son of Man by way of his being lifted up and so drawing *all humanity* to him. The Greeks immediately disappear from the scene, but Jesus implies that their arrival interprets the importance of *all humanity* coming to know him for who he really is. Calvin and Lightfoot, as Hunter and Morris, elaborated this point, declaring that 'the Lord's death will *universalize* His work (italics mine). The day of a national religion, of a select or chosen people, is now over; the Lord will draw all men to Himself. And he will draw them by His submission to and conquest of death on their behalf, thus giving them part in the glory which He shares with the Father, in eternal life'.[170]

This opposes the more particularist arguments of Tenney and Moloney. The cross, an epitome of shame in the Greco-Roman world, becomes for the Son of Man the universal emblem of glorification.[171] John's implied reference for joining the notions of glorification and crucifixion is almost certainly Isa. 52.13 (LXX),

ἰδοὺ συνήσει ὁ παῖς μου καὶ ὑψωθήσεται καὶ δοξασθήσεται σφόδρα ('Behold, my servant shall prosper, he shall be exalted and lifted up, and shall be very high'; הִנֵּה יַשְׂכִּיל עַבְדִּי ירוּם וְנִשָּׂא וְגָבַהּ מְאֹד).

Bultmann understood the crowd's reaction in 12.34 as having important messianic implications. They challenge Jesus on what kind of Son of Man he is discussing. He is speaking of the death of the Son of Man while they understand from their scriptures that the Messiah continues forever. The significant implications are that the crowd associates the Son of Man with the promised Messiah and understands him to have a salvific function. 'The direct identification of the Son of Man with the Messiah shows that

169. Keener, *The Gospel of John*, II, pp. 872-73, 880-81; Hunter, *The Gospel according to John*, pp. 125-28; Lightfoot, *St. John's Gospel*, pp. 251-53.

170. Lightfoot, *St. John's Gospel*, p. 243; Hunter, *The Gospel according to John*, p. 128. Hunter appears to be dependent upon Lightfoot for the observation about the 'lifting up' in crucifixion and resurrection/ascension universalizing the work and impact of the Son of Man. See Morris, *The Gospel of John*, pp. 526-34; and Calvin, *The Gospel according to St John*, II, p. 43. Tenney wishes to emphasize that some will be drawn to the Son of Man for salvation and some for damnation (*The Gospel of John*, pp. 128-31) missing the point of the universalizing perspective of the Johannine text. Likewise, Moloney, *The Gospel of John*, pp. 346-61.

171. Barclay elaborates this point both exegetically and homiletically by emphasizing the triumph without triumphalism of the crucified Son of Man. See Barclay, *The Gospel of John*, II, pp. 123-30. Barclay persuasively cites the poetry of Kipling, Shelley, and Fosdick to make his point.

the question is prompted by their understanding of the Son of Man as the eschatological bringer of salvation'.[172]

This seems to me to press the implications of the question further than the text warrants. They ask: 'We have heard from the Law that the Messiah remains for ever! How can you say that the Son of Man must be lifted up?' There seems to be no reason to draw more from their question than the following two points. First, they know the Messiah is the Son of David who is to reestablish David's kingdom in Jerusalem, turning Israel into a perpetually independent nation of God's people, who will enjoy the eternal 'sure mercies of David':

Δαυιδ ὁ δοῦλός μου ἄρχων αὐτῶν ἔσται εἰς τὸν αἰῶνα, 'David, my servant is to be their king [ruler/leader/judge] forever', Ezek. 37.25.[173]

Second, they express the surprising realization that the Messiah is also the Son of Man.

The only allusion to their associating this with an eschatological figure who brings salvation would be the general understanding that the Son of Man will come as the Eschatological Judge in an end-time *parousia*. However, such an implication seems to be undercut by their reference to the Messiah continuing forever, presumably on David's throne in Jerusalem, in the sense of a newly re-established kingdom of David, lasting throughout history.

What seems most important about their responsive question, however, lies in the fact that according to the text, Jesus has spelled out plainly that he is the one who, when he is lifted up, will draw all humanity to himself. They do not miss a step in immediately acknowledging him as the Son of Man and Messiah. Their only mystification is about how he then could speak of his impending death. Messiahs do not die in Israelite tradition. Mark 8.31ff. strongly indicates that the disciples, themselves, held firmly that the Messiah does not suffer or die in Israelite tradition. At that point in Mark it is clear that Jesus had not yet announced his association of the Messiah with the Son of Man and Sufering Servant. That announcement follows immediately after Mk 8.31. McGrath and Hare,[174] contrary to Higgins,[175] are certain that John here depends upon the Synoptic tradition. Thus, it is all the more interesting that in Jn 12.23 and 32ff. the crowd has no difficulty with Jesus as the Son of Man or with the Son of Man as Messiah, but only with the idea of his dieing, for them an incongruity.

172. Bultmann, *The Gospel of John*, pp. 354-55.

173. See Sloyan, *John*, pp. 156-61.

174. McGrath, *The Gospel according to John*, p. 57; Hare, *Son of Man Tradition*, pp. 106-109.

175. Higgins, *Jesus*, pp. 52f. Hare (*Son of Man Tradition*, p. 107) notes that Higgins confuses and in the end counters his own argument.

10,11,12.3. *Theological Import: Glorified Logos Going Home in Exaltation*

Thus we have in these three Son of Man logia, set in their context in chap. 12, the unquestionable implications that the Son of Man is the *suffering servant*, the *messianic revealer* of God's mysteries, and the *heavenly figure* who is about to be *exalted* to heavenly status, whence he came originally. The ordeal of the crucifixion is inextricably linked to his glorification in his exaltation. The text and context of this pericope also imply the messianic *savior* function of the Son of Man, though they do not spell that out specifically. Presumably, it is for salvation and eternal life, promised by the Son of Man throughout the gospel, that he will draw all humanity to himself in his death and glorification.

13. *The Thirteenth Logion: The Son of Man*

The final Son of Man logion in the Fourth Gospel relates directly to Jesus' declaration in 12.23 that the time for the glorification of the Son of Man has arrived. In 13.31 we read:

Ότε οὖν ἐξῆλθεν λέγει Ἰησοῦς· Νῦν ἐδοξάσθη ὁ υἱὸς τοῦ ἀνθρώπου καὶ ὁ θεὸς ἐδοξάσθη ἐν αὐτῷ ('When he had gone out, Jesus said, "Now is the Son of Man glorified, and in him God is glorified"').

There are no significant variants to the Nestle–Aland text. Some ancient uncials insert a second οὖν between ἐξῆλθεν and λέγει but it does not change the meaning of the sentence. It is generally thought to be an accidental scribal redundancy in an early manuscript source of the Western manuscript family.[176]

13.1. *Context: The Passover, Last Supper, Final Hour*

The context of this logion in 13.31 is the last supper of Jesus and his disciples in the upper room. The statement begins with the observation that Judas has just left the assembly and gone out to betray Jesus to the authorities. Lightfoot, Hunter, Morris and Tenney, therefore emphasize that this logion is Jesus' expressed perception that he is now on the irreversible path to his death. The future tense of the verb, in the sentence immediately following this logion, indicating that God will glorify the Son of Man, suggests to these commentators that Jesus is referring to two events. Now the Son of Man is in the process of being glorified in the immediately impending crucifixion, and subsequently God will glorify him in resurrection and ascension. Hunter emphasizes that the advent of the Spirit at Pentecost is in view here,

---

176. The redundancy appears in A C D W Θ while P[66] and ℵ B L Δ al have the accepted text.

in that Jesus promised in Jn 14.26 that the Holy Spirit of truth, sent from God, would teach the disciples all the truth about the Son of Man.[177]

13.2. *Meaning: Glorification as Death, Resurrection, and Ascent*

Howard and Gossip[178] note that Jesus seems to express himself in this logion as though, with Judas' departure, he has now a sense of relief that, as the Son of Man, he has finally come into his destiny. The gauntlet has been thrown down, and now all is in the hand of God who is about to glorify him with the demonstration that in him God has redemptively changed the world from unrighteousness to salvation. Beasley-Murray holds the similar view, adding that Jesus' reaction to Judas departure is like that to the arrival of the Greeks (12.20-26). In both instances the events do not become occasion for further discourse by the Son of Man, but only constitute the occasion for him to observe that the beginning of the end has been signalled.

The actors are now all in place and the drama is in process, making 'the crucifixion virtually accomplished'. The world of humanity is being drawn to God in the exalted savior, Son of Man.[179] The moment of this logion in 13.31, and its message are confirmed by remembering the similar logion in 12.23ff., where Jesus told the parable of the grain of corn that must die before it can achieve real life, vitality, and fruitfulness. After 13.31 he simply describes the fruitfulness of his being lifted up as evident in the impending spread of a universal community of love and grace.

Barclay observes that it is a strange notion that the ultimate glory of God lies in the incarnation and the cross, but he concludes that there is no glory like that of being cherished in love.[180] Moloney[181] and de Boer[182] agree with Barclay and develop the idea similarly. The incarnation and cross indicate the extent to which God goes to express his love for humankind in the visit of the Son of Man, who in the end is the demonstration that 'no greater love has anyone than that he should lay down his life for his friend[s]' (Jn 15.13). The Son of Man is exalted in the painful transaction of the cross, and in the resurrection and ascension that follow it; and therein is God glorified as the

---

177. Hunter, *The Gosepl according to John*, pp. 138-39; Lightfoot, *St John's Gospel*, p. 267, Morris, *The Gospel of John*, pp. 558-60; Tenney, *The Gospel of John*, p. 141. See Porter (1992) on the scholarly debate on whether the future tense in reference to God glorifying Jesus is a temporal future (pp. 20-45). In private correspondence with this author Porter observes that he does not think the verb is a temporal future in this case.

178. Howard and Gossip, *The Gospel according to St. John*, pp. 690-91.

179. Beasley-Murray, *John*, p. 246.

180. Barclay, *The Gospel of John*, II, pp. 147-49.

181. Moloney, *The Gospel of John*, pp. 381-89.

182. Martinus C. de Boer, *Johannine Perspectives on the Death of Jesus* (CBET, 17; Kampen: Kok Pharos, 1996), pp. 186-89.

God of love that works and grace that heals. Hence it is obvious that those who are loved by the God of grace in the Son of Man should create a universal community of love and grace.

Keener[183] and Barrett[184] see the development of this community of love as the primary manifestation of the divine glory epitomized in the ordeal of the Son of Man: a world of humans who love as God loves them. The context that follows this logion suggests that this development may prove more difficult than the followers of the Son of Man suppose. Nonetheless, in the crucifixion the Son of Man is identified for who he really is; God is revealed as to what he is really doing in the world; and the believing community is inspired to really carry forward that work. This is simultaneously a glory for the Son of Man, for God, and for the fellowship of the faithful.

Hare's interpretation of 13.31 is similar, though he especially wishes to avoid the Docetism that would be implied in focusing this wholly on the glorious return of the Son of Man to his heavenly home. He emphasizes that it is important to let the text speak, particularly in the use of the term, *now*, to grasp the mystifying fact that it is the cross, with its special meaning, that is a glorification.[185] Undoubtedly Hare's caution is appropriate, but the logion itself and its subsequent context urges that the author thinks Jesus had in mind the entire remaining drama of his ordeal, probably from Gethsemane to Pentecost.

Haenchen goes to great pains to demonstrate that this logion does not imply any kind of universalism in the salvation the Son of Man brings. In doing so he departs completely from the text and context in their description of the role and consequence of the Son of Man, apparently in order to preserve a particularist Nicene or post-Nicene theology, missing Johannine (and Pauline) universalism. He asks why the glorification is announced here when Judas departs. His answer is as follows:

> Because this surrender to death, this extreme love, does not apply to everyone [that is, apparently, Judas], but only to those whom God and Jesus have chosen. God may indeed love the world—that does not imply that the whole world will be saved, even if God sacrifices himself for it in Jesus. John knows about the mystery that not everyone comes to faith. At the very moment Jesus is speaking these words, he is convinced that no one really believes in him, not even those who were chosen. If Jesus treats them as though they did believe, that is in anticipation of the future when the spirit will be given to those who are truly chosen.[186]

Haenchen seems to be working here with a theology of double predestination or election, which constitutes eisegesis not exegesis of this thirteenth

183. Keener, *The Gospel of John*, II, pp. 920-23.
184. Barrett, *The Gospel according to St John*, pp. 450-51.
185. Hare, *Son of Man Tradition*, p. 110.
186. Haenchen, *John 1*, II, p. 117.

Johannine Son of Man logion. Even if such a theology were true, this text
cannot be made to say that, nor is it warranted by the context. Few comenta-
tors agree with him regarding this logion. George Caird suggested a number
of potential meanings for God being glorified in the glorification of the Son
of Man. First, through Jesus God is honored by humankind. Second, Jesus
as Son of Man honors God. Third, God has achieved honor for himself in
sending the Son of Man. Fourth, 'God has revealed His glory in Jesus'. He
thinks only the last of these is worthy of the text in 13.31.[187] Calvin agreed
with that conclusion.[188] Brown thought that divine glory is made visible by
the mighty acts of God in history. The historical advent of the Son of Man,
together with his death, resurrection, and ascension, make such glory visible. 'Since Jesus' power is at the same time God's power ... the full meaning
here is to be found in a combination of Caird's second and fourth interpretations'. Brown further stated that Origen 'associates glory with knowing
God and being known by God'.[189] This contemplative perspective does not
do justice to the logion. In a kind of Christian Gnostic sense Origen helle-
nized the text's reference to and description of glory.

13.3. *Theological Import: Divine Glorification*
In the glorification of the Son of Man it is God that is glorified. The Son of
Man is the divinely *exalted one*, a *heavenly figure* in that he is intimate with
God. He is virtually identified with or as God, and he is a *revealer* of God's
mysteries, as well as one to be glorified by God by being *exalted* to heav-
enly status by crucifixion, resurrection, and ascension.

B. *Summary of the Johannine Logia*

In John the predominant characteristic of the Son of Man is that of the
divine *Logos*, the heavenly figure, and savior. Hence he is the revealer of
God's mysteries. This is in keeping with the theological burden of the prologue of this gospel. From the outset of the prologue, the heavenly figure is
not merely heavenly, but is defined as the divine *Logos* who *is* God:

Ἐν ἀρχῇ ἦν ὁ λόγος καὶ ὁ λόγος ἦν πρὸς τὸν θεόν καὶ θεὸς ἦν ὁ λόγος (Jn
1.1).

This divine agent descended to earth as the Son of Man, according to
the Fourth Gospel, and infested a human being, Jesus of Nazareth, with the

---

187. George B. Caird, 'The Glory of God in the Fourth Gospel: An Exercise in Biblical Semantics', *NTS* 15 (1968–69), pp. 265-77. This work is a study specifically
addressed to Jn 13.31.
188. Calvin, *The Gospel according to St John*, II, p. 68.
189. Brown, *The Gospel according to John*, II, p. 606.

divinity and divine agency of the divine *Logos*. It is this incarnated *Logos* and not the man, Jesus of Nazareth, that is the Son of Man in John:

Καὶ ὁ λόγος σὰρξ ἐγένετο καὶ ἐσκήνωσεν ἐν ἡμῖν καὶ ἐθεασάμεθα τὴν δόξαν αὐτοῦ δόξαν ὡς μονογενοῦς παρὰ πατρός πλήρης χάριτος καὶ ἀληθείας (Jn 1.14).

Thus the Johannine Son of Man logia fall into seven main categories: They describe him as the *Logos*, Heavenly Figure, Suffering Servant, Judge, Revealer of the heavenly mysteries, Exalted One, and the Savior. The following figure summarizes this description of the Son of Man.

Figure 1: *The Son of Man in John*

Citation	Logos	Heavenly Figure	Suffering Servant	Savior	Judge	Revealer of God	Divinely Exalted
Jn 1.51		X				X	X
Jn 3.13	X	X				X	
Jn 3.14ff.			X	X			
Jn 5.27ff.		X		X	X	X	X
Jn 6.27		X		X		X	
Jn 6.51-53		X		X		X	
Jn 6.62	X	X		X			X
Jn 8.28			X	X		X	
Jn 9.35-41				X	X	X	
Jn 12.23ff.		X	X	X			X
Jn 13.31ff.		X				X	X

The three dominant designations of the Son of Man in the Fourth Gospel are the *heavenly figure*, the *revealer* of God, and the *savior*. The *heavenly figure* is the descended divine *Logos*, the Anointed One—the Messiah (Christ). As such he is the *revealer* of the heavenly mysteries of God. Because of these characteristics and roles, he is able to be the *savior* of the world. Each is a primary identification in 8 of the 13 Son of Man references. In five of the 13 he is the divinely *exalted* one, *suffering servant* in three, and *judge* in two.

Of course, the Son of Man is inherently the judge. However, his nature and role as savior eclipses his *function* as Eschatological Judge, in the sense of prosecutor. So the Son of Man as judge is mentioned only twice in this gospel, and then is carefully explained in each case. The explanation is consistently as follows, wherever it appears in the gospel.

1. People bring judgment upon themselves by choosing unbelief, in a world in which the judgment is already in process and God endeavors to save everyone.

> Οὐ δύναμαι ἐγὼ ποιεῖν ἀπ᾽ ἐμαυτοῦ οὐδέν· καθὼς ἀκούω κρίνω, καὶ ἡ κρίσις ἡ ἐμὴ δικαία ἐστίν, ὅτι οὐ ζητῶ τὸ θέλημα τὸ ἐμὸν ἀλλὰ τὸ θέλημα τοῦ πέμψαντός με...ταῦτα λέγω ἵνα ὑμεῖς σωθῆτε ('I can do nothing on my own authority: as I hear, I judge; and my judgment is just, because I seek not my own will but the will of him who sent me... I say this that you may be saved', 5.27-47; 3.16-17).

2. The people have had ample opportunity to see and hear the truth God tried to convey to them through the scriptures which they read, through the teachings of Moses whom they admire, and directly through the words and deeds of Jesus who has ministered to them daily. None of this has enlightened them to God's truth and salvation. So Jesus closed 5.27-47 with the rhetorical question,

> Μὴ δοκεῖτε ὅτι ἐγὼ κατηγορήσω ὑμῶν πρὸς τὸν πατέρα; ('Do you think I will accuse you to the Father?')

The implied answer: 'Of course not'. They condemn themselves by failing to follow their own scriptures and Moses.

> (ἔστιν ὁ κατηγορῶν ὑμῶν Μωϋσῆς, εἰς ὃν ὑμεῖς ἠλπίκατε).

They bring themselves under judgement.

3. A similar line of thought is introduced again in 8.15-16 where Jesus declares,

> ἐγὼ οὐ κρίνω οὐδένα. καὶ ἐὰν κρίνω δὲ ἐγώ, ἡ κρίσις ἡ ἐμὴ ἀληθινή ἐστιν, ὅτι μόνος οὐκ εἰμί, ἀλλ᾽ ἐγὼ καὶ ὁ πέμψας με πατήρ ('I judge no one. Yet even if I do judge, my judgment is authentic, for it is not I alone that judge but I and the Father who sent me').

The explanation of this enigmatic statement follows in 8.17-19, to the effect that the available sources of God's truth are having no redemptive effect on his audience, so they are their own condemnation; or as we have it in 3.19, the judgment is that light came into the world but humans preferred the darkness of their own ignorance. In 8.50 Jesus declares that those who embrace the truth he brings are saved and those that fail to embrace it bring themselves under judgment.

Alfred Loisy attempted to resolve the enigma in Jn 8.15-16 by claiming that two different kinds of judgment are intended here, between Jesus' remark that he judged no one, and his comment that if he judged anyone his judgment would be authentic or warrantable, true, and just.[190] Loisy thought

---

190. Alfred F. Loisy, *La quatrième Evangile* (Paris: Nourry, 2nd edn, 1921), p. 288.

that the former kind of judging referred to judgment like that for which the Pharisees were scolded in the forgoing context, namely, an evaluation, assessment, or criticism; while the latter type of judging was that of Jesus, namely, a judgment that involves salvation and condemnation.

Brown took strong issue with Loisy's perspective. Bringing into direct view all of the Johannine references to judgment associated with the Son of Man, Brown asserted that

> the translation of *krinein* as 'condemn' in these passages [3.17; 8.26; 12.47]...is clearly justified by the contrast with 'save'. Nevertheless, the statement that Jesus did not come to condemn does not exclude the very real judgment that Jesus provokes. In the immediate context of the above statements (in iii 19; xii 48) we are told that he who refuses to believe in Jesus condemns himself, while he who believes escapes condemnation (also v. 24). The idea in John, then, seems to be that during his ministry Jesus is no apocalyptic judge ... yet his presence does cause men to judge themselves.[191]

Brown followed this assessment with observations about 9.39 and 5.22:

> Καὶ εἶπεν ὁ Ἰησοῦς· εἰς κρίμα ἐγὼ εἰς τὸν κόσμον τοῦτον ἦλθον ('For judgment I came into this world'); οὐδὲ γὰρ ὁ πατὴρ κρίνει οὐδένα, ἀλλὰ τὴν κρίσιν πᾶσαν δέδωκεν τῷ υἱῷ. ('The Father has turned over all judgment to the Son').

He assures us that these seemingly contradictory statements simply expand the notion that Jesus' presence and proclamation of the mysteries of God provokes self-judgment, as the contexts of all these passages consistently indicate. In Jn 5.15, commented Brown,

> Jesus says that he passes judgment on no one; but 16 recalls that judgment is associated with Jesus' presence. When Jesus says, 'Even if I do judge [real condition, not contrary to fact], that judgment of mine is valid', he seems to mean that the judgment that he provokes among men is one that the Father will accept. It is a judgment that has eternal consequences... The parallel to 'that judgment of mine is valid' is found in v. 30: 'my judgment is honest'. The context in vv. 26-30 is the context of...that judgment which the Father has turned over to him (v. 27), a judgment that is the Father's because Jesus judges only as he hears (v. 30). So also in viii 16 the reason that Jesus can assert that he provokes a valid judgment among men is the supporting presence of the Father.[192]

Brown's view undergirds and amplifies the fact that in the Fourth Gospel Jesus is the Eschatological Judge but will not prosecute, though his presence results in consequences for humans in terms of their posture toward him. This is a judgment humans bring upon themselves because of the way

191. Brown, *The Gospel according to John*, p. 345.
192. Brown, *The Gospel according to John*, p. 345.

in which God the Father has crafted the universe in terms of his determination to save it through the ministry of the Son of Man. The judgment is not a direct act of judgment on the part of God or of Jesus, but a consequence of the structure of the material and moral universes which constitute the context of human existence.

4. The Johannine understanding of what the Son of Man is, moves to a final summary in 12.47-48.

> καὶ ἐάν τίς μου ἀκούσῃ τῶν ῥημάτων καὶ μὴ φυλάξῃ, ἐγὼ οὐ κρίνω αὐτόν· οὐ γὰρ ἦλθον ἵνα κρίνω τὸν κόσμον, ἀλλ' ἵνα σώσω τὸν κόσμον ὁ ἀθετῶν ἐμὲ καὶ μὴ λαμβάνων τὰ ῥήματά μου ἔχει τὸν κρίνοντα αὐτόν· ὁ λόγος ὃν ἐλάλησα ἐκεῖνος κρινεῖ αὐτὸν ἐν τῇ ἐσχάτῃ ἡμέρᾳ ('If anyone hears my sayings and does not keep them, I do not judge him; for I did not come to judge the world but to save the world. He who rejects me and does not receive my sayings has a judge; the word that I have spoken will be his judge on the last day').

Brown took account of this perspective regarding the Son of Man as judge in the Gospel of John. Commenting upon the special passage in John 5 that describes the Son of Man as judge, Brown observed that whereas the primary work of Jesus as Son of Man is the ministry of granting life through illumination and forgiveness of sinners (vv. 19-21), his second most important work is described in 5.22-23.

> Jesus is the judge, for the Father has turned over the power of judgment to the Son. This 'judgment' is to be taken in the common OT sense of vindicating the good (Deut. xxxii 36; Ps xliii 1) and this is complementary to giving life. This salvific judgment which in the OT is the prerogative of Yahweh causes men to honor the Son and to recognize his relation to the Father. Yet, as in iii 19-21, the judgment on behalf of those who believe has its negative side as well; it is at the same time a condemnation of those who refuse the Son sent by the Father. Once again the realized eschatology of this Gospel comes to the fore; judgment, condemnation, passing from death to life (v. 24), are part of that hour which is now here. Just as the royal official listened to Jesus' word and believed in it, thus receiving the life of his son (iv 50), so also those who stand before Jesus and hear his words in the discourse of ch. v have the opportunity to receive life. These words are the source of life for those who are spiritually dead (v. 25).[193]

5. The Johannine Jesus consistently refuses the function of prosecutor. He clarifies that there is a judgment about which to be concerned. However, it is not a threat from God or from Jesus. The intent of God and the role and function of Jesus is simply to save the world by witnessing to the truth of God's grace. Those who cannot grasp it or embrace it are their own judges. Their behavior is its own judgment. Virtue and vice are their own existential rewards.

---

193. Brown, *The Gospel according to John*, p. 219.

6. This Johannine perspective implies that the judgment is past. The 'judgment day' took place before history. Its consequences are in process. God decided in that judgment to save the world. The only open-ended consideration currently extant is the capacity for humans to be open to that divine intervention. History is not awaiting an eschatological *parousia*, a final judgment, or a catastrophic consummation. According to the author of the Fourth Gospel, the Day of the Lord, the day of judgment and salvation, is every day that one encounters the message and ministry of the Son of Man. In such days God does not judge humans, Jesus exercises neither his *exousia* as judge nor as prosecutor, humans judge themselves by their existential response to the presence and the word of the Son of Man.

C. *Conclusion*

In John's Gospel the Son of Man is inherently the Eschatological Judge but suspends his function as prosecutor. He is the divine *Logos* descended from heaven, who in Jesus of Nazareth is the Son of Man, revealing God's mysteries to humankind. In this process as revealer, he is subject to the ordeal of suffering, including crucifixion. As suffering servant and revealer, he becomes the forgiver of sins on earth and the savior of the world. His destiny is to return to his heavenly home as the one exalted by and exalting God.

As we have seen, few scholars have addressed the issue of the identity and function of the Son of Man in the Gospel of John. Those who have addressed these issues, tended to be preoccupied with historical Jesus questions or with whether the term is titular or non-titular in John. Neither of these questions is of direct relevance to this study. Rather, the focus here has been to take the gospel as it stands in the critical edition of Nestle–Aland and ask the question as to what the Son of Man is in John, as one can derive that picture from the Son of Man logia themselves.

On that point, as we have noted exhaustively in this Chapter, Moloney tends to divide the human Jesus from the divine Son of Man, probably reflecting more of a post-Nicene orthodoxy than an objective reading of the logia themselves.[194] The consequence of this posture in Moloney's thought is that the Johannine Son of Man is the active Eschatological Judge and prosecutor in history and in a history-terminating *parousia*. Such a claim is contrary to the findings of this study in which the Son of Man repeatedly sets aside his role or function as prosecutor, and in that sense leaves the judgment of God to carry itself out in the natural consequences of a persons faith response, or lack of it, regarding the Son of Man as the revealer of the

194. Moloney, *The Gospel of John*.

divine mysteries and the savior of the world. On this point regarding the Son of Man as the active Eschatological Judge, Haenschen seems in agreement with Moloney.[195] Burkett felt that at the end of the twentieth century no conclusion could be drawn.[196] Hare conflates the emphases of the four gospels and agrees with Burkett.[197]

Morna Hooker is almost certainly correct in thinking that we can only discern what the Son of Man is in John, or in any other gospel, by seeing that figure through the lens of Second Temple Judaism's traditions regarding the Son of Man.[198] Of course, the question remains, then, as to which of those traditions is the best lens. Traditions potentially related in some degree to the Johannine Son of Man might be drawn from the Psalms, Wisdom Literature, Dead Sea Scrolls, Isaiah, Ezekiel, Daniel 7–9, *1 Enoch* 37–71, *4 Ezra*, and the like. This question will be addressed in Chapter 4 of this work, treating at least the main relevant traditions.

Bultmann saw the Son of Man in John as a post-Easter retrojection of kerygmatic theology into the mythic narrative of Jesus of Nazareth, as he was becoming increasingly the Christ of faith. As such, Bultmann identified the Son of Man logia in John as describing three types or phases of the Son of Man: the revealer of divine mysteries on earth, the suffering savior, and the exalted Lord.[199]

In their commentaries, already amply referenced, Sloyan, Morris, Howard and Gossip, Tenny, Hunter, Beasley-Murray, and Reynolds consistently emphasize the position already held by Calvin and Lightfoot and more exhaustively defended by Brown. They affirm that in John the divine *Logos* is incarnated as the Son of Man in Jesus of Nazareth. Thus, these scholars affirm the fundamental Johannine claim regarding the Son of Man. That claim constitutes the grounding principle upon which this study stands. On that foundation this present analysis has established that in the Gospel of John the Son of Man is the Eschatological Judge, the revealer of the heavenly mysteries, the suffering servant, savior, and the one exalted by God in crucifixion and resurrection, and in his ascension to his heavenly home. The claims of the scholars cited in this paragraph are congenial to these conclusions.

195. Haenchen, *John 1*, pp. 242-67.
196. Delbert Burkett, *The Son of Man Debate: A History and Evaluation* (Cambridge: Cambridge University Press, 1999), pp. 121-24.
197. Hare, *Son of Man Tradition*, pp. 257-82.
198. Morna D. Hooker, 'Is the Son of Man Problem Really Insoluble?', in *Text and Interpretation: Studies in the New Testament, Presented to Matthew Black* (ed. E. Best and R.M. Wilson; Cambridge: Cambridge University Press, 1979), pp. 155-68 (159).
199. Bultmann, *The Gospel of John*.

Chapter 3

THE SON OF MAN IN THE SYNOPTIC GOSPELS

A. *The Son of Man Logia in the Synoptic Gospels*

The Synoptic Gospels have 70 Son of Man logia, plus an additional one in
the second Lukan document at Acts 7.56. Of these 71, Mark has 14, Matthew 30, and Luke–Acts has 27. That is, Mark has approximately the same
number as the Gospel of John, while Matthew and Luke–Acts each contain
approximately twice as many as Mark or John. Numerous logia in each of
the Synoptic Gospels have parallels in the others. Son of Man logia which
appear in the Synoptic Gospels but not in John, as well as their numerous
parallels, account for the aggregate of Son of Man logia in Mark, Matthew,
and Luke, that greatly exceeds the number in the Fourth Gospel.

As Bultmann suggested in the mid-twentieth century, these logia in Mark,
Matthew, and Luke fall into three specific categories: (1) the Son of Man as
a human agent, proclaiming the salvific earthly reign of God; (2) the Son
of Man as Suffering-Servant-Messiah; and (3) the Son of Man in heaven as
exalted Eschatological Judge, whose impending *parousia* will bring in the
final judgment and wrap up history as we know it. In all of these categories
the Son of Man reveals the mysteries of God to humans.

Bultmann believed that originally the Son of Man designation was an
apocalyptic title. He concluded, therefore, that only the specifically apocalyptic Son of Man sayings were actually from the mouth of Jesus himself,
the others being added by the *kerygma* of the post-Easter church.[1] Bultmann
was sure that by the time Matthew's gospel was written, the author of that
gospel no longer remembered the original meaning and employed the title
exclusively as the primary self-designation of Jesus.[2] Tödt is certain that
the evangelists all understood the original apocalyptic freight of the title
and were aware of its roots in Daniel 7 and *1 Enoch* 37–71. Therefore, he

---

1. Bultmann, *The Gospel of John*; see also his *Die Geschichte der synoptischen
Tradition* (Göttingen: Vandenhoeck & Ruprecht, 1921) = *History of the Synoptic Tradition* (trans. J. Marsh; Oxford: Blackwell, 1962); Bultmann, *Theology of the New Testament* (trans. K. Grobel; 2 vols.; New York: Scribner, 1951).

2. Bultmann, *Theology of the New Testament*, I, p. 30. See also Bultmann, *History
of the Synoptic Tradition*, p. 155.

mounted his argument for the radical difference between the Son of Man references to Jesus' earthly ministry and those with apocalyptic content.[3] Reynolds devotes his entire volume to marshalling the evidence which he believes demonstrates that all the Son of Man logia in the Synoptic Gospels that also appear in John's Gospel are apocalyptic in nature and are shaped by Daniel 7–9.

Carsten Colpe, in his definitive article on ὁ υἱὸς τοῦ ἀνθρώπου, contends that only 11 of the Son of Man sayings in the gospels are authentic to Jesus.[4] Paul Stuhlmacher and Viktor Hampel believe that the sayings in all three of Bultmann's categories are authentic to the historical figure, Jesus, as Son of Man.[5] Philipp Vielhauer, in contrast, argues than none of them are.[6] This debate is of interest but not of primary relevance to this study, since the concern here is focused upon the text of the gospels as we have them in their redacted form presented in the Nestle–Aland critical edition. It is neither interested in issues of the historical Jesus nor in whether some of the Son of Man logia are more or less authentic to the gospel narratives than others. This study addresses the Son of Man logia in terms of the three principal composite themes discernible in the way the Synoptic Gospels employ those logia. Those three themes, each of which contains a number of subthemes, can be listed as follow: the Son of Man as Human Proclaimer of the Reign of God and the Forgiver of Sins on Earth; the Son of Man as Messianic Suffering Servant; and the Son of Man, the Heavenly Messiah as Exalted and Enthroned Eschatological Judge.

1. *Human Proclaimer of the Reign of God and the Forgiver of Sins on Earth*

In this first of Bultmann's categories of Son of Man logia in the Synoptic Gospels, that prophetic figure is the human agent who proclaims the fact that the divine kingdom is in the process of breaking in on earth. In that

---

3. Heinz E. Tödt, *The Son of Man in the Synoptic Tradition* (London: SCM Press, 1965), p. 108.

4. Carsten Colpe, 'ὁ υἱὸς τοῦ ἀνθρώπου', in *Theological Dictionary of the New Testament*, VIII, pp. 400-77.

5. Peter Stuhlmacher, *Biblische Theologie des Neuen Testaments* (Göttingen: Vandenhoeck & Ruprecht, 1992), I, pp. 107-25, and Volker Hampel, *Menschensohn und historischer Jesus: Ein Ratselwort als Schlussel zum messianischen Selbstverständnis Jesu* (Neukirchener–Vluyn: Neukirchener Verlag, 1990).

6. Philipp Vielhauer, *Gottesreich und Menschensohn in der Verkündigung Jesu, in Zeit und Geschichte: Dankesgabe an Rudolf Bultmann zum 80. Gegburtstag* (ed. Erich Dinkler; Tübingen: Mohr–Siebeck, 1957), pp. 155-69. See also Philipp Vielhauer, 'Jesus und der Menschensohn: Zur Diskussion mit Heinz Eduard Tödt und Eduard Schweizer', *Zeitschrift fur Theologie und Kirche* 60 (1963), pp. 133-77.

process he is revealed as a human being who has authority and power as the forgiver of sins on earth. In this manner he will subdue evil powers and introduce a redeemed world of God's salvific reign. The relevant logia are of two kinds. First, those that describe the Son of Man as a person who has the authority to overturn the evil human order currently in vogue on earth and to replace it with a new and godly order of righteousness and salvation. Second, in this category of proclaimer of the divine kingdom coming, are the logia that describe the Son of Man as a salvific minister and forgiver of sins on earth. He is a savior of the unrighteous, lost, and broken of humanity.

Table III.1: *Son of Man Logia in the Synoptic Gospels*
Regarding the Proclaimer of the Salvific Kingdom and the Forgiver of Sins

1.1. *Son of Man with authority to overturn evil and establish God's reign: the Proclaimer of the Kingdom*

Mt. 13.37—The Son of Man is the sower of the seed of the word of the kingdom of God;
Mt. 12.8—The Son of Man is Lord of the Sabbath = Mk 2.28; Lk. 6.5;
Mt. 16.13—Some say he is a prophet but he asserts he is more than that, i.e., the messianic Son of Man = Mk 8.27-28; Lk. 9.18-19;

1.2. *Son of Man as minister to the lost and broken: the forgiver of sins on earth and savior*

Mt. 9.6—The Son of Man has power on earth to forgive sins = Mk 2.10; Lk. 5.24;
Mt. 18.11—The Son of Man came to save the lost sheep of Israel;
Mt. 20.28—The Son of Man came to minister, not to be ministered unto = Mk 10.45;
Lk. 9.56—[Variant: The Son of Man came not to destroy human lives but to save them;]
Lk. 12.10—Those who speak against the Son of Man will be forgiven;
Lk. 19.10—[Variant: The Son of Man came to seek and to save the lost;]

2. *Exposition*

2.1. *Proclaimer of the Kingdom*
The vision of the coming reign of God is already explicit in the form of the Lord's prayer recorded by both Matthew (6.9-13) and Luke (11.2-4). Moreover, the succor and salvation of humankind that is associated with that vision is particularly detailed in Lk. 4.18 (cf. Mt. 11.5; 12.18). As Theissen and Merz point out, this quotation from the LXX is Jesus' purported self-identification with the messianic charter of Isaiah 61.1-4 (cf. also Isa.

58.6).[7] The gospel declares that the Son of Man came to preach good news to the poor, bind up the broken-hearted, release the captives, give sight to the blind, free the oppressed, and proclaim the timeliness of Yahweh's salvation. Πνεῦμα κυρίου ἐπ' ἐμὲ οὗ εἵνεκεν ἔχρισέν με εὐαγγελίσασθαι πτωχοῖς, ἀπέσταλκέν με, κηρύξαι αἰχμαλώτοις ἄφεσιν καὶ τυφλοῖς ἀνάβλεψιν, ἀποστεῖλαι τεθραυσμένους ἐν ἀφέσει, κηρύξαι ἐνιαυτὸν κυρίου δεκτόν

רוּחַ אֲדֹנָי יְהוִה עָלָי יַעַן מָשַׁח יְהוָה אֹתִי לְבַשֵּׂר עֲנָוִים
שְׁלָחַנִי לַחֲבֹשׁ לְנִשְׁבְּרֵי־לֵב לִקְרֹא לִשְׁבוּיִם דְּרוֹר וְלַאֲסוּרִים פְּקַח־קוֹחַ:
לִקְרֹא שְׁנַת־רָצוֹן לַיהוָה וְיוֹם נָקָם לֵאלֹהֵינוּ לְנַחֵם
כָּל־אֲבֵלִים:
לָשׂוּם לַאֲבֵלֵי צִיּוֹן לָתֵת לָהֶם פְּאֵר תַּחַת אֵפֶר שֶׁמֶן שָׂשׂוֹן
תַּחַת אֵבֶל מַעֲטֵה תְהִלָּה תַּחַת רוּחַ כֵּהָה וְקֹרָא לָהֶם אֵילֵי
הַצֶּדֶק מַטַּע יְהוָה לְהִתְפָּאֵר:

('The Spirit of the Lord is upon me, because he has anointed me to preach good news to the poor. He has sent me to proclaim release to the captives and recovering of sight to the blind, to set at liberty those who are oppressed, to proclaim the acceptable year of the Lord'). The KJV of Lk. 4.18, though not the RSV, includes the variant, 'to heal the brokenhearted' (Lk. 4.18b), taken from 'to bind up the brokenhearted' (Isa. 61.1b LXX). This variant, ἰάσασθαι τοὺς συντετριμμένους τὴν καρδίαν, is present in A θ ψ and other later and lesser sources.[8] Though the variant is not well attested in the early ancient uncials and papyri, it is congenial to the emphasis in the Synoptic Gospels that depicts the Son of Man as the proclaimer of the new age of righteousness and salvation, as the divine reign is instituted.

Peter Rodgers argues that this variant 'is part of the original text of the gospel'.[9] Walter Grundmann[10] and Heinz Schürmann[11] both agree with Rodgers that the expression is original with Luke, and follows the LXX. Bruce Metzger contends that the variant is 'an obvious scribal supplement introduced in order to bring the quotation more completely in accord with the

7. Gerd Theissen and Annette Merz, *The Historical Jesus: A Comprehensive Guide* (trans. John Bowden; Minneapolis: Fortress Press, 1999), pp. 358ff. = *Der historische Jesus: Ein Lehrbuch* (Göttingen: Vandenhoeck & Ruprecht, 1996).

8. The accepted Nestle–Aland text is witnessed by ℵ B D L W Ξ and f[13] 33. 579. 892. lat sy[s] co Or Eus Did.

9. Peter Rodgers, 'Luke 4.18, To Heal the Brokenhearted', in *The Healing Power of Spirituality: How Religion Helps Humans Thrive* (ed. J. Harold Ellens; 3 vols.; Westport, CT: Praeger, 2009).

10. Walter Grundmann, *Das Evangelium nach Lukas* (THKNT; Berlin: Evangelische Verlagsanstalt, 1966), p. 118.

11. Heinz Schürmann, *Das Lukasevangelium* (THKNT; Freiburg: Herder, 1969), I, p. 229 n. 58.

Septuagint text of Isaiah'[12] Most scholars who comment on this variant agree with Metzger. Joseph Fitzmyer contends that 'the omission…is of little consequence' in view of the import of the other clauses in 4.18 which express the same general pattern of messianic deliverance.[13]

Rodgers, however, thinks that including the variant is essential to the main theological burden of Luke's gospel. This longer reading is certainly compatible with the theme of the Synoptic Gospels, but it also adds an important dimension of psychological healing to this messianic text in Lk. 4.18, indicating clearly that this salvific psychospiritual healing is an inherent part of the proclamation of the impending divine reign. Rodgers notes that Irenaeus, already in the second century CE, quotes Luke's gospel with the variant included; and concludes that the longer reading was established in the Western Manuscript tradition already within a half century after the close of the New Testament canon. Moreover, Rodgers, with James Royce[14] and Peter Head,[15] notes that.

> the possibility of accidental omission by scribes of Luke's gospel has become more attractive in recent years. Whereas earlier studies had emphasized the tendency of scribes to add to their manuscripts, several scholars working on the early papyri have shown that the scribes of these manuscripts were more prone to omit material as they copied.[16]

Bart Ehrman voices a similar conclusion regarding early gospel variants, though he uses it to tease out quite different consequences.[17] Bo Reicke confirms Rodgers' argument for the clause being original to Luke's text.[18]

---

12. Bruce M. Metzger, *A Textual Commentary on the Greek New Testament* (2nd edn; New York: United Bible Societies, 1998), p. 114.

13. Joseph A. Fitzmyer, *The Gospel according to Luke I–IX* (Anchor Bible, 28; Garden City, NY: Doubleday, 1981), p. 532.

14. James R. Royce, *Scribal Habits in Early Greek New Testament Papyri* (Leiden: E.J. Brill, 2007).

15. Peter M. Head, 'Some Observations on Early Papyri of the Synoptic Gospels, Especially concerning Scribal Habits', *Biblica* 71 (1990), pp. 240-47; and Head, 'The Habits of New Testament Copyists: Singular Readings in the Early Fragmentary Papyri of John', *Biblica* 85 (2004), pp. 399-408.

16. Rodgers, 'Luke 4.18', p. 4.

17. Bart D. Ehrman, *The Orthodox Corruption of Scripture: The Effect of Early Christological Controversies on the Text of the New Testament* (New York: Oxford University Press, 1992), p. 62.

18. Bo Reicke, 'Jesus in Nazareth—Luke 4.14-30', in *Das Wort und die Wörter: Festschrift G. Friedrich zum 65 Geburtstag* (ed. Horst R. Balz and Siegfried Schulz; Stuttgart: Kohlhammer, 1973), pp. 47-55. For an extended and erudite discussion of the role of Luke 4 in relationship to the messianic charter of Isaiah 61, see also Stanley E. Porter, 'Scripture Justifies Mission: The Use of the Old Testament in Luke–Acts', in Porter (ed.), *Hearing the Old Testament in the New Testament* (Grand Rapids: Eerdmans, 2006), pp. 104-26.

In any case, this debate and Rodgers' central point are important rein-
forcements of the fact that in the Synoptic Gospels a central theme is the
contention that the Son of Man, in initiating the divine reign on earth, is
the agent of healing and salvation. The Greek word for healing, ἰάομαι, is
a typical term for salvation in the Synoptic Gospels, employed 11 times in
Luke, 4 times in Matthew, and once in Mark. This word for healing is the
key word that links together the entire passage of Luke 4, the entire body of
Synoptic Gospels literature, and their connection with the related Hebrew
Bible and New Testament themes.[19] Moreover, since the quotation of Isaiah 61 in Lk. 4.18 forms the essential content of the proclamation of the
impending messianic kingdom, it is clear that the theme of healing and salvation are constitutent to that proclamation.

The urgent emphasis upon this salvific proclamation of the new reign of
God on earth, in all these practical applied forms, is reinforced in Mt. 12.28
when Jesus is reported to declare that εἰ δὲ ἐν πνεύματι θεοῦ ἐγὼ ἐκβάλλω
τὰ δαιμόνια ἄρα ἔφθασεν ἐφ' ὑμᾶς ἡ βασιλεία τοῦ θεοῦ ('if it is by the spirit
of God that I cast out demons, then the kingdom of God has come upon
you'). Moreover, Mt. 3.2 has John the Baptist declaring that the kingdom of
God is imminent λέγων· Μετανοεῖτε· ἤγγικεν γὰρ ἡ βασιλεία τῶν οὐρανῶν
('Repent, for the kingdom of heaven is at hand'), as he introduces Jesus to
the crowds gathered at the Jordan river.

Luke's corollary report (4.43) adds force to this perspective of king-
dom-proclamation as a characteristic of the Son of Man in the Synoptic
Gospels. The Gospel of Luke tells its readers that Jesus, while 'he was
preaching in the synagogues of Judea', said, ὁ δὲ εἶπεν πρὸς αὐτοὺς ὅτι Καὶ
ταῖς ἑτέραις πόλεσιν εὐαγγελίσασθαί με δεῖ τὴν βασιλείαν τοῦ θεοῦ, ὅτι ἐπὶ
τοῦτο ἀπεστάλην ('I must preach the good news of the kingdom of God to
the other cities also; for I was sent for this purpose'). So it is clear that a
primary characteristic of the Son of Man in the Synoptic Gospels is that of
an Ezekiel-like human being who is commissioned by God to proclaim the
imminent appearance upon earth of the pervasive reign of God, which also
brings with it succor and salvation for humankind.

In his attempt to set Jesus' proclamation of the coming kingdom of God
in the appropriate historical context, Rudolph Otto pointed out that this ministry of the Son of Man was distinctive and in many ways unique, but that
there were many itinerant Galilean preachers of the coming divine kingdom
in Jesus' day.[20] Joseph Klausner reflects the same perspective, declaring that

19. Rodgers notes that it is the word *healing* that ties this verse to the entire quote
from Isaiah 61 about the messianic proclamation, as well as tying all these to Lk. 4.23,
'Doctor, heal thyself', and to the OT stories of Elijah and Elisha referenced in Lk.4.25-
27.

20. Rudolf Otto, *The Kingdom of God and the Son of Man: A Study in the History*

such Galilean Rabbis tended to have a rather regular following of disciples, and were 'Galilean itinerant' preachers.[21] Otto thought that this pattern in the Galilean culture between 100 BCE and 100 CE was influenced by the social mobility and intercommunication between that northern Palestinian province of Galilee, neighboring Syria, and the culture of the eastern Jewish diaspora in Babylon.

He claimed that 'Jesus' message of the kingdom did not fall from the skies as a complete novelty, but had long been prepared for'. It was his assertion that Jesus proclamation of the impending reign of God on earth reflected the influences of Zoroastrian religious ideas upon Galilean thought forms. This was possible, he was sure, because Galilee was, in his view, largely free of the nomistic perspective of the Judaism of Judea and Jerusalem. Moreover, Jewish eschatology and apocalyptic were a special feature of the history of Near Eastern religions, going back far beyond Zoroastrianism and influencing Galilean culture at that time. He observed that 'Jesus' preaching both reflects and transforms' Jewish eschatology and apocalyptic models.[22] It was Otto's notion that the concept of Kingdom of God that played so large a part in Jesus' proclamation was a very ancient construct.[23] Despite these notions, Otto overlooked the degree to which Second Temple Judaic apocalypticism impacted Jesus as Son of Man and his ministry.

On the content of the proclamation of the kingdom by the Son of Man in the Synoptic Gospels, Otto believed he had found the source of Jesus' unique emphasis, his universalism. He observed that Jesus saw himself as commissioned to proclaim the kingdom to the 'lost sheep of the house of Israel', whom Otto thinks were עַם אָרֶץ, τῷ λαῷ τῆς γῆς ('the people of the land'), not exiled to Babylon. That would include the עַם אָרֶץ of Samaria and Galilee. These Israelites had spread widely through the northern neighboring nations so that when Jesus visited the Syrophoenician woman near Tyre and Sidon he was in his mission to those 'lost sheep'.

> Through the conversion of Israel even the nations were some day to attain salvation. Thus...when Jesus was won over by...the faith of such non-Israelites as this woman [of Syrophoenicia] and the centurion of Capernaum, he occasionally exercised his charismatic healing power even on non-Israelites, although he felt it should normally be restricted to the limits of his special mission. In their faith, he glimpsed a higher mandate.[24]

of Religion (trans. Floyd V. Filson and Bertram Lee-Woolf; London: Lutterworth, rev. edn, 1951), p. 13.

21. Joseph Klausner, *Jesus of Nazareth* (London: Lutterworth, 1929), p. 253.
22. Otto, *Kingdom of God*, p. 14.
23. Otto, *Kingdom of God*, p. 14.
24. Otto, *Kingdom of God*, p. 17.

This accounts, in Otto's view, for the frequent association of Jesus with Samaritans, for his championing of the Samaritan in his parable about grace and mercy, and for his being accused in Nazareth of being a Samaritan in the nature of his messianic hope and expectation. Contemporary scholars largely disagree with Otto's perspective on Jesus' identity and the sources of his formative influences. They emphasize, of course, that the Son of Man, who came proclaiming the breaking in of the kingdom of God through his own ministry, derived from a land that had been open to foreign influences. In Capernaum and Bethsaida, the region most frequented by the Son of Man, he would have found a mixed population, as also in the regions in which he travelled: Samaria, Perea, and Syrophoenicia.

In these areas he ministered to Jews and non-Jews, apparently without asking about the ethnicity of his patients or audience. Otto argued rather scandalously that this is 'the harmonious picture of a man who *is not a Jew* in the orthodox and one-sided sense'.[25] Otto's perspective in this regard was shaped by a nefarious socio-political worldview prevailing in Germany in his time. W. Bauer emphasized that while 'The Galilean Jesus represented Judaism in a form inclined to a universal outlook...he certainly felt himself to be a son of the theocracy and was conscious of being sent to his fellow-countrymen, but he did this somewhat in the way in which Paul conceived his apostolate to the Gentiles'.[26]

An essential idea in Second Temple Judaisms' apocalyptic perspectives was certainly the ancient notion of God as a warrior who is engaged in a cosmic conflict with the powers of evil, the kingdom of light against the kingdom of darkness. This may be the root of eschatology in Second Temple Judaisms and in Jesus' proclamation of the divine kingdom. Zoroastrianism foresaw a final cosmic battle in which evil would be definitively defeated, followed by the resurrection of the dead, the final judgment, and the establishment in the world of a 'wondrous new creation', the kingdom of God, otherwise known, as well, as the kingdom of heaven.

This kingdom is not just divine royal dignity, royal sovereignty, or a royal district, realm, people, or a community; but all of these at once. It is 'God's might and holiness and glory, His throne and governing power, His angels and their ordinances, the redeemed holy ones by His throne, the fellowship of the righteous, the triumphant church, the new heaven and earth, the transfigured life and the heavenly salvation, the life of eternity and "God all in all"—these belong together here as a unified whole'. The Synoptic Gospels have Jesus proclaiming such a kingdom as present already in human experience; and its fullness, while still to be anticipated, is imminent.[27]

---

25. Otto, *Kingdom of God*, p. 18.
26. Walter Bauer, *Jesus, der Galilaer* (Tübingen: Mohr–Siebeck, 1924), p. 29.
27. Otto, *Kingdom of God*, pp. 32-32.

As the Son of Man, Jesus is described in the Synoptic Gospels as perceiving that ἡ βασιλεία τοῦ θεοῦ was breaking in because it was operative in his own ἐξουσία and δύναμις against Satan and the βασιλεία of evil. Therefore, and in this sense he is presented by the evangelists as a redeemer, and one who declares with surprising urgency that God's new order is in process of happening. Otto thought that Jesus was less interested in *apocalyptic* perspectives and more certain about the *eschatology* of his world view, the emphasis of the Son of Man being less on the danger of eternal damnation and more upon the call to participation in the kingdom of holiness and healing in time and eternity. Thus Jesus could quote Isa. 61.1-4 as the charter for his proclamation, and proclaim a kingdom of heaven which would reshape life in this mundane world but which would have its ultimate fruitfulness in the heavenly world to come. In this schema, the final judgment is the climactic consummation of the coming kingdom, as we shall consider below.

Mann, commenting on the role of the Son of Man as the proclaimer of the impending salvific reign of God on earth, emphasizes 'that the faithfulness of the Son to the Father's will must be mirrored in' the lives of those who would be part of that divine kingdom of holiness. Mann sees this as the implication of Jesus' caution, in the 'little apocalypse' of Mk 13.37, that humans should be watchful, for the kingdom is immediately impending. The burden of this theme in the Synoptic Gospels is the claim that the presence of the reign of God 'is more certain than the continuance of the physical order... We are...confronted with...the need for immediate decision, judgment in the face of decision, the immediate future, the Reign of God, and the end-time'.

Mann agrees that Mark and Matthew wish here to emphasize mainly immediacy and urgency regarding the kingdom, evident in all the kingdom parables, particularly in the parable of the sower (Mt. 13.37). He sees Luke as diluting the urgency of these expectations of the kingdom breaking in. 'Not for Mark a time of delay and then a manifestation of the risen Jesus in glory: the exhortation to see in passion, death, and resurrection-vindication *the* coming of the master of the house was addressed with urgency to the community for which he wrote'.[28] Mann's view illustrates how contemporary scholars have distanced themselves from much in Otto's perspective, particularly his preoccupation with Iranian and pre-Iranian sources of Second Temple Judaisms and the non-Jewishness of Jesus.

Ulrich Luz agrees with Mann regarding the emphasis the Synoptic Gospels give to the proclamation of the salvific divine reign, focusing particularly upon the implied imperatives for the 'sons of the kingdom'. For Luz, the urgency is in the direct connection between the Son of Man as proclaimer

---

28. C.S. Mann, *Mark: A New Translation with Introduction and Commentary* (Anchor Bible, 27; Garden City, NY: Doubleday, 1986), pp. 539, 541.

of the kingdom and the Son of Man as 'Lord of judgment who accompanies the church on its entire way through lowliness, suffering, and resurrection'. The earthly Jesus is not distinct 'from the judge of the world; [Mt. 13.41] will make clear that the Son of Man has in his hand not only the sowing but also the harvest and thus the entire history of the world'. For Luz, the important thing in the proclamation of the kingdom is the warning.[29]

The Son of Man proclaims the coming of the salvific divine kingdom on earth in many ways. Matthew 5.3 blesses the 'humble hearted' as being inheritors of the kingdom. Those who succor the needy and imprisoned participate thereby in the kingdom (Mt. 25.34-35). Luke 9.62 urges that commitment is the key to entering the kingdom. Jesus clarifies that one must be childlike (Mt. 18.3) in faith and trust in order to recognize the kingdom as it is breaking in all around. The author of each gospel always puts this proclamation in the mouth of Jesus. In Mk 1.15 (= Mt. 4.17) Jesus demands repentence because the kingdom is near.

In Mt. 10.7 (= Lk. 9.2) Jesus instructs the disciples to proclaim that the kingdom of heaven is at hand, as he sends them out on their mission to Israel. In Lk. 21.31 he declares that the kingdom of God is near, in 20.21 he preaches the good news, and in Mt. 22.2 and 25.1 Jesus compares the kingdom of God, that is breaking in as he speaks, with the stories of the marriage feast of the prince, and of the virgins preparing for the bridegroom.

It is interesting that many commentators view the role of the Son of Man as proclaimer of the salvific kingdom as more of a threat than an optimistic anticipation. Richard Trench, for example, picked up the same theme as Mann and Luz and emphasized even more strongly the threat that the 'sons of the kingdom' will, through negligence, lose their status in the kingdom.[30] Of course, it is true that Mt. 13.41 emphasizes the eschatological judgment, which we shall address later in this Chapter; but most of the passages of proclamation indicate the prospect of a new age of righteousness and prospects of blessing.[31] As we have noted already, this is particularly obvious in Lk. 4.18 and 4.43 where Jesus talks about being sent to proclaim the coming kingdom. Luke 8.1 and 16.16 carry forward the same theme rather euphorically as they describe Jesus going through the cities and villages of Judea κηρύσσων καὶ εὐαγγελιζόμενος τὴν βασιλείαν τοῦ θεοῦ ('preaching and proclaiming the good news of the kingdom of God'). This sentence leads into

29. Ulrich Luz, *Matthew 8–20* (trans. J.E. Crouch; Hermeneia; Minneapolis: Fortress Press, 2001), p. 268.

30. Richard C. Trench, *Notes on the Parables of Our Lord* (14th edn; Oxford: Clarendon Press, 1882), pp. 87-88.

31. William D. Davies and Dale C. Allison,, *A Critical and Exegetical Commentary on the Gospel according to Saint Matthew* (ICC, 2; Edinburgh: T. & T. Clark, 1991), pp. 426-31.

the narrative of the sower and the seed, as symbols of the kingdom in the process of being realized on earth (see Lk. 8.4-15; Mt. 13.1-30).

The various kingdom parables of the sowing and harvesting of wheat and tares, as well as those of the mustard seed and the leaven, are, in the view of Davies and Allison, all cut from the same cloth, so to speak. They all stand in continuity with the theme of the pervasive domain of the salvific divine reign that is in the process of unfolding. They see the ultimate triumph of the kingdom as a future hope, expressed in all the gospel passages that proclaim God's reign. Thus:

> For the present the kingdom is a mysterious, hidden entity, whose chief feature seems to be weakness. But according to our similitudes what matters is not the beginning but the end. The kingdom of God may not begin with success, but success is its divinely ordained destiny. If leaven leavens the whole lump, and if a little mustard seed becomes a tree, similarly will the kingdom however obscure now, become, in the end, the measure of all things.[32]

The Son of Man is a subtle but powerful and authoritative kingdom agent in the Synoptic Gospels. That is, he is not only the sower of the seeds of the kingdom. He also has the power and authority as Lord of the Sabbath (Mt. 12.8 = Mk 2.28; Lk. 6.5). In the presence of the Son of Man in time and history, the reign of God is already present on earth. God is taking charge and undoing the opposing powers of evil. Consequently, some see him as a prophet but he asserts he is more than that, i.e., the messianic Son of Man (Mk 8.27-28 = Mt. 16.13; Lk. 9.18-19). Tödt observes, on this point, that

> The action of the Son of Man here appears in a certain light; he acts with supreme authority when bestowing table-fellowship on tax collectors and sinners, when bestowing his fellowship on those with whom the religious man is not allowed to have anything in common; this is what he is come to do. We have to consider this when answering the question whether the name Son of Man...implies a designation of sovereignty. Obviously that action of the Son of Man for which this generation reproaches him...is a specific act of sovereignty superior to the restraints of the Law by virtue of the authority of a direct mission. It is action which befits only an authorized person. It is this distinctive action which is emphasized by the name Son of Man.[33]

Theissen and Merz comment at length upon the import of the Son of Man as proclaimer of the kingdom and its salvific import for humanity. They emphasize that the nature and content of this proclamation is grounded in Jesus' behavior and teaching, not, for example in whether he used or was called by his Christological titles, such as Son of Man, Son of God,

---

32. Davies and Allison, *Commentary*, p. 432.
33. Tödt, *Son of Man in the Synoptic Tradition*, pp. 115-16.

or Messiah. With Bultmann, they declare that as Son of Man, Jesus calls humanity to acknowledge the existential presence of God in life lived under pressure of eternity, and demanding decision regarding the breaking in of God's rule on earth.[34]

Ernst Käsemann is convinced that the central issue in the Son of Man's proclamation is the divine gift of freedom intended for all humanity in the new order. This the Son of Man initiates by the overthrow of the powers of evil and the advent of the reign of God. Käsemann sees this as evidenced by passages like Lk. 6.5 (= Mk 2.28; Mt. 12.8) regarding the Son of Man being Lord of the Sabbath. The call of freedom by the Son of Man is a criticism of oppressive religious regulation and calls into question the ground and principle of all ancient religion.[35]

Bornkamm remarks that in the kingdom proclamation of the Son of Man in the Synoptic Gospels there is evident a unique immediacy.[36] This reflects, on the one hand, the urgent imminence of the advent of the reign of God. However, much more important is the fact that, on the other hand, this sense of immediacy is the expression of an existential presence of the Son of Man himself to his immediate situation. In him, moreover, the divine reign is inescapably present. One's response to him is an alignment or non-alignment with the kingdom. The proclamation by the Son of Man expresses a watershed distinction between *his* proclamation and the apocalyptic casuistry of his environment.

This proclamation, says Ernst Fuchs, is the claim of the love of God for sinners, implemented by means of both the conduct and the message of the Son of Man.[37] Herbert Braun seems to advance and interpret Fuchs' emphasis by pointing to the impact of the ministry of the Son of Man in *initiating* the reign of God. He says that the proclamation, in word and behavior, by the Son of Man in the Synoptic Gospels expresses a 'paradoxical unity of radicalized Torah and radical grace'. In this surprising unity between Torah and divine grace in the proclamation, God's will unfolds, establishes itself, and is enacted in Jesus of Nazareth.[38]

Thus it is plainly evident that in the Synoptic Gospels, the Son of Man is first of all a human person with a calling to proclaim and enact the

---

34. Rudolf Bultmann, 'The Primitive Christian Kerygma and the Historical Jesus', in *The Historical Jesus and the Kerygmatic Christ* (ed. Carl E. Braaten and R.A. Harrisvillec; Nashville: Abingdon Press, 1964), p. 28.

35. Ernst Käsemann, *Jesus Means Freedom* (Philadelphia: Trinity Press International, 1969).

36. Günther Bornkamm, *Jesus of Nazareth* (London: Hodder & Stoughton, 1960).

37. Ernst Fuchs, 'The Quest of the Historical Jesus', in *Studies of the Historical Jesus* (London: SCM Press, 1964), pp. 11-31.

38. Herbert Braun, 'The Meaning of New Testament Christology', *Journal for Theology and the Church* 5 (1959), pp. 89-127.

impending advent of the reign of God in bringing down the powers of evil and establishing the divine kingdom on earth. He does so with authority that transcends that of the Temple and Torah. Fuchs' observation is a key transitional statement. It leads from the emphasis here upon that proclamation, and connects it to the role of the Son of Man as the salvific kingdom agent who forgives sins on earth.

2.2. *Forgiver of Sins on Earth*

In the prophetic role of proclaimer of the divine kingdom on earth, as depicted by the Synoptic Gospels, the Son of Man possesses certain special qualities and abilities. As already indicated, a significant one is that he is given the power and authority (ἐξουσία) to forgive sin. The Synoptic Gospels emphasize the Son of Man as the forgiver of sins on earth (Mark 2; Luke 5) and in that sense, the savior (Mk 10.45; Mt. 20.28). There are repeated suggestions in the Synoptic Gospels that in *the eschatological judgment* the Son of Man will gather all the righteous into the kingdom of God. The redeemed shall be saved while the unrighteous shall be exterminated. Moreover, Mk 3.28-29 (= Mt. 12.31) refers to the fact that every sin and blasphemy shall be forgiven humans except those against the Holy Spirit. While the text does not specifically depict this forgiveness as a saving act by the Son of Man, even this forgiveness of sins is quite obviously associated with his ministry.

Mark, the primary gospel among the Synoptic Gospels, establishes already in his second chapter (2.10) that the Son of Man is the forgiver of sins *on earth*, and Matthew and Luke copy Mark almost verbatim in this claim. Otto emphasizes that until Mk 8.28, Jesus refers to the Son of Man in the third person, as for example in 2.10. However, Otto insists that this circumlocution is merely Jesus' way of introducing the notion of the Son of Man as the agent of the kingdom. In doing so he makes it plain that he uses this method to associate that title with himself. He refers in the *third person* to the Son of Man as forgiver of sins on earth to explain *his act* of curing the paralytic by removing his guilt and shame. Matthew and Luke confirm this identification of Jesus as the Son of Man who forgives sins, by more loosely employing the title with reference to Jesus in the first person, when they copy the narratives of Mark's third-person references.[39] It is obviously of central importance to all three of these evangelists to characterize the Son of Man unequivocally as the *forgiver of sins on earth*.

At the angelic revelation to Joseph in Mt. 1.21, Joseph is instructed to name Mary's expected son Jesus, αὐτὸς γὰρ σώσει τὸν λαὸν αὐτοῦ ἀπὸ τῶν ἁμαρτιῶν αὐτῶν ('For he shall save his people from their sins'). It is not surprising that with such a robust opening Matthew, Mark, and Luke follow up

39. Otto, *Kingdom of God*, pp. 230-35.

on or develop the theme of the Son of Man as savior. This is evident in the nativity story in Luke (2.11), in which the angels inform the shepherds that a savior has been born in Bethlehem. Thus, the theme of savior and forgiver of sins on earth (Mk 2.10; Mt. 9.1-8; Lk. 5.18-26), is significantly present in the Son of Man logia throughout the Synoptic Gospels. Mark 10.45 (Mt. 20.28; Lk. 22.27c) informs the reader that γὰρ ὁ υἱὸς τοῦ ἀνθρώπου οὐκ ἦλθεν διακονηθῆναι ἀλλὰ διακονῆσαι καὶ δοῦναι τὴν ψυχὴν αὐτοῦ λύτρον ἀντὶ πολλῶν ('the Son of Man came not to be ministered unto but to minister and to give his life as a ransom for many').

In a somewhat different context Mt. 18.11 (Lk. 19.10) describes this aspect of the ministry of the Son of Man: 'The Son of Man came to save the lost'.[40] Similar sentiment is found in Mk 2.17 (Mt. 9.13) where Jesus says, αὐτοῖς ὅτι οὐ χρείαν ἔχουσιν οἱ ἰσχύοντες ἰατροῦ ἀλλ᾽ οἱ κακῶς ἔχοντες· οὐκ ἦλθον καλέσαι δικαίους ἀλλὰ ἁμαρτωλούς ('Those who are well have no need of a physician, but those who are sick; I came not to call the righteous, but sinners'). Tödt emphasizes that it is the authority (ἐξουσία) implied in this ministry of healing for the needy and ill that links this ministry of the Son of Man to his ἐξουσία to proclaim the reign of God, supercede the Torah, and forgive sins.[41] Moreover, in the narrative of the healing of the paralytic man in Capernaum, Jesus is said to have healed him by exercising precisely this role and authority as forgiver of sins. It is exactly this power and authority that surprised the crowd and was challenged by the religious authorities.

The narrative appears in Mk 2.1-12 (2.5): καὶ ἰδὼν ὁ Ἰησοῦς τὴν πίστιν αὐτῶν λέγει τῷ παραλυτικῷ Τέκνον ἀφίενταί σου αἱ ἁμαρτίαι ('Then Jesus, seeing their faith [of the man's four friends who brought him] said to the paralytic, "My son, your sins are forgiven"'); with parallels in Mt. 9.1-8 (9.2b): εἶπεν τῷ παραλυτικῷ Θάρσει τέκνον ἀφίενταί σου αἱ ἁμαρτίαι ('He said to the paralytic, "Take heart, my son, your sins are forgiven"') and Lk. 5.18-26 (5.20): καὶ ἰδὼν τὴν πίστιν αὐτῶν εἶπεν· Ἄνθρωπε ἀφέωνταί σοι αἱ ἁμαρτίαι σου ('Seeing their faith, he said, "Man, your sins are fogiven you"').

---

40. The Greek text here is contested. Matthew 18.11 is not present in the primary ancient sources, such as ℵ (Sinaiticus), B (Vaticanus), Θ (Koridethi), and L (Regius-Paris), as well as some ancient Syriac and Bohairic sources, and Eusebius. It is present, however, in D (Bezae Cantabrigiensis), L^mg (Regius Lectionary), Θ^c (Koridethi commentary), the Vulgate, and some Old Latin versions. In any case, it is not a strong parallel for the Markan citation on this issue of the Son of Man as savior. Since this text is well authenticated as original in Luke and is so similar but obviously a late insertion in Matthew, the imperative text-critical conclusion is that a scribe inserted v. 11 into Matthew to bring it into conformity with Luke. Obviously this would have taken place after the major families of manuscripts had been established but before Jerome's Vulgate translation. That would place it at about 350 CE at the latest.

41. Tödt, *Son of Man*, pp. 133-35.

The central point of the story is thrust home after the religious authorities accuse Jesus of blasphemy in claiming God's prerogative of forgiving sins (Mk 2.6), ἦσαν δέ τινες τῶν γραμματέων ἐκεῖ καθήμενοι καὶ διαλογιζόμενοι ἐν ταῖς καρδίαις αὐτῶν ('some of the scribes were sitting there questioning in their hearts'), Mt. 9.3, καὶ ἰδού τινες τῶν γραμματέων εἶπαν ἐν ἑαυτοῖς· Οὗτος βλασφημεῖ ('and, behold, some of the scribes said to themselves, "This person is blaspheming"'), Lk. 5.21, καὶ ἤρξαντο διαλογίζεσθαι οἱ γραμματεῖς καὶ οἱ Φαρισαῖοι λέγοντες· Τίς ἐστιν οὗτος ὃς λαλεῖ βλασφημίας; τίς δύναται ἁμαρτίας ἀφεῖναι εἰ μὴ μόνος ὁ θεός; ('And the Scribes and Pharisees began to discuss and question, saying, "Who is this person that is speaking blasphemies? Who can forgive sins but God alone?"').

So the Synoptic Gospels define the second function of the Son of Man as the forgiver of sins on earth, a feature related as well to the few references to him as savior in these gospels. The critics' challenging question, τίς δύναται ἁμαρτίας ἀφεῖναι εἰ μὴ μόνος ὁ θεός ('Who can forgive sins but God alone?'), is promptly answered by Jesus, Τί ταῦτα διαλογίζεσθε ἐν ταῖς καρδίαις ὑμῶν; τί ἐστιν εὐκοπώτερον, εἰπεῖν τῷ παραλυτικῷ· Ἀφίενταί σου αἱ ἁμαρτίαι, ἢ εἰπεῖν· ἔγειρε καὶ ἆρον τὸν κράβαττόν σου καὶ περιπάτει; ἵνα δὲ εἰδῆτε ὅτι ἐξουσίαν ἔχει ὁ υἱὸς τοῦ ἀνθρώπου ἀφιέναι ἁμαρτίας ἐπὶ τῆς γῆς λέγει τῷ παραλυτικῷ· Σοὶ λέγω ἔγειρε ἆρον τὸν κράβαττόν σου καὶ ὕπαγε εἰς τὸν οἶκόν σου ('Why do you question thus in your hearts? Which is easier, to say to the paralytic, "Your sins are forgiven", or to say, "Rise, take up your pallet and walk? But that you may see that the Son of Man has authority and power (ἐξουσίαν) on earth to forgive sins" he said to the paralytic, "I say to you, rise, take up your pallet, and go home"', Mk 2.8-11; Mt. 9.4-7; Lk. 5.22-24). Theissen and Merz see this demonstration of the saving power and authority of the Son of Man as a direct function of the kingdom breaking in.

> A new legal order prevails in the βασιλεία which is shaped by God's unconditional readiness to forgive, as is shown above all by Jesus' parables (e.g., the merciless creditor in Matthew 18.23ff.; the prodigal son in Luke 15.11ff.). The citizenship of the kingdom of God is made up of forgiven sinners. In return, God expects them also to forgive one another and not to judge (Matthew 6.12; 7.1). What in earthly legal circumstances is embezzlement...is a positive act in the legal order of the kingdom of God. In it, the immoral and disloyal steward becomes a moral hero (cf. Luke 16.1ff.).[42]

Hare observes that when Jesus was asked by the authorities what right he had to go around forgiving sins, an obvious prerogative of God alone, Jesus responded by challenging the assumption at the root of this claim. He demonstrated through a spectacular miracle that God had given him the

---

42. Theissen and Merz, *Historical Jesus*, p. 272.

authority to forgive sins: 'In this respect Mk 2.1-12 constitutes a parallel
to Mk 1.21-28, where Jesus' authority as a God-authorized teacher is confirmed by an exorcism'.[43]

Tuckett agrees, pointing out that were Jesus dependent upon some exte-
rior authority for his role as forgiver of sins, he would have said, 'You should
realize that I am the Son of Man!' Instead he said that in order to make it
plain that the Son of Man had the inherent authority to forgive sins on earth,
i.e., that he possessed that divine prerogative, he would also heal the paralytic: 'The narrative emphasizes that what justifies Jesus' claim to forgive
is not his application to himself of the name "the Son of Man" but his demonstration of the (God-given) power to heal'.[44] The equation is, thus, the
opposite way around. The Son of Man has authority to forgive sins as is
demonstrated by his power to heal; rather than the authority to forgive sins
being obvious because he is the Son of Man.

Tuckett thinks that it makes no difference if we substitute the personal
pronoun for the Son of Man in this text 'But that you may know that I have
the authority to forgive sins on earth...' The meaning is the same. What is
demonstrated in the healing of the paralytic is that it is in the nature of the
Son of Man to save, i.e., to forgive and heal. That Son of Man is already here
identified with Jesus of Nazareth.[45] Norman Perrin was quite certain that
Mark's theological emphasis here is focused upon Jesus' *personal* authority. Mark puts great weight upon both the authority Jesus employs and upon
the claim 'that he exercised that authority as the Son of Man'.[46] Hare[47] and
Tödt[48] generally agree with the content of this part of Perrin's claim, noting that for Mark there is no distinction between the authority of Jesus and
the authority of the Son of Man, but Hare feels that Perrin tends to blur the
subject and predicate of the equation about Jesus authority as Son of Man to
heal and forgive.[49]

Luke inserts at 7.37-50 the narrative of the 'woman of the city, who was a
sinner'. She came into Simon's house where Jesus was dining, and washed,
dried, and anointed his feet. When she was denigrated for doing such a
thing, Jesus commended her and declared that because of her great love
and compassion her sins were forgiven: εἶπεν δὲ αὐτῇ· Ἀφέωνταί σου αἱ
ἁμαρτίαι (7.48). Τίς οὗτός ἐστιν ὃς καὶ ἁμαρτίας ἀφίησιν ('Who is this, who

43. Hare, *Son of Man Tradition*, p. 187.
44. Christopher Tuckett, 'The Present Son of Man', *JSNT* 14 (1982), pp. 48-81 (62).
45. Tuckett, 'The Present Son of Man', p. 62.
46. Norman Perrin, *A Modern Pilghrimage in New Testament Christology* (Phila-delphia: Fortress Press, 1974), p. 89.
47. Hare, *Son of Man Tradition*, p. 190.
48. Tödt, *Son of Man*, pp. 127-28.
49. Hare, *Son of Man*, p. 189.

even forgives sins?'), grumbled those who were at table with him (7.49b). The Synoptic Gospels' Son of Man both proclaims the impending arrival of the divine reign on earth and forgives sins during his earthly sojourn.

Hare, Tödt, Higgins, and Lindars[50] all agree that the issue at stake in the Son of Man logia regarding forgiveness of sins has to do with the ἐξουσία of Jesus, and consequently of the Son of Man. This issue of authority, thus, links the narrative of the healing of the paralytic and that of the woman who bathed Jesus' feet; but it also connects those instances of that authority with Mk 2.28 in which Jesus declares the authority of the Son of Man to be Lord of the Sabbath. This ἐξουσία is not only expressed in the power to heal but also in the authority over the interpretation of the Torah. Tödt observes.

> How is the *exousia* of the Son of Man conceived in Mark 2.10? According to Mark 2.5b-10 Jesus by granting to an individual person the forgiveness of his sins utters a claim which must seem blasphemous to his opponents (v. 7), 'For by forgiving sins Jesus not only places himself at variance with the existing Law which demands the punishment of the sinner but also assumes that very place at which according to Jewish belief and knowledge God alone can stand'. Seeing Jesus standing at this place, the community calls him Son of Man. This is unparalleled and unprecedented; neither in the synoptic nor in the Jewish apocalyptic tradition is there any other indication that the Son of Man forgives sins. This ascription to Jesus of the power of forgiving sins is thus not inspired by attributes of the *transcendent* Son of Man [emphasis added]. Rather is the reverse process recognizable; by calling Jesus in his unique authority Son of Man and conceiving of Jesus' authority as including the forgiveness of sins, the community can formulate the saying that the Son of Man has the *exousia* to forgive sins on earth.[51]

The Son of Man logia in the Synoptic Gospel narratives confirm this role of Jesus as proclaimer of the impending divine reign, and in that context his function as forgiver of sins on earth: 'The forgiveness of sins, which Jesus according to Mk 2.10 claims as part of his activity on earth, is part of his way of acting with a mission, part of his authority. How are the *exousia* in general and the authority to forgive sins in particular correlated? Jesus' preaching of the coming of God's reign not only summoned men to turn round in repentance in face of this coming but also included the assurance of God's forgiveness'.[52] Entry into the divine kingdom does not just carry with it the promise of transcendental forgiveness at the last

50. See Hare, *Son of Man Traditon*, pp. 190-92; Tödt, *Son of Man*, pp. 125-33; Angus J.B. Higgins, *Jesus and the Son of Man* (Philadelphia: Fortress Press, 1964), pp. 26-30; Barnabas Lindars, *Jesus, Son of Man: A Fresh Examination of the Son of Man Sayings in the Gospels* (Grand Rapids: Eerdmans, 1983), pp. 46, 176.

51. Tödt, *Son of Man*, p. 129.

52. Tödt, *Son of Man*, p. 129.

judgment. He also offers the more surprising, and for Jesus' audience more offensive, notion that 'already here on earth' humanity's sins are forgiven, implying present existential salvation.

3. *Son of Man as Messianic Suffering Servant*

The second of Bultmann's categories contains a number of Son of Man logia that describe in various ways the necessary and impending suffering of this messianic figure. They are a compact set of very similar statements about the Son of Man.

Table 2

3.1. *Son of Man* Logia *in the Synoptic Gospels Regarding the Suffering Servant*

Mt. 8.20—The Son of Man has nowhere to lay his head = Lk. 9.58;
Mt. 12.40—The Son of Man will be three days and nights in the belly of the earth;
Mk 8.31 The Son of Man must suffer = Mk 9.12; Lk. 9.22;
Mt. 17.22—The Son of Man is betrayed and delivered into the hands of wicked men = Mk 9.31; Lk. 9.44; Lk. 24.7;
Mt. 20.18—The Son of Man is betrayed = Mk 10.33-34a, Lk. 18.31-33;
Mt. 26.2 and 45—The Son of Man is betrayed to be crucified/betrayed into the hands of wicked men = Mk 14.41;
Mt. 26.24a—The Son of Man goes as prophetically predicted = Mk 14.21a, Lk. 22.22a;
Mt. 26: 24b—Woe to betrayer of the Son of Man = Mk 14.21b, Lk. 22.22b;
Lk. 22.48—He asks Judas in Gethsemane 'Do you betray the Son of Man with a kiss?'
Lk. 6.22—The disciples are blessed if they are persecuted for the Son of Man's sake.

3.2. *Exposition*

The Synoptic Gospels make much of this role of the Son of Man as the Suffering Servant. Mark 8.31 typifies those suffering servant passages, and has Jesus' explanation that as Son of Man he must suffer much at the hands of the religious authorities who will kill him (Καὶ ἤρξατο διδάσκειν αὐτοὺς ὅτι δεῖ τὸν υἱὸν τοῦ ἀνθρώπου πολλὰ παθεῖν καὶ ἀποδοκιμασθῆναι ὑπὸ τῶν πρεσβυτέρων καὶ τῶν ἀρχιερέων καὶ τῶν γραμματέων καὶ ἀποκτανθῆναι). The parallels in Matthew and Luke are interesting. Matthew 16.21 declares: Ἀπὸ τότε ἤρξατο ὁ Ἰησοῦς δεικνύειν τοῖς μαθηταῖς αὐτοῦ ὅτι δεῖ αὐτὸν εἰς Ἱεροσόλυμα ἀπελθεῖν καὶ πολλὰ παθεῖν ἀπὸ τῶν πρεσβυτέρων καὶ ἀρχιερέων καὶ γραμματέων καὶ ἀποκτανθῆναι ('From that time Jesus began to show his disciples that he must go to Jerusalem and suffer many things from the elders and chief priests and scribes, and be killed'). Luke 9.22 expresses it in this way: εἰπὼν ὅτι δεῖ τὸν υἱὸν τοῦ ἀνθρώπου πολλὰ παθεῖν καὶ ἀποδοκιμασθῆναι ἀπὸ τῶν πρεσβυτέρων καὶ ἀρχιερέων καὶ γραμματέων καὶ ἀποκτανθῆναι ('The Son of man must suffer many things, and be rejected by the elders and chief priests and scribes, and be killed').

The disciples resist this role and identity for the Son of Man and rebuke him through the voice of Peter. To this Jesus responds by reemphasizing the fact that suffering is the destiny of the Son of Man. In Mk 9.12, 31; 10.33; and 14.41b Jesus describes his impending suffering and death. The parallels in Matthew and Luke make virtually the same prophetic statements (Mk 9.31 = Mt. 17.12; Lk. 9.44; Mk 10.33 = Mt. 20.18-19; Lk. 18.32-34; Mk 14.41b = Mt. 26.45b): ἰδοὺ ἤγγικεν ἡ ὥρα καὶ ὁ υἱὸς τοῦ ἀνθρώπου παραδίδοται εἰς χεῖρας ἁμαρτωλῶν ('The Son of man will be delivered into the hands of sinful men').

Mark 8 is the watershed chapter in the Synoptic's story of Jesus of Nazareth as the Son of Man and Suffering Servant. The context of this narrative depicts Jesus as having arrived at a point at which he felt great ambivalence about his ministry. He had just fed the 4000 (Mk 8.1-10). Then he had had an argument with the Pharisees that seemed to trivialize his ministry because people were fixing only on the miracles and missing the message (8.11-13). Immediately thereafter he is protrayed as distressed over his disciples misunderstanding him, and sharply chides them with the denigrating rhetorical question (8.14-21), καὶ ἔλεγεν αὐτοῖς· Οὔπω συνίετε ('Do you not *yet* understand?', 8.21). There follows Jesus' healing of a blind man (vv. 22-26). However, in the same breath, so to speak, he negatively charges the blind man not to re-enter his own village or tell anyone of his healing. Obviously, Jesus is intentionally depicted as having no trust in or patience with the crowds who had become enamored of his miracles but immune to his message.

Then (vv. 27-33) Jesus challenges his disciples as to whether they understand who he really is, whether they perceive what he intends in his ministry, and whether they discern the real nature and mission of the Son of Man. It seems like a situation contrived by the author of the gospel to announce Jesus messianic role as Son of Man and Suffering Servant. Jesus asks who the crowds take him to be. The disciples' answers are varied: John the Baptist *redivivus*, Elijah *redivivus*, or another one of the ancient prophets. Then Jesus focuses on the disciples directly. Who do they take him to be? Peter responds, 'You are the Christ' (ἀποκριθεὶς ὁ Πέτρος λέγει αὐτῷ· Σὺ εἶ ὁ Χριστός).

Immediately Peter receives a severe scolding, informing him and the disciples that they should, under no circumstances, use that kind of language or say anything like that to anyone. It is of interest that Matthew's account implies surprise regarding Jesus severe and austere response to Peter's 'profession'. Matthew (16.16-17) turns the scene into a positive picture. He has Peter responding: σὺ εἶ ὁ χριστὸς ὁ υἱὸς τοῦ θεοῦ τοῦ ζῶντος ('You are the Christ, the Son of the living God'), in response to which Matthew has Jesus highly commending Peter as having received such insight directly from God alone: ἀποκριθεὶς δὲ ὁ Ἰησοῦς εἶπεν αὐτῷ· μακάριος εἶ, Σίμων Βαριωνᾶ, ὅτι σὰρξ καὶ αἷμα οὐκ ἀπεκάλυψέν σοι ἀλλ᾽ ὁ πατήρ μου ὁ ἐν τοῖς οὐρανοῖς ('And Jesus answered him, "Blessed are you, Simon Barjona, for flesh and blood has not revealed this to you but my Father who is in heaven"').

Otto observes that ancient popular messianism and the transcendental messianism of Second Temple Judaism traditions were synthesized long before the time of Jesus. However, in Jesus' allusions to the Suffering Servant Messiah in Mk 8.31-33, a new synthesis was being proposed, the contours of which had not been worked out in Jewish traditions. It was not only mystifying to Jesus' audiences, including his disciples, but it was obviously seen as blasphemous, according to the gospel narratives (Mk 14.61-2; Mt. 26.63-4; Lk. 22.66-71):

> The gospel tradition…shows with sufficient clearness that after a certain time [Mk 8.27-31] Christ's preaching underwent a change occasioned by some new teaching. This new teaching is briefly summarized in the simple sentence: 'The Son of Man must suffer'… The suffering was not a tragic accident which befell him as a man. … It was the suffering which would befall him as Son of Man, and this meant that it was part and parcel of his Messianic calling. As the Son of Man he must suffer. It was part and parcel of the saving work committed to him. It was redemptive suffering. It was thereby the last consequence of his logical eschatology. The saving of the lost for the eschatological order was, as such, and as a whole, the meaning of his person and message.[53]

Obviously in Mark's version, Jesus perceived that for Peter and the disciples, as for the crowds at the time, the term Christ (Messiah or Anointed One) meant Son of David. That would have implied that Peter was identifying Jesus as an ordinary man with an extraordinary lineage, namely, the line of David, and a regal destiny. Peter saw Jesus as a person who would restore the throne and dynasty of David in Israel. The implications would be that Jesus, like the Maccabees, would lead a revolution to regain for Israel the status of an independent nation, free from foreign imperial domination; in this case, throwing out the Romans.

Jesus' response to this was vigorous and intensely negative. Mark (8.31-33) and the parallels (Mt. 16.21-23; Lk. 9.22) tell their readers that Jesus' ministry took a sinister turn from this point forward. In 8.31-32a we read: Καὶ ἤρξατο διδάσκειν αὐτοὺς ὅτι δεῖ τὸν υἱὸν τοῦ ἀνθρώπου πολλὰ παθεῖν καὶ ἀποδοκιμασθῆναι ὑπὸ τῶν πρεσβυτέρων καὶ τῶν ἀρχιερέων καὶ τῶν γραμματέων καὶ ἀποκτανθῆναι…καὶ παρρησίᾳ τὸν λόγον ἐλάλει ('He began to teach them that the Son of Man must suffer many things, and be rejected by the elders and the chief priests and the scribes, and be killed…and he said this plainly').

53. Otto, *Son of Man*, pp. 247-48.

Peter's response to Jesus' references to the Son of Man as Suffering Servant, must have confirmed that Jesus' suspicion was correct. Peter and the disciples, in Mark's account, were thinking of the Son of Man as a political messiah and not as the suffering servant. They thought the Son of Man was a heroic human figure, the Son of David, who was on the way to being crowned king of Israel in Jerusalem. Thus, as the crowd in the Johannine story (12.32-34), so Peter, as spokesman for the disciples in Mark's narrative, is mystified—even angered—by Jesus talk of his Suffering Servant role.

Peter expressed his mystified anger by taking Jesus aside and rebuking him for associating the messianic Son of Man with suffering and death. We can discern that to the disciples that sounded like a defeatist attitude, just as they were catching their stride in preparing for the revolution. Jesus' rebuke is also his explanation: Ὕπαγε ὀπίσω μου, σατανᾶ, ὅτι οὐ φρονεῖς τὰ τοῦ θεοῦ ἀλλὰ τὰ τῶν ἀνθρώπων ('Get behind me, Satan, for you are not expressing the sentiments of God, but of men').

When Jesus' declaration in Mk 9.12, regarding the Son of Man as Suffering Servant, provoked opposition, he responded by asking how, if the Son of Man were not to be the Suffering Servant, the scripture could, nonetheless, have claimed that the messianic Son of Man needed 'to suffer many things and be treated with contempt'. This implied that Jesus' was consciously referring to Isaiah 53 and presenting the paradox of his being both the Son of Man and Suffering Servant. The gospel narratives present a Son of Man who was clearly aware, Otto believed, that he was commissioned as an *expiatory* suffering servant of God as in Isaiah's prophecy. Otto took the reference to necessity in this passage to mean that Jesus was convinced of a divine predestination of the expiatory death of the Son of Man. Aside from Otto's implied reference to atonement theology, his emphasis was upon the defining fact of Jesus ministry, i.e., that Jesus saw the role of Suffering Servant as inherent to the identity of the Son of Man.

Otto linked this notion of the suffering servant of Isaiah 53 to Jesus' identification of himself in Mk 10.45 and Mt. 20.28. In these passages he is represented as the Son of Man who must give his life as a ransom for many, καὶ γὰρ ὁ υἱὸς τοῦ ἀνθρώπου οὐκ ἦλθεν διακονηθῆναι ἀλλὰ διακονῆσαι καὶ δοῦναι τὴν ψυχὴν αὐτοῦ λύτρον ἀντὶ πολλῶν Otto emphasized that the term λύτρον has a long history in Iranian and Jewish traditions but its ancient uses do not afford us a discriminating definition. He thought it had a legal implication of paying for an unmet obligation but also an emotional import as something useful to cover and conceal a wound or a breach of some expectation:

> If the Son of Man gives his life as a ransom for many, he gives it as a means of their consecration and sanctification, in the divine kingdom of holiness... With this ... deeply numinous element are associated ideas of

forgiveness and pardon… If a fault is covered by expiation, it is also forgiven, pardoned…which can belong only to divine forgiveness… In a righ-
tous man's intercession for those who belong to him there lies atoning and
expiatory power.[54]

Otto contended that Jesus, as Son of Man, did not offer a new theory of
atonement or a new concept of God. He simply indicated that through his
role as Suffering Servant those who identified with him would gain inclu-
sion in the covenant of the coming kingdom. This concept of the divine
kingdom and of a holy nation was only brought to fullbloom in the religion
of Israel. Otto completed his comments on this matter with the apparently
apologetic point that no religion has developed this insight so completely,
profoundly, and to so powerful an expression as Christianity.[55] Contemporary Son of Man scholars of the four gospels do not readily align themselves
with that kind of apologetic dogmatism but endeavor a more objective focus
on the literary data.

The crisis of spirit and message reported by the gospels at this point in
the Jesus-narrative is followed in Mark's account by a kind of rhetorical
peroration in which Jesus' apparently depressive assessment of things is
strikingly underlined. He paints the picture of discipleship in his mission as
bearing a cross. He declares that there is no meaning in life except to lose
one's life for this mission. He insists that earthly gain is worthless and only
heavenly gain is of value, and he declares that the world is full of worthless,
adulterous sinners. The job of disciples is to witness against that world, and
if they do not they betray the Son of Man to their own damnation. One gets
the impression that Jesus was lucky that later he was drawn out of this preoccupation by a mountain top experience, the transfiguration (Mk 9.2-8).

The Son of Man as Suffering Servant, in any case, is a dominant theme
throughout the Synoptic Gospels from this point in Jesus' odyssey onward
to the end of it. After the transfiguration pericope, the story has Jesus'
descending from the mountain and speaking of the Son of Man rising
from the dead. This seems to have mystified the disciples even more, but
they kept their quandary to themselves. After Mk 9.12 (= Mt. 17.12) has
Jesus' oblique reference to Isaiah 53, Mark follows in 9.31 (= Mt. 17.22-
23; Lk. 9.22, 44) with a further elaboration: ἐδίδασκεν γὰρ τοὺς μαθητὰς
αὐτοῦ καὶ ἔλεγεν αὐτοῖς ὅτι ὁ υἱὸς τοῦ ἀνθρώπου παραδίδοται εἰς χεῖρας
ἀνθρώπων καὶ ἀποκτενοῦσιν αὐτόν ('For he was teaching his disciples,
saying to them, "The Son of Man will be delivered into the hands of men,
and they will kill him"').

54. Rudolf Otto, *The Idea of the Holy: An Inquiry into the Non-Rational Factor in
the Idea of the Divine and its Relation to the Rational* (trans. John W. Harvey; New
York: Oxford University Press, 1958), p. 56. See also Otto, *Kingdom of God*, p. 257.
55. Otto, *Kingdom of God*, p. 261. See also Otto, *The Idea of the Holy*, p. 56.

As the final week of Jesus life drew near, Mark has Jesus warning his disciples that all this tragedy is about to actually happen. In 10.33-34 (= Mt. 20.17-19; 26.2; Lk. 18.32-33) Jesus declares: Ἰδοὺ ἀναβαίνομεν εἰς Ἱεροσόλυμα, καὶ ὁ υἱὸς τοῦ ἀνθρώπου παραδοθήσεται τοῖς ἀρχιερεῦσιν καὶ τοῖς γραμματεῦσιν καὶ κατακρινοῦσιν αὐτὸν θανάτῳ καὶ παραδώσουσιν αὐτὸν τοῖς ἔθνεσιν καὶ ἐμπαίξουσιν αὐτῷ καὶ ἐμπτύσουσιν αὐτῷ καὶ μαστιγώσουσιν αὐτὸν καὶ ἀποκτενοῦσιν ('Behold, we are going up to Jerusalem; and the Son of Man will be delivered to the chief priests and the scribes, and they will condemn him to death, and deliver him to the Gentiles; and they will mock him and spit upon him, and scourge him, and kill him').

Mark 14 presents the story of the last day of Jesus life before the crucifixion. In v. 21 (= Mt. 26.24; Lk. 22.22) Jesus observes that he will now surely be killed, as it was predestined, but the person responsible for it is in great spiritual or eternal jeopardy. As Judas and the band approach him in Gethsemane, Jesus observes to the disciples that he is at the point of being betrayed 'into the hands of sinners' (14.41 = Mt. 26.45; Lk. 24.7).

Lindars notes that the importance of these passion logia for Mark, all of which are taken over by Matthew and Luke, may be discerned from Mark's mentioning of them in nine of his Son of Man logia, while the combination of all other characteristics of the Son of Man in Mark only appear in five.[56] Lindars sees three (Mk 8.31; 9.31; 10.31f.) of the nine Markan passion predictions to be the key to the entire set. Mark's use of the verb, παραδίδοται (he is to be delivered) in 9.31 and 10.31f., Lindars thinks, reinforces the connection of the passion predictions with the suffering servant in Isaiah. In a corollary manner, the use of the verb ἀποδοκιμασθῆναι (to be rejected) in 8.31 and 12.10 links them to the Psalms, particularly 118.22: אֶבֶן מָאֲסוּ הַבּוֹנִים הָיְתָה לְרֹאשׁ פִּנָּה (λίθον ὃν ἀπεδοκίμασαν οἱ οἰκοδομοῦντες οὗτος ἐγενήθη εἰς κεφαλὴν γωνίας, 'The stone which the builders rejected has become the head of the corner').

Moreover, Lindars observes that in 9.12, in Jesus' instructions following the transfiguration experience, Mark has Jesus declaring that he will suffer many things and be treated with contempt (πολλὰ πάθῃ καὶ ἐξουδενηθῇ). The use of those two verbs, conclusively links the passion narratives to Isa. 53.3 specifically. Matthew actually uses the word, ὁ υἱὸς τοῦ ἀνθρώπου παραδίδοται εἰς τὸ σταυρωθῆναι ('the Son of Man is to be delivered up to be crucified'). The Son of Man in the Synoptic Gospels is the Suffering Servant of the Hebrew Bible. Lindars sees all these passion logia in the Synoptic Gospels, particularly those in which Jesus is said to have spoken of the necessity of his departing, as indicating an early memory of the post-Easter church regarding the suffering servant nature of the Son of Man.[57]

---

56. Lindars, *Jesus, Son of Man*, pp. 60-84.
57. Lindars, *Jesus, Son of Man*, pp. 74-76.

For Lindars the logia that predict the passion are linked to Mk 10.45 and its parallel in Lk. 22.27: καὶ γὰρ ὁ υἱὸς τοῦ ἀνθρώπου οὐκ ἦλθεν διακονηθῆναι ἀλλὰ διακονῆσαι καὶ δοῦναι τὴν ψυχὴν αὐτοῦ λύτρον ἀντὶ πολλῶν ('For the Son of man also came not to be served but to serve, and to give his life as a ransom for many'). In both Mark and Luke this logion is a response to the disciples' argument about the prominence of each in the coming kingdom, which they apparently expect to be a revolutionary new government of an independent Israel, centered in Jerusalem. Moreover, this is conceptually linked to the foot washing episode at the Last Supper (Jn 13.4-17) and the 'offering for sin' in Isa. 53.10. While the noun λύτρον, is not used in the LXX of Isa. 53.10, the concept of laying down one's life as a sacrifice for others is implied in that entire Hebrew Bible prophecy and in the Synoptic Gospels' concept of the Son of Man as Suffering Servant.

Lindars is not alone in discerning this suffering servant theme as a primary feature of the Son of Man in the Synoptic Gospels. Higgins[58] and Vincent Taylor[59] largely agree with the perspective of Lindars.

Hare concludes, in contrast to Tödt[60] and Hooker[61] that these logia regarding the Suffering Servant Son of Man are not about issues of Jesus' authority but about the fact that the Christ suffers 'in accordance with scriptural necessity'. Hare places the sources of these Synoptic Gospel logia of the Suffering Servant Son of Man in an ancient collection with such pre-Pauline kerygma as, 'Christ died for our sins in accordance with the Scriptures' (1 Cor. 15.3).[62]

Tödt is mainly interested in the relationship between the passion predictions, that is, the Suffering Servant Son of Man logia, and those about his resurrection and exaltation. He attempts to clarify the problem that arises from these two sets of logia being so different, and for many scholars, unrelated and incongruous. Tödt acknowledges that the Son of Man's suffering is formative and essential in the composition of the Markan narrative; and that Mk 8.31 is the watershed incident that turns the Son of Man from simply a proclaimer of the impending divine reign into the Suffering Servant. Moreover, Tödt points out that the suffering Son of Man passages in 8.27–10.52 and 14.1-42 lead directly into the narratives of Jesus' trial and crucifixion, constituting the main frame of the gospel, so to speak. He endorses Wellhausen's defining comment that this shift to the suffering Son of Man is Mark's *theologia crucis*.[63]

58. Higgins, *Jesus*, pp. 30-54.

59. Vincent Taylor, *The Gospel according to St Mark* (New York: Macmillan, 1952), p. 436.

60. Tödt, *Son of Man*, p. 178.

61. Morna Hooker, *The Son of Man in Mark* (London: SPCK, 1967), pp. 108ff.

62. Hare, *Son of Man Tradition*, pp. 195-96.

63. Tödt, *Son of Man*, pp. 145, 148.

Tödt agrees with Bultmann's notion that Mark regarded the logia about the suffering servant and those about resurrection and exaltation as separate and unrelated sets. These are not in unconnected juxtaposition, but connected and related, as Lohmeyer thought. Lohmeyer argues that the three phases of the Son of Man in the Synoptic Gospels are parts of a whole. The proclaimer of the impending divine reign is the suffering Son of Man who will resurrect and ascend to the heavenly status of eschatological judge. In Mk 8.27–10.52, and its Matthean and Lukan parallels, the Son of Man constantly informs the disciples, in one breath, so to speak, of his impending suffering as constituent to the coming of the divine reign.

Moreover, this is the setting for the emphasis upon the suffering awaiting the disciples as a condition of their entry into τὴν βασιλείαν: 'In this way the evangelist leads the reader from Mk 8.31 to 8.38 and 9.1. He first guides the view towards the Son of Man's suffering, then to the disciples' following through suffering, and finally to their future participation in the glory of the transcendent Son of Man'.[64] While in Mark these are only loosely connected in a soteriological emphasis, in Luke's version the suffering Son of Man logia and those describing his transcendent exaltation are more closely connected.

We may summarize this section with the observation, therefore, that the suffering servant theme of Isaiah 53 is dominant in all of the Synoptic Gospels. The identification of that Suffering Servant with the Son of Man and the Heavenly Messiah is clearly established in all of them.

4. *The Son of Man, Heavenly Messiah, as Exalted and Enthroned Eschatological Judge*

The Son of Man logia in the Synoptic Gospels depict the earthly Son of Man becoming the Eschatological Judge. In this unfolding drama he achieves that exalted heavenly status through his ordeal of proclaiming the impending divine reign on earth and through his ordeal of suffering. These gospels see that judge as enthroned in heaven, awaiting his immediately impending *parousia*. That event will bring in completely God's reign on earth, effect the final judgment of the righteous and unrighteous, and wrap up history as we know it. The Son of Man logia depicting this third and final phase of the drama fall into four categories; the resurrection of the Son of Man, the enthronement of the Son of Man, the cosmic signs accompanying the surprising drama of his *parousia*, and the judgment of the righteous and unrighteous.

64. Tödt, *Son of Man*, p. 148.

Table 3

4.1. *Son of Man* Logia *in the Synoptic Gospels Regarding the Exalted and Enthroned Eschatological Judge*

4.1.1. *The resurrection of the Son of Man*
Mt. 17.9—He shall rise from dead = Mk 9.9;
Mt. 20.19b—After three days he shall rise from the dead = Mk 10.34b, Lk. 18.33b;

4.1.2. *The enthronement of the Son of Man*
Mt. 19.28—The Son of Man shall sit on his glorious throne;
Mt. 25.31—When the Son of Man shall come he shall sit on his glorious throne;
Mt. 26.64—Hereafter you shall see the Son of Man seated on his glorious throne = Mk 14.62; Lk. 22.69;
Acts 7.55-56—Stephen envisioned heaven opened and saw the Son of Man standing on the right hand of God.

4.1.3. *The signs accompanying the* parousia *and the arrival of the Son of Man*
Lk. 11.30—As the sign of Jonah, so shall the Son of Man be to this generation;
Lk. 17.24—As light flashing from sky to sky so will be the day of the Son of Man;
Lk. 17.26—As in the days of Noah, so will be the day of the Son of Man;
Lk. 17.30—So will be the day when the Son of Man is revealed;
Mt. 24.27-31 (3)—There will be dramatic cosmic signs of the Son of Man and he will come with power and glory = Mk 13.24-27; Lk. 21.25-28;
Mt. 24.39—So shall the coming of the Son of Man be;
Mt. 10.23—The disciples will not have gone through Israel before the Son of Man returns;
Mt. 24.44—In such an hour as you think not, shall the Son of Man come = Lk. 12.40;
Mt. 25.13—You know not the day or the hour;
Lk. 17.22—Sometimes you will desire to see the day of the Son of Man and will not;
Mt. 16.27, 28—The Son of Man shall come in the glory of the Father and humankind shall see this happen;

4.1.4. *The judgment expedited by the Son of Man and his angels*
Mt. 13.41—Son of Man will send his angels to gather the righteous and unrighteous;
Mk 8.38—Of those ashamed of him in life, he will be ashamed when he comes = Lk. 9.26;
Lk. 12.8—He who confesses the Son of Man in life, him shall the Son of Man also confess at his coming;
Lk. 18.8—When the Son of Man comes will he find faith in the earth?
Lk. 21.36—People should pray that we are worthy to stand before the Son of Man at his coming.

5. *Exposition*

5.1. *The resurrection of the Son of Man*
In the Synoptic Gospels two phases of the exaltation of the Son of Man are noted: resurrection from the dead and ascension to heavenly status. The

former is explicitly described, though surprisingly infrequently and with-out major emphasis. It is referred to explicitly only five times in the gospels of Mark, Matthew, and Luke, combined. The ascension is implicit in the scenes that describe the Son of Man in his heavenly status, from which his return to earth in 'the day of the Son of Man' is impending (Lk. 17.22-30). In Mk 9.9, 31 (= Mt. 17.9) Jesus is reported to have spoken of his antici-pated resurrection from the dead. However, he did not develop the theme in that pericope, closing it rather with a remark about the disciples' mystifica-tion regarding what Jesus could possibly have had in mind in his reference to the Son of Man rising from the dead.

Mark 10.34 and its parallels (Mt. 20.19; Lk. 18.33) promise the resur-rection of the Son of Man on the third day, following his mistreatment and murder by the authorities in Jerusalem: ἐμπαίξουσιν αὐτῷ καὶ ἐμπτύσουσιν αὐτῷ καὶ μαστιγώσουσιν αὐτὸν καὶ ἀποκτενοῦσιν, καὶ μετὰ τρεῖς ἡμέρας ἀναστήσεται ('they will mock him, and spit upon him, and scourge him, and kill him; and after three days he will rise'). The parallel passages have more similar formulaic wording than is the case with most of the other Son of Man logia in the Synoptic Gospels.

Tödt expresses surprise that Mark does not make more of the resurrec-tion story than he does: 'Evidently he did not feel this to be necessary, since he had made *Jesus himself* solemnly announce his rising in the weighty say-ings on the Son of Man's suffering in 8.31; 9.31; 10.33ff.; 9.9'.[65] Luke adds a parallel narrative in 24.7 with equal emphasis upon the resurrection. In all of his references to the suffering of the Son of Man, Jesus concludes with the promise of the resurrection on the third day. Scholars so uniformly agree upon the testimony, weight, and meaning of the resurrection references in these Son of Man logia of suffering and resurrection in the Synoptic Gos-pels that they seldom comment upon the resurrection. Hare has more than fifty pages devoted to the Son of Man logia, dealing with his suffering, and ending with the phrase, 'on the third day rise again'. In none of them does he deal significantly with that culminating triumphal phrase. The treatment is similar in Theissen and Merz, Higgins, and Lindars.

It is the general scholarly consensus that the resurrection narratives are derived from the *kerygma* of the post-Easter church in its attempt to discern the meaning of the unanticipated and premature death of the Son of Man. The church came surprisingly quickly to understand resurrection Christol-ogy as an inherent part of the advent of the divine reign on earth. They per-ceived it as the inevitable outcome of the prophetic narrative of the Son of Man. He had been emphasizing it frequently throughout his ministry.

Geldenhuys explicates this by pointing out how the certainty of the res-urrection of the Son of Man permeates the entire New Testament. Each

---

65. Tödt, *Son of Man*, p. 148.

of the Synoptic Gospels emphasizes it. The suffering servant Son of Man died but Luke–Acts, for example, is a story of how a small company of disciples moved from despondency and powerlessness to confidence and vigor in spreading throughout the known world the proclaimed reign of God. The empowerment they experienced arose from their confidence that the Son of Man's promises of resurrection had been fulfilled. Alongside the death of the Son of Man, his resurrection and exaltation took up a central place in the life of that believing community.[66] While the narratives of resurrection appearances and of the empty tomb differ, there can be no question that all of the Synoptic Gospels, including the short form of Mark, assume throughout the claim of the resurrection of the Son of Man.

5.2. *The enthronement of the Son of Man*

Perhaps the most explicit expression of the exaltation of the Son of Man in the Synoptic Gospels is in Mt. 19.28: ὁ δὲ Ἰησοῦς εἶπεν αὐτοῖς· Ἀμὴν λέγω ὑμῖν ὅτι ὑμεῖς οἱ ἀκολουθήσαντές μοι, ἐν τῇ παλιγγενεσίᾳ, ὅταν καθίσῃ ὁ υἱὸς τοῦ ἀνθρώπου ἐπὶ θρόνου δόξης αὐτοῦ, καθήσεσθε καὶ ὑμεῖς ἐπὶ δώδεκα θρόνους κρίνοντες τὰς δώδεκα φυλὰς τοῦ Ἰσραήλ ('Jesus said to them, "Truly, I say to you, in the new world, when the Son of Man shall sit on his glorious throne, you who have followed me will also sit on twelve thrones, judging the twelve tribes of Israel"'). Matthew 25.31-32a affirms the same picture of transcendental expectation: Ὅταν δὲ ἔλθῃ ὁ υἱὸς τοῦ ἀνθρώπου ἐν τῇ δόξῃ αὐτοῦ καὶ πάντες οἱ ἄγγελοι μετ' αὐτοῦ, τότε καθίσει ἐπὶ θρόνου δόξης αὐτοῦ· καὶ συναχθήσονται ἔμπροσθεν αὐτοῦ πάντα τὰ ἔθνη ('When the Son of Man comes in his glory, and all the angels with him, then he will sit on his glorious throne. Before him will be gathered all the nations').

Jesus promises (Mk 14.62; Mt. 26.64b, Lk. 22.69) that the crowds present in Caiaphas's judgment hall, and hence humanity in general, will see the Son of Man seated on the right hand of Power (deity). Luke's reference states that ἀπὸ τοῦ νῦν δὲ ἔσται ὁ υἱὸς τοῦ ἀνθρώπου καθήμενος ἐκ δεξιῶν τῆς δυνάμεως τοῦ θεοῦ ('From now on the Son of Man is to be seated on the right hand of the power of God'). The exaltation of the Son of Man in the Synoptic Gospels is a stage event to move the main character in the drama from his human ordeal as proclaimer of the divine kingdom, earthly forgiver of sins, and suffering servant, to the status of heavenly Messiah, from which 'he shall come to judge the living and the dead'.

In these three gospels the title, Son of Man, is the title of one destined to *become* the heavenly *Messiah*, exalted by God to transcendental status.

---

66. Norval Geldenhuys, *Commentary on the Gospel of Luke* (The International Commentary on the New Testament; Grand Rapids: Eerdmans, 1954), p. 622.

This is a role toward and into which the Son of Man moves progressively in the earthly odyssey of Jesus, narrated in Mark, Matthew, and Luke. Having begun his ministry as a prophetic human figure he increasingly *becomes* associated with the notion that he will progress to a messianic role with an ultimate transcendent or heavenly status. This status is confirmed by the association of the Son of Man with the angelic host (Mt. 16.27a, 28b): μέλλει γὰρ ὁ υἱὸς τοῦ ἀνθρώπου ἔρχεσθαι ἐν τῇ δόξῃ τοῦ πατρὸς αὐτοῦ μετὰ τῶν ἀγγέλων αὐτοῦ, ...εἰσίν τινες τῶν ὧδε ἑστώτων...ἴδωσιν τὸν υἱὸν τοῦ ἀνθρώπου ἐρχόμενον ἐν τῇ βασιλείᾳ αὐτου ('The Son of Man is to come with his angels in the glory of his Father...there are some standing here who will...see the Son of Man coming in his Kingdom').

This description of the exaltation of the Son of Man is plainly the point made by Mt. 25.31: Ὅταν δὲ ἔλθῃ ὁ υἱὸς τοῦ ἀνθρώπου ἐν τῇ δόξῃ αὐτοῦ καὶ πάντες οἱ ἄγγελοι μετ' αὐτοῦ, τότε καθίσει ἐπὶ θρόνου δόξης αὐτου ('When the Son of man comes in his glory, and all the angels with him, then he will sit on his glorious throne').

It is of immense surprise that virtually none of the commentaries that treat the texts in the Synoptic Gospels and Acts regarding the enthronement of the Son of Man give any attention to that enthronement. They all concentrate their efforts upon the final clause of the texts, namely, the enthronement of the disciples. However, volumes on Biblical Theology such as the work of Vincent Taylor treat the enthronement of the Son of Man as the primary issue in these logia. Taylor views the promises of enthronement as evidence that the authors of the gospels believed that the confidence empowering Jesus to face and endure the ordeal of crucifixion was well founded. They were sure that he really believed he would be exalted after his ordeal on the cross. They were, therefore, confident that what had appeared to them as a tragedy, terminating their revolutionary vision, was in fact the mainspring of a profound transcendental hope for the consummation of the kingdom of God.

> The importance of the entire [enthronement] saying is the revelation which it gives of the strong consciousness of authority which Jesus possessed in relation to the Kingdom; He is endowed by the Father with the powers of royal rule. Equally clear is His certainty concerning the consummation of the Kingdom and His right to assign to the disciples the part they are to play in its life; invested with power, He can give them their place and set them their task in the New Age. Few sayings of His breathe such an air of certainty and authority. But the full significance of the words is that they are uttered in the prospect of rejection and death. In the light of this fact no theory is tenable which implies any opposition to be overcome between Himself and God, which interprets His death as defeat, or which limits its meaning to narrowly individual relationships. Jesus goes to death in the assurance that His Father has given Him lordship, that the Kingdom will be perfected, and that His disciples will share in its joys and its duties. That

> such convictions should be expressed in such an hour is inexplicable unless
> He believes that His suffering and death manifest His lordship and in some
> way are necessary to the consummation of the Divine Rule.[67]

Thomas Manson takes a similar stance. 'Finally, when it becomes apparent that not even the disciples are ready to rise to the demands of the ideal, he stands alone, embodying in his own person the perfect human response to the regal claims of God'.[68] He will be vindicated by God, and the travail he endures in the meantime is not demeaning tragedy but an empowering enthronement in which God himself will be exalted as well.

Theissen and Merz consider it crucial to take the Son of Man synoptic enthronement passages as eschatological in two senses. First, they set the pre-conditions for his *parousia* as Eschatological Judge. Second, they imply an authoritative heavenly imperative for the disciples, as they press forward the cause of the kingdom on earth. The context of the enthronement passages is the discourses on the disciplines and challenges of discipleship. The disciples are empowered by Jesus to drive out demons, heal the sick, bless the houses that receive them, and those that do not they are instructed to curse with the threats of the final judgment.

They are instructed like the Greek Cynic philosophers[69] as to how and with what equipment to travel as they proceed with the kingdom harvest. They disseminate an aura of eschatological salvation and judgment. Their reward is that, as the Son of Man is to be enthroned, they too shall be enthroned to judge the twelve tribes of Israel. They have an eschatological destiny as surely as does he! The Son of Man is promising this to them in advance. 'Common to the apocalyptic and primitive Christian texts is their socio-mythical parallelism: the fate of the Son of Man stands in parallel to the fate of his followers; the authority and outsider role of the Son of Man, his suffering and his exaltation, correspond to the experiences and hopes of the followers of Jesus'. [70]

Of course, contrary to the claims of Burton Mack,[71] neither Jesus nor his disciples are Jewish Cynic philosophers. Rather, discipleship means participation in the eschatological promises. They endure the ordeal of proclaiming the kingdom, suffering reproach for their innovative nonconformism *vis*

67. Vincent Taylor, *Jesus and his Sacrifice: A Study of the Passion-Sayings in the Gospels* (London: Macmillan, 1959), p. 190.

68. Thomas W. Manson, *The Teaching of Jesus: Studies in its Form and Content* (Cambridge: Cambridge University Press, 1959), pp. 227-28.

69. F. Gerald Downing, *Christ and the Cynics: Jesus and the Other Radical Preachers in First-Century Traditions* (Sheffield: Sheffield Academic Press, 1988).

70. Theissen and Merz, *Historical Jesus*, p. 548.

71. Burton Mack, 'Q and a Cynic-Like Jesus', in *Whose Historical Jesus?* (ed. William E. Arnal and Michel Desjardins; Studies in Christianity and Judaism, 7; Waterloo, Ontario: Wilfrid Laurier University Press, 1997), pp. 25-36.

a vis Torah traditions, and await their exaltation. Implied in Jesus' impending exaltation, the disciples see the promise of their exalted positions in
the end-time. Enthroned in heaven, they will judge with the Son of Man,
the heavenly judge. The Psalms of Solomon prophesy (17.26), 'He will
gather a holy people whom he will lead in righteousness; and he will judge
the tribes of the people that have been made holy by the Lord their God'.
The disciples celebrate the enthronement of the Son of Man as the warrant for their achievement of messianic authority. 'They are to form a Messianic collective. Jesus transforms the traditional messianism into a group
messianism'.[72] As one would expect, Theissen and Merz, as well as Taylor
and Manson, see these enthronement texts as based upon Second Temple
Judaism traditions of the heavenly Son of Man. That issue will be treated at
length in Chapter 4.

In his treatment of the enthronement passages, Tödt expresses surprise
that so little attention is given to the pre-existence of the Son of Man. He
declares, 'When we call to mind how quickly the conviction spread in the
primitive community that Jesus is the pre-existent Son of God who became
man, it is surprising that there is not a single Son of Man saying within the
synoptic tradition which links up with the concept of pre-existence from
apocalyptic literature...the synoptic Son of Man sayings have nothing to do
with this concept'.[73] It is unclear what data Tödt is citing or what prompts
this argument and his surprise at this absence of preexistence in Mark, Matthew, and Luke. The Synoptic Gospels nowhere propose a pre-existent Son
of Man, and that notion of his preexistence apparently appears only in the
Fourth Gospel, in the late first or early second century.

Hamerton-Kelly argued, however, that such logia as Mt. 8.20 (Lk. 9.58)
echo more ancient Wisdom sayings and imply that Jesus consciously called
himself Son of Man with the awareness that the title implied his preexistence. Jesus presented himself as comparable to preexistent Wisdom of
Hebrew tradition. Hamerton-Kelly contends that 'for Matthew Jesus was
Wisdom Incarnate'.[74] Hammerton-Kelly's data is thin, his argument unpersuasive, his conclusions not clearly related to the picture the Synoptic Gospels consistently paint, as this study organizes the matter. Hare observes
that Hamerton-Kelly's argument presupposes the view that preexistence is
an essential characteristic of the Enochian Son of man and that consequently

72. Theissen and Merz, *Historical Jesus*, p. 216.
73. Tödt, *Son of Man*, pp. 284-85.
74. Robert G. Hamerton-Kelly, *Pre-existence, Wisdom, and the Son of Man: A Study
of the Idea of Pre-existence in the New Testament* (SNTSMS, 21; Cambridge: Cambridge University Press, 1973), pp. 61 n. 2, 100ff.; see also Jack M. Suggs, *Wisdom,
Christology, and Law in Matthew's Gospel* (Cambridge, MA: Harvard University
Press, 1970), p. 71.

the term implies preexistence when applied to Jesus. Hare sets aside this line of thought out of hand.

Bauernfeind held a view similar to Tödt on this matter, 'The possibility of introducing the concept of pre-existence and the setting for it were in fact provided when the designations Son of Man, Messiah, Son of God, *Logos* and others were used for Jesus'.[75] However the Synoptic Gospels do not treat of the *Logos* nor does their use of the reference, Son of God, imply deity or transcendence. On the basis of standard usages in Mark, Matthew, or Luke, there would be no occasion to think of preexistence as related to the titular nomenclature Bauernfeind mentions. In the end Tödt accounts for the lack of the notion of pre-existence in the enthronement Son of Man logia in the Synoptic Gospels on the basis of the fact that the authors of those documents were

> intent on continuing the teaching of Jesus. In this teaching the concept of pre-existence was as absent as the concept of an itinerary by means of which an eschatological figure would have been described as proceeding in his course leading the way to salvation, according to the pattern of *4 Ezra* 13. The immunity of the synoptic Son of Man sayings from the concepts of pre-existence and itinerary cannot be explained more conclusively, so far as we see, than by assuming that these sayings are dependent on Jesus' preaching.[76]

The Jesus of the Synoptic Gospels has no concept of his preexistence.

Tödt then raises the question as to whether the references in the Synoptic Gospels to exaltation and enthronement are to be taken for face value. He argues that while Lk. 24.26 clearly indicates that the trajectory of the Son of Man 'leads through suffering into glory', it is primarily in Luke–Acts that the emphasis is upon this exaltation. Tödt argues that the exaltation of a human to the dignity of a heavenly Son of Man was a notion of which Jewish doctrine had not yet conceived. However, such exaltation seems very much the point of Daniel 7–9 and *1 Enoch* 37–71, as we shall see more explicitly in Chapter 4.

Reynolds[77] and Casey[78] argue erroneously that in *1 Enoch* (*4 Ezra* and Dan. 7.13), the Son of Man of Second Temple Jewish tradition is both

---

75. Otto Bauernfeind, *Die Apostlegeschichte* (Religion in Geschichte und Gegenwart, 4; Tübingen: Mohr–Siebeck, 1957), col. 1385.

76. Tödt, *Son of Man*, p. 285.

77. Reynolds, *Apocalyptic Son of Man*, pp. 45, 48-49, 54-55, 69. Unfortunately, Reynolds arguments are characterized by frequent incautious generalizations and eisegesis, importing into specific texts and *logia* notions from the general corpus of related writings or concepts, resulting in frequent imprecision regarding the exegesis of the specific texts themselves.

78. Maurice Casey, 'The Use of the Term "Son of Man" in the Similitudes of Enoch', *JSJ* 7 (1976), pp. 11-29 (13). See also Casey, *Son of Man: The Interpretation and Influence of Daniel 7* (London: SPCK, 1979); Casey, *The Solution to the 'Son of Man'*

preexistent and exalted to heavenly status, a model on which the gospels draw for their Son of Man concepts. They are correct about the Son of Man's exaltation and incorrect about his preexistence, apparently confusing trancendental status with preexistence. Manson[79] and VanderKam[80] argue correctly that the preexistence claim for Enoch is untenable. We will treat this matter more extensively in Chapter 4.

Tödt's perplexity about this matter of exaltation seems to arise out of a peculiar distinction he makes between the status of the Son of Man in the exalted posture at the right hand of God, and the process of his getting there and being installed in that place. He agrees that the status is well attested in the synoptic Son of Man logia, but the process of getting there is not.

> We do not intend to dispute here the fact that in the Palestinian primitive community Jesus was conceived of as the exalted one. What we are discussing now is rather the problem whether the concept of exaltation is associated with the sayings about the coming Son of Man and whether it is originally connected with them. We will leave aside also the problem whether and how far the resurrection is considered to be identical with the exaltation or whether the exaltation is an independent aspect additional and subsequent to the resurrection. There is no stereotyped and clear expression of the concept of exaltation to be found in the synoptic texts, not even in Luke, whose way of thinking had an affinity to this concept (cf. 22.62), but who nevertheless described the ruling function of the exalted one indirectly rather than directly by pointing to his activity in the post-Easter present.

For the purposes of this study, we have consistently taken the texts as they stand, without any attempt to discern differences between primitive and redactional forms of the documents. Consequently, it is the conclusion of this analysis that the Synoptic Gospels, in every text referring to the Son of Man's resurrection, exaltation, and heavenly status, assert, imply, or leave room for the association or even identification of exaltation in both resurrection and heavenly status. Two claims are made in those logia. Jesus rose from the dead and Jesus is presented in a status on

Problem (LNTS, 343; New York: T. & T. Clark, 2007); Casey, 'General, Generic and Indefinite: The Use of the Term "Son of Man" in Aramaic Sources and in the Teaching of Jesus', *JSNT* 29 (1987), pp. 21-56; Casey, 'Method in our Madness, and Madness in their Methods: Some Approaches to the Son of Man Problem in Recent Scholarship', *JSNT* 42 (1991), pp. 17-43; Casey, 'Idiom and Translation: Some Aspects of the Son of Man Problem', *NTS* 41 (1995), pp. 164-82; Casey, *Is John's Gospel True?* (London: Routledge, 1996).

79. Thomas W. Manson, 'The Son of Man in Daniel, Enoch and the Gospels', *BJRL* 32 (1950), pp. 171-93 (181-85).

80. James C. VanderKam, 'Righteous One, Messiah, Chosen One, and Son of Man in 1 Enoch 37–71', in *The Messiah: Developments in Earliest Judaism and Christianity* (ed. James H. Charlesworth; Minneapolis: Fortress Press, 1992), pp. 169-91 (179-82).

the right hand of God. Both of these are consistently described in these gospels as standing in contrast with his ordeal of humanness, humiliation, suffering, and death.

It is not a complex matter to divide the issue plainly in this fashion, while it is difficult to agree with the manner in which Tödt poses it, an enigma from which he seems in the end unable to extricate himself. Hare agrees with my critique of Tödt's position. He states it in a rather forthright way by pointing out Tödt's claims that the traditions of the earthly Son of Man and those regarding the heavenly Son of Man were separate and unrelated traditions from pre-Markan formulations to the characterizations in Luke–Acts. Consequently, Tödt has a problem with the notion that it is the earthly Son of Man who is exalted, since no trajectory is described in the Synoptic Gospels for the itinerary from one to the other. Moreover, he also has a problem with connecting a resurrection of the earthly Son of Man with the identification of the figure that appears in heavenly status, claiming that the Son of Man logia do not give us enough information to make this connection. As indicated above, the question is whether the resurrection of the earthly Son of Man is part of the exaltation of which Jesus prophesies, or whether the exaltation has to do with a separate and later issue, namely, the identification of a figure at God's right hand. Hare believes Tödt's attempt to divide the tradition rather arbitrarily is consistently wide of the mark, in his address to such logia as Lk. 22.28-30; Acts 7.55ff., Mt. 19.28, and Mark 8. He observes

> Apparently Tödt cannot believe that [the evangelist] would understand 'the Son of man' to function in the same way in these…very different sayings. This appears to be Tödt's problem, not [the evangelist's]. The evangelist uses the phrase in sayings that imply Jesus' mortal nature as well as in logia concerning his destined heavenly glory without perceiving that one use is more appropriate than the other.[81]

Hans Conzelmann agrees with the perspective taken in this study. He emphasizes that the Son of Man is described throughout the Synoptic Gospels as an independent agent on earth and also as an agent of God and eschatological judge, when in heavenly status. On the one hand, therefore, he has a commission from God and carries out his mandate on his own volition and in terms of his own independent judgment, in his ministry on earth. On the other hand, the Son of Man logia indicate that he is raised from the dead and placed in an exalted heavenly status by a direct act of God and not on his own authority as Son of Man.

Sometimes Jesus is the subject of the action and sometimes God is. 'From this we see that the status of Jesus is something that is bestowed upon him entirely by God. It expresses on the one hand his subjection to God, and on

---

81. Hare, *Son of Man Tradition*, p. 198.

the other hand his special preeminence in relation to the world'.[82] The two types of Son of Man logia thus express this relationship, one set describing his earthly ministry and ordeal and the other describing his triumph over or deliverance from it. Conzelmann describes the trajectory, or in Tödt's terminology, the itinerary, as moving from the humanness of the Son of Man in his earthly ministry to the status of the Heavenly Judge in his exaltation. Contrary to Tödt, this picture is as clear in Mark and Matthew as it is in Luke–Acts.[83] The Son of Man is always subordinate to God but that distinction decreases in size and importance as the Son of Man progresses along the trajectory of his itinerary to Heavenly Messiah.[84]

Hare declares that Matthew, for example, 'would have grave difficulty in comprehending' Tödt's distinctions; and he believes that the evangelists were conscious of the fact, as they wrote the narrative of the Son of Man, that Jesus' predictions regarding the exaltation of the Son of Man by resurrection and assignment to heavenly status, were combined as a direct fulfillment of the prophecy of Ps. 110.1.

It cannot be doubted that the authors of the Synoptic Gospels saw the promised enthronement of the Son of Man as an integral aspect of the proclaimed and impending divine reign. It was their confident hope and their untrammeled expectation. Jesus, as the Son of Man, was vindicated by an act of God in the form of resurrection from the dead and heavenly exaltation. The disciples saw this as a surety of their own impending eternal life and enthronement. The Stephen-narrative in Acts 7.55-56 is their testimony to the conviction that their hope was not merely vain or mythic. They had hard data. Stephen had seen the Son of Man standing on the right hand of God.

5.3. *The signs accompanying the* parousia *and the appearance of the Son of Man*

The heavenly status of the exalted Son of Man is described in many ways and in numerous passages in the Synoptic Gospels. That status is amply documented in the narratives. Nonetheless, the return of the Son of Man as judge will be sudden and surprising. Matthew, Mark, and Luke describe the *parousia* of the Eschatological Judge as arriving as a thief in the night. Without warning, but with great drama he will arrive. The signs of Jonah and Noah, and remarkable cosmic disturbance will coincide with his spectacular descent from heaven to earth (Lk. 11.30; 17.24; Mt. 24.27-31; Mk 13.24-27; Lk. 17.26; and 21.25-28). It will be an astounding day of

82. Hans Conzelmann, *The Theology of St Luke* (trans. Geoffrey Buswell; New York: Harper, 1960), p. 176.
83. Tödt, *Son of Man*, pp. 284-92.
84. Tödt, *Son of Man*, pp. 175-78.

revelation regarding the Son of Man that will be beyond description (Lk. 17.30; Mt. 24.39). He will come with divine power and with the heavenly host.

Undoubtedly, both Matthew and Luke borrow this narrative from Mark, and hence are parallels to the somewhat more austere report of Mk 8.38-9.1. The key element of this passage in Mark does not allude to the final judgment, as do Matthew and Luke, but only presents the heavenly status and authority of the exalted Son of Man, together with his surprising impending *parousia*, Καὶ ἔλεγεν αὐτοῖς Ἀμὴν λέγω ὑμῖν ὅτι εἰσίν τινες ὧδε τῶν ἑστηκότων οἵτινες οὐ μὴ γεύσωνται θανάτου ἕως ἂν ἴδωσιν τὴν βασιλείαν τοῦ θεοῦ ἐληλυθυῖαν ἐν δυνάμει ('And he said to them, "Truly I say to you that there are some of those standing here who shall not see death until they see that the kingdom of God has come with power"').

In his pre-trial hearing and juridical examination by Caiaphas before the Sanhedrin (Mk 14.53-65), Jesus is described as stating the definition of his role as heavenly Messiah. According to Mark's narrative, when ὁ ἀρχιερεὺς ἐπηρώτα αὐτὸν καὶ λέγει αὐτῷ Σὺ εἶ ὁ Χριστὸς ὁ υἱὸς τοῦ εὐλογητοῦ ('the highpriest asked him and said to him, "Are you the Christ, the Son of the Blessed?"'), Jesus declared, Ἐγώ εἰμι καὶ ὄψεσθε τὸν υἱὸν τοῦ ἀνθρώπου ἐκ δεξιῶν καθήμενον τῆς δυνάμεως καὶ ἐρχόμενον μετὰ τῶν νεφελῶν τοῦ οὐρανοῦ ('I am, and you will see the Son of Man sitting at the right hand of Power, and coming with the clouds of heaven'; see also Mk.13.26; Mt. 24.30b, Lk. 21.27).

Theoretically Jesus might have answered Caiaphas truthfully in a great variety of ways. He is presented in the narrative as obviously choosing, consciously and intentionally, to answer in the specific manner in which he did. He directly defined the Messiah (Christ, the Son of the Blessed) as the Son of Man with the exalted status of the Heavenly Messiah. The Matthean (26.63-4) and Lukan (22.67-69) parallels are worded similarily to the phraseology of Mark.

Luke presents this scene as Jesus debating with the religious authorities. This distinctiveness of the Lukan version is important for our emphasis upon the Son of Man as the Heavenly Messiah because of the more vigorous statement about that which is put into Jesus' mouth by Luke. The assembly of authorities accosted him (22.67), Εἰ σὺ εἶ ὁ Χριστός εἰπὸν ἡμῖν ('If you are the Christ, tell us'). Jesus' response is definitive (22.69) and has an enduring finality about it, εἶπεν δὲ αὐτοῖς Ἐὰν ὑμῖν εἴπω οὐ μὴ πιστεύσητε ἐὰν δὲ ἐρωτήσω οὐ μὴ ἀποκριθῆτε πὸ τοῦ νῦν δὲ ἔσται ὁ υἱὸς τοῦ ἀνθρώπου καθήμενος ἐκ δεξιῶν τῆς δυνάμεως τοῦ θεοῦ ('He said to them, "If I tell you, you will not believe; and if I ask you, you will not answer. However, from now on the Son of Man is seated at the right hand of the power of God"'). This response clearly intends to strengthen the emphasis upon the permanent heavenly status of the Son of Man's exaltation.

Bultmann argued that the logion in Mk 8.38 refers to the Son of Man in the third person and thus it distinguishes between Jesus and the Son of Man. It must, therefore, be authentic to Jesus. The early church would not have crafted such a bifurcation, having come quickly after Easter to conclusively coalesce Jesus and the Son of Man.[85] Tödt argues for a radical separation between the Son of Man logia about Jesus on earth *versus* the apocalyptic Son of Man whose dramatic and cataclysmic return is imminently anticipated by the evangelists.[86] Because this passage and Mk 13.26 use apocalyptic titles, Schmithals argues that they are pre-Markan Son of Man logia, the only two in any of the gospels.[87] Hare says that Bultmann has failed to notice or afford adequate weight to Mark's consistent use of the third person in all fifteen Son of Man logia in his gospel. In that sense, they all seem to imply a distinction between Jesus and the Son of Man, but the important fact is that all of them are set in such contexts that imply a solid identification between the two figures as being the same person.

> For example, even if it could be demonstrated beyond doubt that Mark 13.26 derives from a pre-Christian Jewish apocalyptic pamphlet, its placement in the Gospel of Mark is inconceivable apart from the implied identification of Jesus with the one there referred to as the Son of man. The statement would otherwise be unusable for Christian proclamation...the possibility of Markan creativity here cannot be ruled out... If, as Schmithals argues, Mark was capable of creating all the passion predictions, where 'the Son of man' occurs in statements regarding Jesus' human suffering and subsequent vindication by resurrection, there was certainly nothing to prevent him from creating a saying concerning Jesus' future destiny as eschatological judge. That is, if Mark regarded 'the Son of man' as an appropriate self-designation for 'earthly' and 'suffering' sayings of Jesus, he could naturally extend that usage to 'future sayings...'.[88]

Moreover, Hare criticizes Tödt and Schmithals for failing to read the logia in their theological and narrative contexts.

The point is that in the logia that refer to the signs of the *parousia* of the Son of Man Mark asserts without equivocation that it is the Jesus whom they all knew on earth who is the Son of Man that will return on the clouds in a startling drama. Moreover, Matthew and Luke not only copy the text of Mark, but confess the same eschatological claim. It is this figure, Jesus, the proclaimer of the divine kingdom on earth who will bring in that reign of God with a cosmic spectacle. Lightning will flash across the heavens.

85. Rudolf Bultmann, *The History of the Synoptic Tradition* (Oxford: Blackwell, 1963), pp. 151ff.

86. Tödt, *Son of Man*, pp. 144-46.

87. Schmithals, 'Die Worte', p. 442.

88. Hare, *Son of Man Tradition*, p. 197.

World-reshaping changes will overwhelm the inhabitants of the earth as in the days of Noah. Attention-demanding challenges associated with the descent of the Son of Man will confront all humanity, as Jonah confronted Nineveh in his day and caused radical spiritual renovation. All this will happen to everyone while they are busy making other plans. Humans will all be overtaken in the middle of their work and thoroughly persuaded that a divine intervention has brought the Son of Man into their presence as the final judge of the good and the evil.

As Kümmel writes and Higgins agrees, 'Jesus, in the course of the hearing before the Sanhedrin after his arrest, gave his assent to the question about his Messiahship and illustrated it by pointing to the future coming of the Son of Man in divine glory. Without doubt it follows from this that Jesus expected that his future installation into the full messianic office would be the necessary preliminary to his participation in the coming judgment'.[89] Higgins continues with the observation that the most formatively influential gospel, Mark, reflects a theological development regarding Jesus that has moved far enough along so that what the community remembers Jesus having said about his earthly ministry, death, and resurrection, 'has been radically affected by utterances about the Son of man's future activity as counsel or judge'.[90]

Who is the Son of Man in the Synoptic Gospels? He is the man from Nazareth, commissioned to be the proclaimer of the divine kingdom, who has suffered the ordeal of human life, rejection, and death; who has become the Heavenly Messiah whom God has exalted. Moreover, he is the one who, when heaven is opened for all to see the comprehensive divine drama, will descend with awesome accompaniment, to implement the terminal event of history.

When in Mk 13.26, and its twin in Mk 14.62, this Son of Man of the impending dramatic *parousia* is described as coming in clouds with great power and glory, the context is the narrative about false and true Christs. 'The Son of man saying does not provide new information about Jesus' identity; its function is to point…to the final, public vindication of Jesus and of the faith of those who confess him to be the true Christ'.[91] This is the messianic Son of Man whose coming we anticipate, the evangelists uniformly testify. The Synoptic Gospels speak with vigor and without hesitation or ambiguity of Jesus as the Son of Man. The Proclaimer of the Divine Kingdom; the Suffering Servant; and the Forgiver of Sins on Earth is the

89. Werner G. Kümmel, *Promise and Fulfillment: The Eschatological Message of Jesus* (Studies in Biblical Theology, 23; Naperville, IL: Allenson, 1957), p. 50.

90. Higgins, *Jesus*, p. 75.

91. Donald Juel, *Messiah and Temple: The Trial of Jesus in the Gospel of Mark* (Missoula, MT: Scholars Press, 1977), p. 92.

enthroned Heavenly Messiah whose impending dramatic descent will radically change everything in this world.

5.4. *The judgment expedited by the Son of Man and his angels*

Throughout the Synoptic Gospels, references to the exaltation of the Son of Man to the heavenly status of power and glory generally associate him with the angelic hosts. The declaration of exaltation is also almost always associated with the promise of his *parousia* as the Eschatological Judge. He is exalted and he shall come with power and glory, with the angelic host, to carry out the final judgment of the righteous and unrighteous. Through this dramatic event of judgment, he will fully bring in the divine kingdom he had always proclaimed. He will accomplish that by exterminating all evil and gathering the righteous into God's fold.

His judgment comes in many forms. The passage in Mark, regarding the sudden and spectacular nature of the *parousia*, is set in the context of Jesus' remark that ὁ υἱὸς τοῦ ἀνθρώπου ἐπαισχυνθήσεται αὐτὸν ὅταν ἔλθη ἐν τῇ δόξῃ τοῦ πατρὸς αὐτοῦ μετὰ τῶν ἀγγέλων τῶν ἁγίων ('The Son of Man will be ashamed of him, when he comes in the glory of his Father with the holy angels'). This first form of judgment will be for those who provoke the disappointment of the Son of Man, shaming him by being ashamed of him.

Matthew 16.27b describes his judgment in another way, μέλλει γὰρ ὁ υἱὸς τοῦ ἀνθρώπου ἔρχεσθαι ἐν τῇ δόξῃ τοῦ πατρὸς αὐτοῦ μετὰ τῶν ἀγγέλων αὐτοῦ, καὶ τότε ἀποδώσει ἑκάστῳ κατὰ τὴν πρᾶξιν αὐτοῦ ('For the Son of man is to come with his angels in the glory of his Father, and then he will repay every man for what he has done') This second description of the final judgment as vengeance is more common in the Synoptic Gospels.

Matthew 24.31 (Mk 13.27; Lk. 21.27) is a detailed narrative about the appearance of the Son of Man for positive judgment regarding the righteous, a third kind of judgment at his coming, ἀποστελεῖ τοὺς ἀγγέλους αὐτοῦ μετὰ σάλπιγγος μεγάλης, καὶ ἐπισυνάξουσιν τοὺς ἐκλεκτοὺς αὐτοῦ ἐκ τῶν τεσσάρων ἀνέμων ἀπ' ἄκρων οὐρανῶν ἕως τῶν ἄκρων αὐτῶν ('He will send out his angels with a loud trumpet call, and they will gather his elect from the four winds, from one end of heaven to the other'). The following chapter in Matthew carries forward the same theme, corollary to the 'little apocalypse' of Mark 13 (Mt. 25.32-33), καὶ συναχθήσονται ἔμπροσθεν αὐτοῦ πάντα τὰ ἔθνη, καὶ ἀφορίσει αὐτοὺς ἀπ' ἀλλήλων, ὥσπερ ὁ ποιμὴν ἀφορίζει τὰ πρόβατα ἀπὸ τῶν ἐρίφων,καὶ στήσει τὰ μὲν πρόβατα ἐκ δεξιῶν αὐτοῦ, τὰ δὲ ἐρίφια ἐξ εὐωνύμων ('Before him will be gathered all the nations, and he will separate them one from another as a shepherd separates the sheep from the goats, and he will place the sheep at his right hand, but the goats at the left').

Matthew virtually duplicates Mark, though the latter describes an even more catastrophic termination of history, than the former, to be expected upon the descent of the Son of Man as Eschatological Judge. It speaks of many false messiahs and false prophets, persecution of the followers of the Son of Man, an ordeal for God's community on earth, internecine warfare, intrafamilial hatred, violation and desecration of sacred spaces, extermination of humans by natural devastations, tribulations that cause hordes of fleeing refugees, and massive disturbances of the sun and other heavenly bodies (Mk 13.26-27) καὶ τότε ὄψονται τὸν υἱὸν τοῦ ἀνθρώπου ἐρχόμενον ἐν νεφέλαις μετὰ δυνάμεως πολλῆς καὶ δόξης καὶ τότε ἀποστελεῖ τοὺς ἀγγέλους καὶ ἐπισυνάξει τοὺς ἐκλεκτοὺς αὐτοῦ ἐκ τῶν τεσσάρων ἀνέμων ἀπ ἄκρου γῆς ἕως ἄκρου οὐρανου ('And then they will see the Son of Man coming in clouds with great power and glory. And then he will send out his angels, and gather his elect from the four winds, from the ends of the earth to the ends of heaven'). Here it is clear that a judgment of evaluation is to take place and an assignment of differing status to the righteous and unrighteous. All people and things will be weighed in the divine balances. One might identify this as a fourth form of judgment.

Matthew 13.40-43 is even more colorfully explicit about the judgment that the Son of Man will wreak upon humankind, ὥσπερ οὖν συλλέγεται τὰ ζιζάνια καὶ πυρὶ κατακαίεται οὕτως ἔσται ἐν τῇ συντελείᾳ τοῦ αἰῶνος· ἀποστελεῖ ὁ υἱὸς τοῦ ἀνθρώπου τοὺς ἀγγέλους αὐτοῦ καὶ συλλέξουσιν ἐκ τῆς βασιλείας αὐτοῦ πάντα τὰ σκάνδαλα καὶ τοὺς ποιοῦντας τὴν ἀνομίαν καὶ βαλοῦσιν αὐτοὺς εἰς τὴν κάμινον τοῦ πυρός· ἐκεῖ ἔσται ὁ κλαυθμὸς καὶ ὁ βρυγμὸς τῶν ὀδόντων Τότε οἱ δίκαιοι ἐκλάμψουσιν ὡς ὁ ἥλιος ἐν τῇ βασιλείᾳ τοῦ πατρὸς αὐτῶν ('Just as the weeds are gathered and burned with fire, so will it be at the close of the age. The Son of Man will send his angels, and they will gather out of his kingdom all causes of sin and all evildoers, and throw them into the furnace of fire; there men will weep and gnash their teeth. Then the righteous will shine like the sun in the kingdom of their Father').

The image of Eschatological Judge is one of the most important, perhaps *the* most important of the images of the Son of Man in the Synoptic Gospels. It defines his nature and identity as he is to appear in the *parousia* at the *eschaton*. All three of these gospels strongly emphasize that in his role as judge the Son of Man will mete out the eternal destiny of humankind and bring history to its new age. This cosmic reorganization is a fifth type of judgment that the Son of Man will carry out. He will gather the righteous into the fulfilled kingdom of God and exterminate the unrighteous as well as all forms of institutionalized evil: ἀποστελεῖ ὁ υἱὸς τοῦ ἀνθρώπου τοὺς ἀγγέλους αὐτοῦ, καὶ συλλέξουσιν ἐκ τῆς βασιλείας αὐτοῦ πάντα τὰ σκάνδαλα καὶ τοὺς ποιοῦντας τὴν ἀνομίαν ('The Son of man will send his angels, and they will gather out of his kingdom all causes of sin and all evildoers', Mt. 13.41).

We have noted previously that Jesus declares in Mt. 19.28, ὁ δὲ Ἰησοῦς εἶπεν αὐτοῖς Ἀμὴν λέγω ὑμῖν ὅτι ὑμεῖς οἱ ἀκολουθήσαντές μοι ἐν τῇ παλιγγενεσίᾳ ὅταν καθίσῃ ὁ υἱὸς τοῦ ἀνθρώπου ἐπὶ θρόνου δόξης αὐτοῦ καθήσεσθε καὶ ὑμεῖς ἐπὶ δώδεκα θρόνους κρίνοντες τὰς δώδεκα φυλὰς τοῦ Ἰσραήλ ('Truly, I say to you, in the new world, when the Son of Man shall sit on his glorious throne, you who have followed me will also sit on twelve thrones, judging the twelve tribes of Israel'). It is worth noting that here the role of Eschatological Judge which defines the Son of Man in the Synoptic Gospels, is extended to define those, as well, who are identified with the Son of Man. This is true at least for the twelve disciples on their twelve thrones.

The Lukan parallel (22.28-30) to that passage elaborates the message in an interesting manner, ὑμεῖς δέ ἐστε οἱ διαμεμενηκότες μετ᾽ ἐμοῦ ἐν τοῖς πειρασμοῖς μου· κἀγὼ διατίθεμαι ὑμῖν καθὼς διέθετό μοι ὁ πατήρ μου βασιλείαν ἵνα ἔσθητε καὶ πίνητε ἐπὶ τῆς τραπέζης μου ἐν τῇ βασιλείᾳ μου καὶ κάθησθε ἐπὶ θρόνων τὰς δώδεκα φυλὰς κρίνοντες τοῦ Ἰσραήλ ('You are those who have continued with me in my trials. As my Father appointed a kingdom for me, so do I appoint for you that you may eat and drink at my table in my kingdom, and sit on thrones judging the twelve tribes of Israel').

This enthronement of the Eschatological Judge is a common metaphor in Matthew, Mark, and Luke, as for example in Mt. 25.31-34, 41, Ὅταν δὲ ἔλθῃ ὁ υἱὸς τοῦ ἀνθρώπου ἐν τῇ δόξῃ αὐτοῦ καὶ πάντες οἱ ἄγγελοι μετ᾽ αὐτοῦ τότε καθίσει ἐπὶ θρόνου δόξης αὐτοῦ· καὶ συναχθήσονται ἔμπροσθεν αὐτοῦ πάντα τὰ ἔθνη καὶ ἀφορίσει αὐτοὺς ἀπ᾽ ἀλλήλων ὥσπερ ὁ ποιμὴν ἀφορίζει τὰ πρόβατα ἀπὸ τῶν ἐρίφων καὶ στήσει τὰ μὲν πρόβατα ἐκ δεξιῶν αὐτοῦ τὰ δὲ ἐρίφια ἐξ εὐωνύμων τότε ἐρεῖ ὁ βασιλεὺς τοῖς ἐκ δεξιῶν αὐτοῦ Δεῦτε οἱ εὐλογημένοι τοῦ πατρός μου κληρονομήσατε τὴν ἡτοιμασμένην ὑμῖν βασιλείαν ἀπὸ καταβολῆς κόσμου ... Τότε ἐρεῖ καὶ τοῖς ἐξ εὐωνύμων Πορεύεσθε ἀπ᾽ ἐμοῦ κατηραμένοι εἰς τὸ πῦρ τὸ αἰώνιον τὸ ἡτοιμασμένον τῷ διαβόλῳ καὶ τοῖς ἀγγέλοις αὐτοῦ ('When the Son of Man comes in his glory, and all the angels with him, then he will sit on his glorious throne. Before him will be gathered all the nations, and he will separate them one from another as a shepherd separates the sheep from the goats, and he will place the sheep at his right hand, but the goats at the left. Then the king will say to those at his right hand, "Come, O blessed of my Father, inherit the kingdom prepared for you from the foundation of the world"...then he will say to those on his left hand, "Depart from me, you cursed, into the eternal fire prepared for the devil and his angels..."').

Similar sentiments are expressed by the Lukan passages which are somewhat parallel to this Matthean pericope (Lk. 21.27, 36). There the disciples or the crowd are cautioned to insure that they will be able to stand before the Son of Man at his appearing, presumably as the judge of their eternal destiny: τότε ὄψονται τὸν υἱὸν τοῦ ἀνθρώπου ἐρχόμενον ἐν νεφέλῃ μετὰ δυνάμεως καὶ δόξης πολλῆς ἀγρυπνεῖτε δὲ ἐν παντὶ καιρῷ δεόμενοι ἵνα κατισχύσητε ἐκφυγεῖν ταῦτα πάντα τὰ μέλλοντα γίνεσθαι καὶ σταθῆναι ἔμπροσθεν τοῦ υἱοῦ τοῦ ἀνθρώπου. ('Then you will see the Son of Man coming on the clouds with power and great glory. So be watchful at all times, praying that you may have the strength to escape all these things that will take place, and to be able to stand before the face of the Son of Man'.) So here we have a sixth form of judgment, one must be able to stand morally and spiritually before the judgment, presumably without the fear, guilt, or shame to which the previous types of judgment refer explicitly or implicitly.

Higgins perceives, with Bultmann,[92] Vielhauer,[93] Schweizer,[94] and Jeremias,[95] a tension between the logia regarding the judgment, as in the first five forms listed above, and the cautionary logion that describes the sixth form of judgment here identified. These scholars uniformly agree that this tension reflects the struggle in the early church to come to terms with the delayed *parousia*. On the one hand, the evangelists emphasize confidently that the arrival of the Son of Man in power and glory will be a blessed advent for those who are faithful to their committment to the Son of Man. On the other hand, they must be continually watchful so that they can stand in the judgment. Undoubtedly, behind this sixth form of judgment lies the earlier text, πλὴν ὁ υἱὸς τοῦ ἀνθρώπου ἐλθὼν ἆρα εὑρήσει τὴν πίστιν ἐπὶ τῆς γῆς ('Nevertheless, when the Son of man comes, will he find faith on earth?', Lk. 18.8b). Trust in the promises of the Son of Man and confidence regarding the nature of the *parousia* is one thing, but in the face of this new reality of the delayed *parousia*, endurance is quite another thing.[96]

> The eschatological outlook of the passage is…conditioned by the problem of the delay of the parousia, 'That day' (v. 34) will still come suddenly, but it is not near. Meanwhile life continues on its usual course; and although the suddenness of the irruption of 'that day' is stressed, in view of this expectation the life of the Christian must be regulated by unceasing watchfulness in prayer in order that he may be able to escape 'all these things that will take place', that is, the trials and tribulations immediately preceding the end, and 'to stand before the Son of man'.[97]

92. Bultmann, *History*.

93. Vielhauer, *Gottesreich*, p. 57.

94. Eduard Schweizer, 'Der Menschensohn (Zur eschatologischen Erwartung Jesu)', *ZNW* 50 (1959), pp. 185-209 (192).

95. Joachim Jeremias and Walter Zimmerli, *The Servant of God* (2nd edn; Studies in Biblical Theology, 20; London: SCM Press, 1954).

96. Higgins, *Jesus*, pp. 92-96.

97. Higgins, *Jesus*, p. 93.

Hare says Luke's question implies that appropriate faith exists among the disciples at the time of the writing of the gospel. However, he or the faith community is beginning to think that sufficient time is likely to transpire before the return of the Son of Man for faith to erode to the vanishing point. Such a decline in eschatological expectation may result from persecution, heresy, the cares of this world, indifference, or the decline in the assurance of any *parousia* at all because there are no signs indicating its impending urgency or advent.[98]

Hare observes that such pessimism seems far removed from Luke's sources and from Luke–Acts itself, which throbs with the triumphalism of the gentile expansion of the church. This negative mood can only be accounted for on the basis of a generalized development in the believing community of mystification about the failure of Jesus eschatological promise in such passages as Mt. 10.23 and 16.28: ἀμὴν γὰρ λέγω ὑμῖν, οὐ μὴ τελέσητε τὰς πόλεις τοῦ Ἰσραὴλ ἕως ἂν ἔλθῃ ὁ υἱὸς τοῦ ἀνθρώπου ('I say to you, you will not have gone through all the towns of Israel, before the Son of man comes') and ἀμὴν λέγω ὑμῖν ὅτι εἰσίν τινες τῶν ὧδε ἑστώτων οἵτινες οὐ μὴ γεύσωνται θανάτου ἕως ἂν ἴδωσιν τὸν υἱὸν τοῦ ἀνθρώπου ἐρχόμενον ἐν τῇ βασιλείᾳ αὐτοῦ ('Truly, I say to you, there are some standing here who will not taste death before they see the Son of man coming in his kingdom', Mt. 16.28).

The point to be distilled from all this is the confidence and clarity that the early Christian community obviously had, at the time of the composition of the Synoptic Gospels, regarding the nature and certainty of the Son of Man's return to earth, with heavenly power and authority, as the Eschatological Judge. The surprise is their obvious tenacity in spite of the delay of the *parousia*. They were sure that Son of Man is the heavenly commander of the angelic host (Mt. 13.41), the angels are *his angels*, (ἀποστελεῖ ὁ υἱὸς τοῦ ἀνθρώπου τοὺς ἀγγέλους αὐτοῦ καὶ συλλέξουσιν ἐκ τῆς βασιλείας αὐτοῦ πάντα τὰ σκάνδαλα..., 'The Son of Man will send *his* angels, and they will gather out of his kingdom all causes of sin'). The angels will, at his command, impose the divine reign upon the world of humankind. They will assemble the righteous into the kingdom of God. There can be no doubt that they shaped their world view around the expectation that a new world order was about to be imposed by God, in which the proclaimed divine reign would be realized and the exalted Son of Man would be in charge. His delay merely required of them a more valliant form of faith and faithfulness.

---

98. Hare, *Son of Man Tradition*, p. 67.

B. *Summary of the Identity and Function of the Son of Man in the Synoptic Gospels*

Figure 2a: *Son of Man in the Synoptic Gospels*

Citation		Forgiver of Sin on Earth and Savior	Suffering Servant	Exalted to Heavenly Status
Mk 2.9-11 = Mt. 9.1-8 Lk. 5.17-26		X		
Mk 2.27-28 = Mt. 12.7-8 Lk. 9.22; cf. v. 2b			X	
Mk 8.31 = Lk. 9.22			X	
Mk 8.38 = Lk. 9.26			X	X
Mk 9.9 = Mt. 17.9 cf. v. 2b				
Mk 9.12 = Mt. 17.12b			X	
Mk 9.31 = Mt. 17.22-23 Lk. 9.44			X	
Mk.10.33-34 = Mt. 20.18 Lk. 18.31-33			X	
Mk 10.45 = Mt. 20.28			X	
Mk 13.26-27 = Mt. 24.30b Lk. 21.27				X

Citations				
Mk 14.21 = Mt. 26.24 Lk. 22.22			X	
Mk 14.41 = Mt. 26.45b			X	
Mk 14.62 = Mt. 26.64 Lk. 22.67-69				X
Mt. 12.40			X	
Mt. 26.2			X	
Lk. 12.8				X
Lk. 12.10		X		
Lk. 22.48			X	
Lk. 24.7			X	

Figure 2b: *Son of Man in the Synoptic Gospels*

Citations	Eschatological Judge	Forgiver of Sins on Earth and Savior	Exalted by his Resurrection
Mk 2.27-28 = Mt. 12.7-8 Lk. 9.22			
Mk 8.31			X
Mk 8.38	X		
Mk 9.9 = Mt. 17.9			X
Mk 9.31 = Mt. 17.22-23			X
Mk 10.33-34 = Mt. 20.18			X
Mk 10.45 = Mt. 20.28		X	

Reference				
Mk 13.26-27 = Mt. 24.30b Lk. 21.27	X			
Mk 14.62 = Mt. 26.64 Lk. 22.67-69	X			X
Mk 8.38 = Mt. 16.24-28 Lk. 9.26	X			
Mt. 10.23 Mt. 12.40 Mt. 13.41-43	X X			X
Mt. 18.11 Mt. 19.28 Mt. 24.27 Mt. 24.44	 X X X	X		
Mt. 25.13 Mt. 25.31-46	X X			
Lk. 12.40 Lk. 17.22-30 Lk. 19.10	X X	 X		
Lk. 21.36 Lk. 24.7	X			X

Three factors are predominant regarding the Son of Man in the Synoptic Gospels. First, his identity as the *Eschatological Judge* is indicated in 20 of the 69 logia in Mark, Matthew, and Luke. If we combine this feature with that of the 9 logia that characterize him as the *Exalted Heavenly Man*, a combination that is natural and fitting to the narrative content, we have 29 such Son of Man passages. The Son of Man in these three gospels does not merely have a function, or authority and power, as Eschatological Judge. In the Synoptic Gospels the Son of Man *is* the Eschatological Judge. It is not just a function but his identity. Nine additional logia also anticipate that Jesus will be exalted in the sense of being resurrected, the event that is precursor to his becoming the Exalted Heavenly Man.

Second, we can assume the coalescence of the forgiver of sins and savior. In 5 Son of Man logia he is referred to as *Savior* and 4 emphasize that Jesus, as Son of Man, is the *Forgiver of Sins*. Combined we have 9 dealing with his function as forgiver and savior. In every case that Jesus forgives someone or refers to his salvific role, that function is carried out on earth. No reference is made to his forgiving sins in his exalted heavenly status as Eschatological Judge, or in the *eschaton* at the *parousia*. Moreover, Jesus himself specifically declares that he healed the paralytic by forgiving his sins so the crowd might 'know that the Son of Man has authority to forgive sins on earth'.

Third, in 23 logia the Son of Man is identified as the *Suffering Servant*. This is an unusual element in the Son of Man traditions of Second Temple Judaisms. As we have in Jesus' discussion with the crowd (Jn 12.27-36a), the connection of the Son of Man with the Messiah (Isa. 61.1-3 and Isaiah 53) had been made. The connection of both with the *Suffering Servant* was obviously innovative for the Synoptic Gospels, as well as John.

C. *Conclusion*

The Synoptic Gospels present the Son of Man similarly as a prophetic figure with a sense of divine commission to declare in word and deed that God is in the process of instituting a new order for the history of humanity and God's created world. The Son of Man is the champion of this new order and understands himself in terms of the messianic charter of Isaiah 61. Humans are challenged to engage with him in the divine enterprise to bring an end to evil and initiate a reign of grace, freedom, forgiveness, and goodness on earth. This requires an individual decision on the part of each person. The method for this is clear. One is required to commit oneself in trust and faith to the Son of Man and his cause. This Son of Man, Jesus of Nazareth, champions a renewal of the people of God by expanding a new operational freedom in interpreting the Torah.

The consequence of his innovative challenge to the more rigid interpretation of the Torah by the established religious authorities is the precipitation of a collision course with them. The Son of Man, as a result, must concede to the *modus operandi* of the Judaism of his time, or suffer for maintaining his trajectory of non-conformity in worldview and behavior. In fulfillment of specific messianic texts of the Hebrew Bible he chooses to suffer and comes to envision himself as the Suffering Servant of Isaiah 53. Scholars differ markedly on how conscious Jesus was of the ancient roots of Jewish apocalypticism associated with the figure and title, Son of Man. In the end, the resolution of that issue is not crucial. Regardless of what Jesus's self-understanding might have been, the gospels present him in his unwavering commitment to follow his divinely ordered destiny as the messianic Son of

Man. According to the gospel narratives, the trajectory of that destiny will escalate his suffering unto death on a cross.

As his trajectory becomes increasingly lethal his concept of being the messianic Son of Man also escalates into a vision of a divine rescue from his suffering, crucifixion, and death. This rescue develops in the form of a vision of God exalting the Son of Man by resurrection, ascension, and enthronement in heaven, at the right hand of God. In this exaltation, God is also exalted in that this is not merely a rescue of the Son of Man from death but a rescue of the divine reign throughout the created world. Because the cause of the Son of Man cannot, therefore, fail, God's cause of instituting the universal kingdom of God on earth must triumph, and *vice versa*. That triumph will be demonstrated in the fact that the exalted Son of Man will be assigned the identity, mandate, power, and authority of the Eschatological Judge. As such he will descend from his heavenly status, in divinely accorded power and glory, with the heavenly angelic host at his command. He will judge and exterminate the wicked and every evil thing, and send his angels to gather the righteous into the new world of God's kingdom.

As we have noted throughout this Chapter, scholars disagree on some of the details of the Son of Man narratives in the Synoptic Gospels. The similarities and differences of the claims, statements, content, and style of the Synoptic Gospels is the occasion for a continuing dialogue. The stronger scholarly consensus, however, is focused upon the coherent, relatively uniform, claim of all three regarding the Son of Man's ministry of proclamation of the divine reign and salvific forgiveness of sins on earth, his suffering and death, his exaltation in resurrection and heavenly status as Eschatological Judge.

The concern of this study is what the Son of Man is in the Gospel of John. To clarify the answer to that question, this Chapter has evaluated the nature of the Son of Man in the Synoptic Gospels. That prepares for a comparison of the testimony of Mark, Matthew, and Luke, on the one hand, with the Fourth Gospel, on the other. That analysis will be made against the background of the Son of Man traditions of Second Temple Judaism. That comparison is the burden of Chapter 4.

Chapter 4

COMPARISON OF THE SON OF MAN IN JOHN AND IN THE
SYNOPTIC GOSPELS, IN THE LIGHT OF SECOND TEMPLE
JUDAISM SON OF MAN TRADITIONS

When comparing the figure of the Son of Man in John and the Synoptic
Gospels, scholars have reached different, if not opposite, conclusions. Maddox held that 'In spite of considerable differences of vocabulary and imagery, the fundamental significance of the title "the Son of Man" in John is not
different from that which it has in the Synoptic Gospels'.[1] Morris suggests
that this is a deficient assessment since in regards to 'the Fourth Gospel one
or two additions should be made. In this Gospel the term is always associated either with Christ's heavenly glory or with the salvation he came to
bring. Thus there are references to him as having access to heaven or even
being in heaven (1.51; 3.13; 6.62). The first of these (1.51) carries the idea
that he brings heaven to people on earth... Twice Jesus refers to the Son of
Man as being lifted up (3.14; 8.28; cf. 12.34), and twice to his being glorified (12.23; 13.31)'. Moreover, Morris urges that the Johannine Son of Man
brings and is the bread from heaven which permanently nourishes those
identified with him (6.27, 53). The sum of all this, in Morris's view, is that
the Johannine Son of Man is the revealer of the divine truth, the heavenly
mysteries, and the fact of salvation through belief in him (3.12-18).

   Sloyan points out that the Son of Man in John's Gospel, for example in
1.51, is definitely not the Son of Man of the Synoptics. The Son of Man in
the Synoptic Gospels

> is always a simple human being or a present sufferer or a future reigning
> apocalyptic figure. John's Son of Man is a person on whom angels ascend
> and descend from the open heavens. He is God's man, even as the Jacob
> of the ladder was the man who became 'Israel' and gave that name to his
> people. There is already a sense of mystery about Jesus' calling to which
> every phrase in the first chapter contributes. He is more than and greater
> than all the claims that are being made in his favor. Jesus is interchangeable

---

1. Robert Maddox, 'The Function of the Son of Man in the Gospel of John', in
Reconciliation and Hope: Festschrift for L.L. Morris (ed. Robert J. Banks; Exeter:
Paternoster Press, 1974), p. 203.

with the whole Jewish people, and they with him. He is the contact point on
earth with the myriads of heavenly messengers.[2]

It is my contention that such a complex problem as the relation between
the Son of Man in John and in the Synoptics cannot be addressed in isolation from the first-century Jewish context in which the debate took place.
It was not an intra-Christian debate but rather an intra-Jewish debate and
it involved other traditions outside the Gospels. While the description
of the Son of Man as 'Judge' shows some awareness of the Synoptics'
perspective,[3] the dissimilarities in the depiction of the Son of Man in John
and in the former gospels reflect different influences upon them by the
Second Temple Judaism Son of Man traditions. Three prominent Jewish
traditions shaped Second Temple Jewish notions of the Son of Man: the
prophecy of Ezekiel, the prophecy of Daniel, and the *Parables of Enoch* (*1
En.* 37–71). To what extent these traditions directly influenced any of the
four canonical gospels, and particularly the Gospel of John, is a question
that requires exploration.

The concern of this Chapter is to discern how and to what degree the
author of the Fourth Gospel particularly, may have elaborated his or her
understanding of the Son of Man from the three indicated traditions, as
compared to the influence of those traditions on the first three canonical
gospel narratives. It is also of interest here to examine to what extent the
Synoptic Gospels may have influenced the shape of the Son of Man in the
Gospel of John as we have it today. The question is the extent to which these
traditions of Second Temple Judaisms, and their mediation through the Synoptic Gospels, may have shaped the six dominant facets of the identity and
function of the Son of Man as presented in the Fourth Gospel. Those six
facets are (1) the Son of Man as the Heavenly Figure of the Divine Logos
descended as the incarnate one, (2) the Son of Man as Revealer of the Mysteries of God, (3) the Son of Man as Suffering Servant, (4) the Son of Man
as Savior of the World, (5) the Son of Man as Judge, and (6) the Son of Man
as God's Exalted One.

---

2. Gerard S. Sloyan, *John* (Interpretation: A Biblical Commentary for Teaching
and Preaching; Atlanta: John Knox Press, 1988), pp. 25-26.

3. Phillip Munoa, in personal correspondence with this writer, urges that John's
author was aware of the Synoptic Son of Man and was specifically focused upon continuing and advancing what the Synoptics had done. However, it is the argument of
Sloyan, Hare, Reynolds, and others, as well as the discernment of this study that there
is no explicit indication in John's gospel that its author was citing or referring to the
texts of the Synoptic Gospels. Whether he was familiar with the Synoptics or simply
aware of similar perspectives afloat in the early Christian community, John's gospel is
a conscious move beyond the human who becomes the heavenly man and Eschatological Judge, to the divine *Logos* who descends, saves, and ascends.

A. *Ezekiel and the Gospel of John*

As noted above, the Son of Man in Ezekiel is merely a man, albeit, a man with a priestly and prophetic call. He is commissioned to proclaim the imminent advent of the divine kingdom on earth (e.g., Ezek. 36–37). This seems to resonate with the view of the Synoptic Gospels. In them the structure, as we have noted before, is similar to that of the book of Ezekiel, which in turn takes its form from the Levitical liturgy for ordination of priests (Lev. 8–9). Moreover, in the Synoptic Gospels, the Son of Man, at least until Mk 8.27-33 (Mt. 16.13-23; Lk. 9.18-22), is simply a human proclaimer of the coming reign of God on earth. That reign is to be anticipated in the form of the human experience of forgiveness and *Shalom* (Mt. 10.11-14): peace and prosperity in body, mind, and spirit.

In his recent publication of the summary of his life's work, Casey, a specialist in the Aramaic that was the *lingua franca* of first-century Palestine, argued that all use of the term Son of Man in Second Temple Judaisms was a reference to a mere mortal, as in Ezekiel.[4] Casey writes as though in commenting on the gospels he is dealing with the historical Jesus, not merely with a character in literary documents. Since Jesus' mother tongue was Aramaic, he declares, he could never have meant anything more with his use of the term, Son of Man, than a reference to himself as a mere or ordinary human. Casey believes that even in the Gospel of John, Jesus self-identification as the Son of Man, in so far as those Johannine logia depend upon Jesus own words, originally could have meant only 'ordinary person'.

It was the gospel writer's formulation of Jesus' original usage in their Greek gospel narratives that prompted and permitted them to turn Son of Man into an exalted title. Mark, Matthew, Luke, and John each conspired to employ the term with a Greek definition, to make the theological point that was the burden of each individual gospel, argues Casey. The capstone of Casey's claim is his declaration that the Son of Man logia in the most theological of all the gospels, the Gospel of John, each fit precisely into that gospel's line of thought to confirm the Johannine Christology.

Owen, Shepherd, and others[5] have pointed out significant flaws in Casey's work, noting especially that he completely overlooked the work of Dalman,[6] the nineteenth-century Aramaic specialist who came to precisely opposite

---

4. Maurice Casey, *The Solution to the 'Son of Man' Problem* (LNTS, 343; New York: T. & T. Clark, 2007).

5. Paul L. Owen and David Shepherd, 'Speaking up for Qumran, Dalman and the Son of Man', *JSNT* 81 (2001), pp. 81-222. See also Paul L. Owen, 'Review: Maurice Casey, *The Solution to the 'Son of Man' Problem*', in *RBL* February, 2009.

6. Gustaf Dalman, *Die Worte Jesu: Mit Berücksichtigung des nachkanonischen jüdischen Schrifttums, und der aramäischen Sprache* (Leipzig: Hinrichs, 1898).

conclusions than Casey. Moreover, Casey does not take into consideration the insights, quite different from his own, that were offered more recently by the work of such twentieth-century scholars as Black, Jeremias, Fitzmyer, and Larry Hurtado. The critique of Casey's work by Owen and Shepherd noted many of these deficiencies and offered a substantially different perspective, more in line with Dalman and the cited twentieth-century scholars. In his *magnum opus* in 2007, Casey did not take up their critique to counter it, though he had responded to it in a journal article somewhat earlier.[7]

In any case, Casey's attempt to separate Jesus' personal Aramaic usage from that of the Greek of the New Testament gospels fails on a third count. It is not the historical Jesus with whom we have to do in those gospels, but a literary character in four different narratives. Thus the Son of Man in each of those gospels is what he is in that Greek gospel. Moreover, the use of the term, ὁ υἱὸς τοῦ ἀνθρώπου, was an infelicitous term in Greek, having been derived as Casey argued, from Aramaic. Moreover, at least at the beginning of the Synoptic Gospel narratives, Jesus is depicted (Mk 1.1–8.13) as a mere human who, like Ezekiel, is commissioned to proclaim the coming kingdom of God. Their Greek usage of the term has not corrupted its original meaning as in Ezekiel. It is what becomes of the term and the figure it identifies, as they develop in the gospel narratives, that really counts, not Casey's data about the original Aramaic meanings.

The gospel authors must have been quite sure that their use of the Greek translation of the Aramaic term was authentic or they would not have preserved such an infelicitous Greek usage and used it as a pillar of their narratives. We have no way of recovering the historical Jesus, or his linguistic usages, but we must deal with gospels in which Jesus is presented in the story as though the authors believed they were dealing correctly with historically valid terminology. The biblical meanings of the term, Son of Man, were disposed of immediately after the completion of the Gospel of John, only to be misundertood and misinterpreted by the Greek Church Fathers already in the mid-second century, as noted in the Introduction to this present work.

Casey raises a genuine point of concern, of course, since the Son of Man in Ezekiel is a mere human and so our understanding of Second Temple Judaisms' usages of the term must take that into account. Moreover, it is possible that Casey is correct about Aramaic meanings of Son of Man in the period of 100 BCE to 100 CE in Palestine, however, it is unlikely that he can determine precisely what weight each person or movement in Second Temple Judaism gave to the term. The weight given it in Ezekiel, Daniel, and *1 Enoch*, differs remarkably, case by case.

---

7. Maurice Casey, 'Aramaic Idiom and the Son of Man Problem: A Response to Owen and Shepherd', *JSNT* 25 (2002), pp. 3-32.

In any case, there is none of the Levitical, Ezekiel, or Synoptic Gospel imagery in the Fourth Gospel, since in John, as the incarnation of the Son of Man, Jesus is a divine heavenly figure from the outset and throughout. Despite incarnation of the *Logos* in the man, Jesus of Nazareth, the Son of Man continues to present throughout John's gospel as the divine *Logos* from heaven (1.1 Ἐν ἀρχῇ ἦν ὁ λόγος, καὶ ὁ λόγος ἦν πρὸς τὸν θεόν, καὶ θεὸς ἦν ὁ λόγος, 'In the beginning was the *Logos*, and the *Logos* was with God, and the *Logos* was God'; 1.14 Καὶ ὁ λόγος σὰρξ ἐγένετο καὶ ἐσκήνωσεν ἐν ἡμῖν, ...πλήρης χάριτος καὶ ἀληθείας, 'And the *Logos* became flesh and dwelt among us, ...full of grace and truth; 3.13, καὶ οὐδεὶς ἀναβέβηκεν εἰς τὸν οὐρανὸν εἰ μὴ ὁ ἐκ τοῦ οὐρανοῦ καταβάς, ὁ υἱὸς τοῦ ἀνθρώπου, 'And no one has ascended into heaven but he who descended from heaven, the Son of Man').

Moreover, this Johannine Son of Man has not come merely to proclaim the impending reign of God, but to save the world in a transcendental and spiritualized or heavenly sense (3.16-17, οὕτως γὰρ ἠγάπησεν ὁ θεὸς τὸν κόσμον, ὥστε τὸν υἱὸν τὸν μονογενῆ ἔδωκεν, ἵνα πᾶς ὁ πιστεύων εἰς αὐτὸν μὴ ἀπόληται ἀλλ᾽ ἔχῃ ζωὴν αἰώνιον. οὐ γὰρ ἀπέστειλεν ὁ θεὸς τὸν υἱὸν εἰς τὸν κόσμον ἵνα κρίνῃ τὸν κόσμον, ἀλλ᾽ ἵνα σωθῇ ὁ κόσμος δι᾽ αὐτοῦ, 'For God so loved the world that he gave his unique Son, that whoever believes in him should not perish but have eternal life. For God sent not the Son into the world to condemn the world, but that the world might be saved through him').

Both Ezekiel and the Johannine Son of Man are called and commissioned to proclaim the impending arrival of God's reign on earth and the consequent reordering of earthly affairs. However, beyond that similarity, it is difficult to find much of the Ezekiel tradition of the human Son of Man in the Gospel of John. Instead, he is described as the heavenly light that illumines all humans (1.5, 8-9), a heavenly teacher (3.2), the revealer of heavenly things (3.12), the salvific Lamb of God (1.29), the possessor and dispenser of the divine spirit (1.33b), and the bridge between the mundane and celestial worlds (1.51). Jesus himself, as Son of Man, claims in the narrative of the Fourth Gospel that he is the Messiah (4.25-26), he descended from heaven (3.13; 6.38a; 48-51), he reveals and enacts the divine will on earth (5.17-37a; 6.38b), he is one and the same with God (10.30; 17.21; see also 1.1), and by his exaltation God is exalted (17.1, 5).

Five of the six characteristics that shape the Johannine figure are not present in the Ezekiel tradition. The Son of Man as the Heavenly Figure of the Divine Logos and descended to earth as the incarnate one, is not present in Ezekiel. Ezekiel is depicted as the Son of Man who reveals some of the divine mysteries regarding God's intent to rebuild and purify his kingdom on earth; but Ezekiel is nowhere in his prophecy a literal Suffering Servant Son of Man, as in John. Nor is he ever the Son of Man as Savior of the

World. While Ezekiel's mission entails pronouncing many things regarding what God wants and intends in his renewal of his world, Ezekiel, as Son of Man, is not described as a judge. The Son of Man in Ezekiel is never exalted to a heavenly status, much less that of the divine Exalted One that we encounter in John's gospel. The Johannine theme of divine exaltation and glorification seems more in tune with the tradition of Daniel and the *Parables of Enoch* than with the narratives of the Prophecy of Ezekiel.

B. *Daniel and the Gospel of John*

Daniel 7.13 is the specific site at which the Son of Man appears in that document. His story stretches from chap. 7 to chap. 9. He makes his appearance by being ushered with a cloud into the heavenly presence of God, the Ancient of Days. He is referred to as 'one like unto a son of man'. The unique form of this appellation has led to a great deal of scholarly debate about the essential nature and function of the Son of Man in Daniel. John Collins argues that this is not the figure of a man at all, but rather of the angel Michael, the champion of the nation of Israel.

In making this claim, Collins suggests that each of the beasts in Daniel 7–12 symbolically represents the evil (beastly) nations or empires for which they stand and which will be defeated by the field forces of the Son of Man. Therefore, argues Collins, the one like unto a Son of Man must also be the symbolic figure who stands for God's people, the righteous ones who carry out God's will on earth. These are styled in the prophecy of Daniel as 'The People of the Holy Ones of the Most High'. Because Michael is referred to in Daniel 12 as the one who, in the *eschaton*, will deliver Israel from trouble, Collins transfers this allusion to the role of the Son of Man in Dan. 7.13 and concludes that the Son of Man in Daniel 7 is the archangel Michael.[8] Stefan Beyerle[9] and Reinhard Kratz agree with this position.[10]

Other considerations have led scholars to different conclusions on the identity of the Son of Man in Dan. 7.13ff. It is good and well that in the end, Michael will save Israel from the travail of her earthly pilgrimage (Dan.

---

8. John J. Collins, *The Apocalyptic Imaginagion: An Introduction to Jewish Apocalyptic Literature* (Grand Rapids: Eerdmans, 1984), pp. 88, 110-15; Collins, *Between Athens and Jerusalem: Jewish Identity in the Hellenistic Diaspora* (Grand Rapids: Eerdmans, 2000), pp. 148-49; John J. Collins and Peter W. Flint, *The Book of Daniel: Composition and Reception* (2 vols.; Leiden: E.J. Brill, 2001), I, pp. 191-92; II, p. 431; see also John J. Collins, *Daniel* (Hermeneia; Minneapolis: Fortress Press, 1993), pp. 304-10.

9. Stefan Beyerle, 'The Book of Daniel and its Social Setting', in Collins and Flint, *The Book of Daniel*, p. 219.

10. Reinhard Kratz, 'The Visions of Daniel' in Collins and Flint, *The Book of Daniel*, p. 97.

12.1: 'At that time shall Michael arise, the great prince who has charge of your people' [RSV]; or, 'At that time shall Michael stand up, the great prince which standeth for the children of thy people' [KJV]. καὶ κατὰ τὴν ὥραν ἐκείνην παρελεύσεται Μιχαηλ ὁ ἄγγελος ὁ μέγας ὁ ἑστηκὼς ἐπὶ τοὺς υἱοὺς τοῦ λαοῦ σου [LXX]. The ancient Hebrew is not altogether clear on the precise import of this passage.

וּבָעֵת הַהִיא יַעֲמֹד מִיכָאֵל הַשַּׂר הַגָּדוֹל העֹמֵד עַל־בְּנֵי עַמֶּךָ [BHS-WTT]).

However, there is no implication here that the one like unto the Son of Man in 7.13 is an angelic or angelomorphic personage. Nor is there any direct reason in the text to associate Michael in 12.1 with the Son of Man in 7.13, since they are in separate pericopes with different literary structures and style; apparently taken from different source narratives; probably written by different authors; certainly derived from different time-settings, and the issue at stake is different in each case, 7.13 and 12.1.

It is not readily apparent why Collins imports Michael from chap. 12 back into Daniel's dream-vision in 7.13-14, in view of the fact that Collins, himself, in keeping with the argument of Martin Noth, declares that 'The dream report [7.13ff.] constitutes a unit in itself and is not imbedded in a larger narrative in the way Nebuchadnezzar's dreams are embedded in the court tales' (in chaps. 2 and 4). Collins thus acknowledges that the Son of Man pericope in Daniel 7 is not to be treated as an inherent part of the imagery of the two separate narratives in Daniel 1–6 and 8–11. One should, therefore, conclude that Dan. 7.13-14 is obviously not to be treated as belonging to the unrelated narrative in chap. 12; that quite different narrative that is even more remote from 7.13 in the text than is 8–11, and that has very different imagery.[11]

In his chapter, 'The Social Setting of the Aramaic and Hebrew Book of Daniel', in Collins's book, Rainer Albertz reinforces this point in declaring that the visions in Daniel 7 and 12 differ definitively.

> Both visions have in common, following the nadir of deterioration, the final collapse of the Hellenistic empire. In Dan. 7.11-12 this is brought about by God's judgement, but in Dan. 12.1 by the victory of the archangel Michael. From this point onwards the two visions differ completely: whereas the former expects the establishment of God's Kingdom and its operations by the community of the pious [the Son of Man's field forces on earth, i.e., The People of the Holy Ones of the Most High], the latter envisages the resurrection of the dead, God's judgement on the pious and the wicked, one to eternal life the other to eternal shame, and finally the elevation of the pious teachers (מַשְׂכִּלִים) as ever-shining stars in God's heavenly world (Dan. 12.2-3).[12]

11. Collins, *Daniel*, p. 277.
12. Rainer Albertz, 'The Social Setting of the Aramaic and Hebrew Book of Daniel', in Collins and Flint, *The Book of Daniel*, pp. 191-92.

The phrase Son of Man appears only one other time in the prophecy of Daniel (8.17). There it specifically refers to a man, namely, Daniel, himself. The angel Gabriel is referred to as a man in 8.15 and 9.21. However, no one is referred to in Daniel as a Son of Man, except (1) Daniel in a reference to a mortal as in Ezekiel, and (2) the figure who looks like a human being that is presented to God in 7.13-14. It is important to consider that in Daniel, Son of Man, means an *Anthropos* of some kind.

Kvanvig argued that Daniel's dream-vision corresponds in all of its key formal elements to a seventh-century BCE Akkadian narrative, *The Vision of the Netherworld*.[13] In that document one of the five primary elements of similarity is the fact that the action agent in the story is a man, a *Anthropos* whom the king of the gods commissions with full responsibility and authority to execute judgment and salvation. Kvanvig's thesis provides a strong alternative to Collins's position.[14]

Collins declares that Daniel refers to a Son of Man who stands in correlation and contrast to the beasts from the sea. While those beasts represent reprehensible rulers of powers and empires on earth, the one like a Son of Man is an ideal ruler to whom is given the divine eschatological kingdom. On the other hand, the Akkadian vision is of a redeemer figure who is 'the exalted shepherd…to whom the king of the gods gives full responsibility' for curbing evil and advancing godliness. The similarity of the two narratives seems far more remarkable than the dissimilarity. However, Collins finds it impossible to acknowledge the similarity or concede the possibility of Dan. 7.13-14 depending upon the more ancient Akkadian story, for that would undercut Collins's claim that the 'one like a Son of Man' in Daniel is an angel, specifically the archangel Michael of 12.1, and not a *Anthropos* as a straightforward reading of the text would urge.

The text of Daniel 7 describes two essential matters. First, the Son of Man is a *Anthropos*. Second, the Son of Man is introduced to God, who promptly assigns him dominion, power, and authority (ἐξουσία). God also assigns him, by implication, a heavenly status and location. Nickelsburg develops at length the relationship between Daniel 7 and the *Parables of Enoch* (*1 En.* 37–71), particularly with regard to the role and status of the Son of Man in both traditions.[15] While he distinguishes carefully between the judicial role of Michael in Daniel 10 and 12, on the one hand, and the

13. Helge S. Kvanvig, 'An Akkadian Vision as Background for Daniel 7', *StTh* 35 (1981), pp. 85-89. See also Kvanvig, *Roots of Apocalyptic: The Mesopotamian Background of the Enoch Figure and of the Son of Man* (WMANT, 61; Neukirchen–Vluyn: Neukirchener Verlag, 1988), pp. 390-91.

14. Collins, *Daniel*, pp. 284-86.

15. George W.E. Nickelsburg, 'Son of Man', in *Anchor Bible Dictionary* (ed. David N. Freedman; New York: Doubleday, 1992), VI, p. 138.

non-judicial role of the one like a Son of Man in Daniel 7, he points out, nonetheless, that 'The heavenly enthronement of the one like a Son of Man [Dan. 7.13ff.] will involve Israel's earthly supremacy over all the nations'. This supremacy is reminiscent of the messianic destiny of Israel in Isa. 61.5-9.

However, it is of significant importance to this Danielic Son of Man tradition that, contrary to the claims of Nickelsburg, the Son of Man in Daniel is neither enthroned nor assigned the identity or function of Eschatological Judge, though he is commissioned and directed to use his power and authority, to subdue the evil kingdoms, empires, and beastly rulers and powers of the earth.

וְלֵהּ יְהִיב שָׁלְטָן וִיקָר וּמַלְכוּ וְכֹל עַמְמַיָּא אֻמַיָּא
וְלִשָׁנַיָּא לֵהּ יִפְלְחוּן שָׁלְטָנֵהּ שָׁלְטָן עָלַם דִּי־לָא יֶעְדֵּה
[BHS] וּמַלְכוּתֵהּ דִּי־לָא תִתְחַבַּל[16]

καὶ ἐδόθη αὐτῷ ἐξουσία καὶ πάντα τὰ ἔθνη τῆς γῆς κατὰ γένη καὶ πᾶσα δόξα αὐτῷ λατρεύουσα καὶ ἡ ἐξουσία αὐτοῦ ἐξουσία αἰώνιος ἥτις οὐ μὴ ἀρθῇ καὶ ἡ βασιλεία αὐτοῦ ἥτις οὐ μὴ φθαρῇ [LXX], 'And to him was given dominion and glory and kingdom, that all peoples, nations, and languages should serve him; his dominion is an everlasting dominion, which shall not pass away, and his kingdom one that shall not be destroyed [RSV]'). He is to bring an end to evil mundane powers and replace them with the universal reign of God. Moreover, though God is the judge and the Son of Man is not formally enthroned in Daniel 7, the Son of Man is to bring in the divine reign through the work on earth of the People of the Holy Ones of the Most High.

In Daniel, the Son of Man never leaves his heavenly *locus* or state. The work of deploying the divine reign on earth is carried out by his field forces. Therefore, to them are also delegated the required (ἐξουσία) dominion, power, and authority to carry out the mission (Dan. 7–9). Thus the one like a Son of Man becomes the heavenly epitome of The People of the Holy Ones of the Most High who are on earth. Conversely, they become the earthly epitome of the exalted and heavenly Son of Man. God is the Judge. God has already made the judgment. Thus, the Son of Man is assigned the role and function of God's agent, the implementer or prosecutor of the judgment. His field forces on earth are those who prosecute God's judgment and bring in his reign.

Just as the beasts in Daniel 7–12 represent vicious, repugnant, and inhumane imperial leaders of the empires of the earth, *human figures* known for their *beastliness* and who must be destroyed, so the Son of Man in the same passage represents a redemptive and perhaps messianic leader of

16. The original composition of Daniel 7 is in Aramaic.

the kingdom of God on earth, *a human figure* who is to be known for his *humane godliness* and who will establish a reign of goodness that shall never be destroyed. The correlation of images requires this equivalence of figures.

Moreover, if the text intended to refer to an angelic or angelomorphic figure, it would have said so, as it does later in other regards in 12.1. The text goes out of its way to make very clear that what we have in view here is a figure immediately recognized as human. The sense of surprise or wonder implied in the way the passage is worded is not the surprise of seeing near God an angel looking like a man, but rather of seeing a man appearing in the angelic realm and being presented directly to God.

The setting is heavenly, the context other worldly, the mission divine, and the vision ethereal. If that human figure were an angel, there would have been every reason in the world for the author to say so. Something angelic or angelomorphic would have much more readily fit the setting. Thus the author takes pains not to say that, indeed, to say rather carefully exactly the opposite. The vision was not about an angel or angelomorphic figure but about an anthropomorphic figure. That is after all what it says. It says so because that is what the figure was. That personage was a *Anthropos*; and an individual human, not a collectively symbolic figure.

Much is lost from the narrative in Collins' rationale that claims the figure is angelic. The entire point of the passage is that at the end times *humans* will undertake the cause of God in establishing God's reign on earth and shall in the process bring down evil *human* structures of power and oppression and will establish in the earth, instead, a *human* order of godly style and humane virtue. This will be accomplished by a *heavenly human* and those under his command who operate on earth. One can hardly miss the messianic connection of this model with that in Isaiah 61. Thus one can hardly avoid seeing in Dan. 7.13-27 some messianic overtones associated with the Son of Man in Second Temple Judaism traditions, despite the fact that the Son of Man in Daniel is never overtly or clearly designated as *the* Messiah, *a* messiah, or a messianic character.

Was the author of the Fourth Gospel aware of and influenced by the potentially meaningful associations, messianic and otherwise, that we can discern in Dan. 7.13-27? That is difficult to determine. However, a number of things are clear regarding the possibility that he was so aware and so influenced. The Danielic Son of Man has six distinct features. (1) He is a figure with heavenly status who appears with the Ancient of Days (God). (2) He manifests as a human being. (3) He holds significant power and authority (ἐξουσία), accorded him by God directly. (4) He has the commission to destroy the powers of evil but he does not act in the role or function of judge. (5) He has the mission, authority, and responsibility to see that God's work and purpose of judgment and salvation are prosecuted and the divine reign is established on earth. (6) In this latter sense, the Son of Man in Daniel is also eschatological but does not anticipate a descent to earth in a terminal *parousia*. Daniel does not anticipate such an apocalyptic event at the end of history.

The Gospel of John maintains from the outset that the Son of Man (1) is a heavenly figure who was with God (Jn 1.1-5). (2) Descending to earth (Jn 1.14), he manifested as an individual human being, Jesus of Nazareth (Jn 1.17-23, 29-34; 6.33-35) and not a collective or symbolic figure. (3) He holds significant power and authority (ἐξουσία, LXX Dan. 7.14; Jn 5.27) accorded him by God directly. This is noted throughout John's gospel (Jn 4.34: λέγει αὐτοῖς ὁ Ἰησοῦς· ἐμὸν βρῶμά ἐστιν ἵνα ποιήσω τὸ θέλημα τοῦ πέμψαντός με καὶ τελειώσω αὐτοῦ τὸ ἔργον, 'Jesus said to them, "My food is to do the will of him who sent me, and to accomplish his work"'; 5.30: Οὐ δύναμαι ἐγὼ ποιεῖν ἀπ᾽ ἐμαυτοῦ οὐδέν· καθὼς ἀκούω κρίνω, καὶ ἡ κρίσις ἡ ἐμὴ δικαία ἐστίν, ὅτι οὐ ζητῶ τὸ θέλημα τὸ ἐμὸν ἀλλὰ τὸ θέλημα τοῦ πέμψαντός με 'I can do nothing on my own authority; as I hear, I judge, and my judgment is just, because I seek not my own will but the will of him who sent me'; 6.38: ὅτι καταβέβηκα ἀπὸ τοῦ οὐρανοῦ οὐχ ἵνα ποιῶ τὸ θέλημα τὸ ἐμὸν ἀλλὰ τὸ θέλημα τοῦ πέμψαντός με, 'For I have come down from heaven, not to do my own will, but the will of him who sent me;' 17.4: ἐγώ σε ἐδόξασα ἐπὶ τῆς γῆς τὸ ἔργον τελειώσας ὃ δέδωκάς μοι ἵνα ποιήσω, 'I glorified thee on earth, having accomplished the work which thou gavest me to do'). (4) In John's gospel, as we have seen in Chapter 2 above, the Son of Man has the authority and function of judge (5.27) but never exercises that role or the role of prosecutor (5.28-47). (5) Instead he uses his authority and power (ἐξουσία) to see that God's will and work of salvation is carried out in the world (3.16-18). (6) Finally, the Son of Man in the Fourth Gospel is eschatological only in the sense that he is ultimately glorified while his minions on earth are commissioned to put down evil powers and bring in the divine reign of love that works and grace that heals. As in Daniel, John's exalted Son of Man does not anticipate a descent to earth in a terminal *parousia* and an apocalyptic end of history. Through the exaltation of the Son of Man God is exalted, and in that exaltation the salvific destiny of the whole world is insured and consummated.

There is strong reason to conclude that in regard to these six key characteristics of the Son of Man, the author of the Gospel of John knew and was influenced by the Son of Man tradition in Daniel 7–9. Moreover, in the Fourth Gospel the Son of Man anticipates a triumphal re-ascent to the heavenly realm after his tenure on earth is complete (Jn 14.2-3, 12b, 28; 16.5; 17.13). The gospel reinforces this claim by reporting the assertion, put in Jesus' own mouth, that no one ascends into heaven except the one who has descended from heaven, even the Son of Man (Jn 3.13: καὶ οὐδεὶς ἀναβέβηκεν εἰς τὸν οὐρανὸν εἰ μὴ ὁ ἐκ τοῦ οὐρανοῦ καταβάς, ὁ υἱὸς τοῦ ἀνθρώπου). In this reference, Jesus seems aware of the heavenly Son of Man in Daniel, or at least of a Jewish tradition of such a man who originates in heaven and completes his work by retaining his *status* and *locus* in heaven. In the same breath Jesus asserts that Enoch cannot be the Son of Man because his real *locus* is on earth and he ascends to heaven before he descends from heaven again, as we will discuss more extensively below.

It is significant that in both Daniel and John the Son of Man begins his life's odyssey in heaven. He simply appears in heaven with God and in both narratives he is immediately associated definitively with earthly affairs, unseating evil and establishing the kingdom of God on earth. However, because the Danielic Son of Man never descends from heaven to earth he does not anticipate a subsequent ascent into heaven. The Son of Man in John first descends from heaven and secondly anticipates a return to heaven.

While the Son of Man of the Fourth Gospel is also the heavenly director of earthly forces that will bring down abusive empires and the evil powers of the earth, he, nonetheless, visits the human realm to initiate this process himself.[17] In this regard he differs from the Danielic Son of Man. Though he has the function and authority to judge evil persons and forces (Jn 5.27), he consistently refuses to undertake or exercise that role (Jn 5.28-47; 3.17; 8.15-17; 12.47-48). He is specifically described in John as one who does not condemn but who saves the whole *world* (Jn 3.16-17), not just the righteous, while in Daniel it is only the righteous that are gathered into the divine kingdom. In Daniel the Son of Man sends his field forces to destroy the unrighteous and save the righteous. In John the Son of Man sends his field forces, the disciples, 'as sheep among wolves', to do the work of kingdom-building on earth for the purpose of saving the whole world. Moreover, he insists that they are to do it, not by judgment and prosecutorial power, but by servanthood.

17. Surely in Heb. 1.1 it is evident that the early church made much of this direct identification of their notion of the Son of Man with the Danielic Son of Man. Clearly they noted the fact that their Son of Man performs exactly as the Danielic Son of Man does, but goes one step further. They held to a Son of Man who visits the earthly domain of God to proclaim the reign of God, as did the man, Ezekiel, thus initiating the work of putting down the evil powers and of bringing in the kingdom. In Hebrews the author declares, Πολυμερῶς καὶ πολυτρόπως πάλαι ὁ θεὸς λαλήσας τοῖς πατράσιν ἐν τοῖς προφήταις ἐπ' ἐσχάτου τῶν ἡμερῶν τούτων ἐλάλησεν ἡμῖν ἐν υἱῷ, ὃν ἔθηκεν κληρονόμον πάντων, δι' οὗ καὶ ἐποίησεν τοὺς αἰῶνας ('God, who in bits and pieces, now and then, spoke in ancient times to our ancestors through the prophets, has in these last days visited us in his Son, whom he made to be heir of all things, and by whom he also created the world'.) The coincidence in the pattern of the odyssey of these two Son of Man figures indicates a close connection between the two in the late first century church, a possible backdrop to the later formulations of the Fourth Gospel. This awareness is of special interest because the Synoptic Gospels, written at approximately the same time as the Epistle to the Hebrews, have a remarkably different perspective.

Thus there is reason to conclude that the author of the Fourth Gospel was aware of a Second Temple Judaism tradition of some kind that featured the Son of Man as a heavenly personage. The six corollaries between the Danielic and Johannine Son of Man seem strong indications that John's author was specifically aware of and to some extent dependent upon Daniel. The coincidence in the pattern of the odyssey of these two Son of Man figures in John and Daniel indicates a close connection between the two in the perception of some communities of the early church. Apparently some early Christian communities saw the coincidence between the two figures and John's apparent dependence on Daniel, despite the differences between the Danielic and gospel traditions. Indeed, the early church went one step further than Daniel in the declaration that the heavenly Son of Man descended to visit the human community on earth, thence returning to his heavenly home as his final exaltation.

Hunter confirms that we ought not to be surprised by this implied connection in the mind of the church between the Son of Man in John and that in Daniel. In Caesarea Philippi, on the occasion of Peter's assertion that Jesus is the Messiah, Jesus shifted the title from Messiah to Son of Man. This has the specific import of associating him with and placing him in the Danielic tradition: 'What we can be sure of is that the Son of man is not... merely a poetical synonym for "man". On the contrary, it was about the most pretentious piece of self-description that any man in the ancient East could possibly have used... For "the Son of man", a title ultimately derived from Dan. 7.13, is a mysterious Man who receives a kingdom from God and is destined to reign as God reigns. With this majestic figure Jesus identifies himself...'.[18]

Reynolds weights heavily the reference in both Daniel and John to seeing, suggesting that it sets this logion in tandem with the gospel's frequent emphasis upon believing. He asserts that this is a key to discerning the apocalyptic quality of this logion but his argument is rather opaque. He also urges that 'the "apocalyptic Son of Man" in Jn 1.51 is...also *the Messiah*' [emphasis added]. Reynolds grounds this claim on the fact that Jn 1.51 is, in his judgment, directly dependent upon the image of the one like a Son of Man in Dan. 7.13. He also contends that regarding the Aramaic, Theodosian Daniel, and less so the Old Greek text, the general scholarly opinion agrees that Daniel's Son of Man is the Messiah.[19]

However, it is an open question whether Daniel's Son of Man is represented as the Messiah in 7.13. Moreover, it is perhaps over-stated to suggest

18. Archibald M. Hunter, *Introducing New Testament Theology* (Philadelphia: Westminster, 1957), p. 19.

19. Benjamin E. Reynolds, *The Apocalyptic Son of Man in the Gospel of John* (WUNT, 2/249; Tübingen: Mohr–Siebeck, 2008), pp. 90-91.

that this is the general position of scholars. For example, while Geza Vermes allows for the suggestion,[20] Collins alludes to an ancient rabbinic contention that Daniel's figure on the cloud is messianic, but neither endorses it nor suggests elsewhere in his extensive work on this passage that the one like a Son of Man in Dan. 7.13 is to be described as *the* Messiah. Collins remarks that there was a rabbinic tradition that the reference to a figure on the clouds was always a reference to deity or to the Messiah. However, Collins makes nothing of this rabbinic curiosity.[21]

The perspective is quite different in the Synoptic Gospels. As we noted in Chapter 3, Otto was certain that the notion of the kingdom that the Son of Man proclaimed was derived from Iranian influences and their sources; and mediated into the gospels through the ideas that derived from Second Temple Judaisms. These notions in Second Temple Judaisms were in turn derived from the exilic and post-exilic exposure of the Israelites to Babylonian ideologies. With Gerhard von Rad,[22] he perceived, just as Hunter concluded, that the special apocalyptic distinction made in the Synoptic Gospels between the present ministry of the Son of Man and his future eschatological destiny derived directly from the Prophecy of Daniel. Otto thought the Jesus Movement and its apocalyptic narratives in the gospels were shaped by the Persian influences upon the eschatology of Daniel 7–9.[23]

He further asserts that it is the imagery of Dan. 7.13 that shaped the shift in the Synoptic Gospels. At first they describe the concept of the kingdom of God as breaking in on earth in the proclamation by a human Son of Man. This is a divine reign in the form of an earthly ethical and spiritual renewal of Israel. As the trajectory of the gospel narratives unfolds, this shifts toward the 'purely transcendental' notion of the kingdom of heaven. To this heavenly kingdom the Son of Man ascends and becomes the Eschatological Judge, awaiting his spectacular descent in the *parousia*: 'God's royal claim will be fulfilled, and the judgment will be at hand, …the kingdom of heaven will descend from above, … the world will undergo a marvelous transformation. Such expectations are put into a concrete form in the later ideas of a Jerusalem that comes down from heaven; they form the inevitable connotations surrounding all preaching of the coming of the kingdom of God, and

20. Geza Vermes, *Jesus the Jew: A Historian's Reading of the Gospels* (rev. edn; Minneapolis: Fortress Press, 2001), p. 171. See also Chrys C. Caragounis, *The Son of Man* (WUNT, 38; Tübingen: Mohr–Siebeck, 1986), p. 134.

21. Collins, *Daniel*, p. 311. Collins refers to *Tanhuma Toledoth* 20: *Targum I Chronicles* 3.24; see also Hermann L. Strack and Paul Billerbeck, *Kommentar zum Neuen Testament aus Talmud und Midrasch* (Munchen: Beck, 1928), I, p. 67.

22. Gerhard von Rad, *Theologisches Wörterbuch zum Neuen Testament* (Göttingen: Vandenhoeck & Ruprecht, 1952), Volume ???, p. 569.

23. Otto Eissfeldt, *Einleitung in das Alte Testament* (Tübingen: Mohr–Siebeck, 1943), p. 36.

of every prayer for it'. This proves progressively to be the theme in the gospels, in the early church, and in much of the church's history ever since.[24] These kingdom concepts, expectations, and prayers are rooted, says Otto, in the transcendent vision of the heavenly status and commission of the Son of Man in Dan. 7.13, as elaborated in the Synoptic Gospels.

This picture would mean that both John's Gospel and the Synoptic Gospels were influenced by the tradition ultimately deriving from Daniel 7–9. However, contrary to John's perspective, this influence took the form in the Synoptic Gospels of an emphasis upon an earthly Son of Man who ascends to the Ancient of Days, God in heaven, at the end of his earthly ministry; and there is commissioned as in Daniel 7 to be the one who brings down evil earthly kingdoms and people, and shepherds the people of God into a divine domain. Thus, there are also radical differences between the Son of Man in Mark, Matthew, and Luke–Acts from the figure in Daniel.

Reynolds devotes his entire volume to the argument that the Gospel of John is wholly dependent on Daniel 7 for its Son of Man imagery and much of its Son of Man theology. Moreover, as noted in chapters two and three of this work, the trajectory of his argument is, consistently and throughout, the claim that Daniel 1–9 is composed of apocalyptic passages and this makes all the Johannine Son of Man logia apocalyptic. Reynolds over-reaches the textual data in this latter claim. However, he has focused scholarly dialogue on the evidence for Johannine awareness of and dependence upon Daniel. Reynolds notes critically that Burkett 'dismisses Dan. 7.13-14 and *4 Ezra* 13 as possible backgrounds for the 'son of Man' title on the grounds that ὁ υἱὸς τοῦ ἀνθρώπου is not found in either of these texts...'.[25]

Burkett noted that first-century authors have widely differing views of the Son of Man, using such traditions in diverse ways so that it is difficult to discern which ones were aware of the Danielic Son of Man, and perplexing to discover just how they intended to use his narrative, if aware of it. Reynolds expands this theme, emphasizing that 'in early Christian literature, the Danielic son of man is interpreted with the same common features that were found in the Jewish apocalyptic interpretations of this figure. The Christian authors understood the Danielic son of man to be a heavenly figure, to have some kind of preexistence, to be the Messiah, to be involved in judgment and salvation, to share descriptions and actions with God, to gather the righteous, and to be recognized'.[26] Reynolds acknowledges that these characteristics in themselves do not prove his case that all the Johannine Son of Man

24. Eissfeldt, *Einleitung*, p. 37.
25. Reynolds, *Apocalyptic Son of Man*, p. 7.
26. Reynolds, *Apocalyptic Son of Man*, p. 85.

logia are apocalyptic, but do constitute the basis for Mark, Matthew, and Luke to emphasize that he is both a present and future Son of Man, as well as a dying and rising figure.

In comparison with the Synoptic Gospels, however, in Daniel's prophecy there is no description of the Son of Man beginning his professional trajectory on earth and from there ascending to heaven. He simply appears on a cloud before God in heaven at the outset of his messianic action. While there is much scholarly debate about whether the Son of Man in Daniel is messianic in character, it is clear that he is commissioned with messianic tasks described in Isaiah 61. It is significant to keep in mind our observation in chapters two and three that in Daniel 7–9, God is the judge, and the Son of Man is only the prosecutor or director of the field forces who bring in the kingdom on earth. Moreover, in Daniel, contrary to the Synoptic Gospels, there is no anticipation of an eschatological *parousia* in which the Son of Man descends to earth with the angelic host to execute the judgment which he is responsible to carry out. If that notion of the Son of Man as heavenly Eschatological Judge, in the Synoptic Gospels, and of his impending *parousia*, came from Second Temple Judaism traditions, they are ideas that must come from other sources than Daniel.

The influence of Daniel 7 on the Gospel of John, however, took the form of a Son of Man who begins in heaven with God, as in Daniel, descends to earth quite unlike the Son of Man in Daniel, but ascends again into heaven to his proper exalted status with God, as shepherd of God's people. In this he is again like the figure in Daniel. However, in Daniel, as in the Synoptic Gospels, the Son of Man remains an *Anthropos*, while in John he is the divine *Logos-Theou*. So in this essential identity and in his descent and ascent he differs from Dan. 7.13. These quite different characteristics of the Son of Man must derive from elsewhere if they are in some way dependent upon or derived from Second Temple Judaism traditions.

To what degree then can we discern in the Danielic Son of Man the six primary features of the comparable Johannine figure? As previously indicated, those six facets are (1) the Son of Man as the Heavenly Figure of the Divine Logos descended as the incarnate one, (2) the Son of Man as Revealer of the Mysteries of God, (3) the Son of Man as Suffering Servant, (4) the Son of Man as Savior of the World, (5) the Son of Man as Judge, and (6) the Son of Man as God's Exalted One.

(A) Daniel's Son of man is, indeed, and exclusively a Heavenly Figure from beginning to end. However, in no way is he characterized as having a divine identity or role. Nothing in his nature and role would identify him as or with the *Logos-Theou*; nor does he descend to earth. He does not become man. He begins as a *Anthropos* and remains such throughout his odyssey. (B) Daniel's Son of Man might be thought of in a certain sense as revealing heavenly, even divine, mysteries, in the sense that presumably he commands and communicates with The People of the Holy Ones of the Most High. However, even that action seems to be mainly an act of God, delegating the power and authority of the Son of Man to the field forces on earth. (C) The Danielic Son of Man is in no sense the Suffering Servant, even if we should judge that he has some implied messianic characteristics. (D) The 'one like unto a Son of Man' in Dan. 7.13 does perform a kind of salvific role and so might be considered a model of a savior figure, in that he is commissioned to put down the powers of evil and raise up the divine kingdom. (E) In Daniel the Son of Man is not a judge but he is commissioned to carry out and apply operationally the results of God's already completed judgment to destroy evil and establish the divine reign in the company of the righteous and in righteousness. (F) Finally, the Danielic Son of Man is God's exalted Son of Man, and not as the result and consummation of his ardors on earth in establishing the divine reign, as in the Synoptic Gospels, but as the nature of his inherent status as the heavenly man, a model much closer to the Johannine image.

The facts that suggest possible influence of Daniel 7–9 upon the Gospel of John are, therefore, easily summarized. First, both Son of Man figures are heavenly figures from beginning to end, though John's Son of Man descends for a salvific tenure on earth as the Suffering Servant of Isaiah 52–53. Second, both figures have a salvific role and commission. That is, both carry out a solution to the problem of evil and the destiny of the saved community. Reynolds gives considerable emphasis to this similarity.[27] Third, both are revealers of the divine mysteries. Fourth, both save rather than judge, though this is an ambiguous comparison because Daniel's Son of Man only saves the righteous while the Johannine figure saves the world. Otto, as we observed above, thought this universalism was the key and center of the Johannine narrative. Fifth, both are exalted by God. Here Reynolds correctly observes that while both are exalted to heavenly status with God, only the Johannine Son of Man is said to be glorified.[28] However, he points out that the *Parables of Enoch*, *2 Baruch*, and the Synoptic Gospels, indicate that the glorification of the Johannine Son of Man corresponds to the various Second Temple Jewish interpretations of the Danielic Son of Man.[29] It

27. Reynolds, *Apocalyptic Son of Man*, p. 143.
28. Reynolds, *Apocalyptic Son of Man*, pp. 198-213.
29. Reynolds, *Apocalyptic Son of Man*, p. 211: '"glory" is a common characteristic of the "one like a son of man" in the interpretations of this figure in Jewish apocalyptic and early Christian literature. The Danielic son of man receives dominion, honor, and a kingdom…or only authority…from the Ancient of Days (7.14). In the Similitudes of Enoch, the son of man figure is glorified and is seated upon a throne of glory (45.3; 51.3; 55.4; 61.8; 62.2,3,5; 69.27-29). In 2 Bar. 30.1, the Messiah returns to heaven in glory. The Synoptic Son of Man is also associated with glory (Mk 8.38; 13.26; Mt. 16.27; 19.28; 24.30; 25.31; Lk. 9.26; 21.27) as is the son of man figure in Revelation

appears that the author of the Fourth Gospel is at least very much aware of the Danielic Son of Man tradition in Second Temple Judaism, and in key ways influenced by it.

C. *The Parables of Enoch and the Gospel of John*

Is the Son of Man concept in the Gospel of John shaped by the Son of Man tradition from *1 Enoch* 37–71?[30] This document from Second Temple Judaism's Son of Man traditions speaks of Enoch being caught up in a whirlwind into the heavenly spheres (37.3; 71.1, (5)) where he surveys the place of the eternal destiny of the wicked and the righteous (37.4–41.1; 52.1–66.1; 67.4-12). He is enthroned in heaven, communes with the heavenly host of angels (48.4–51.5b, 71.1-14), and appears to enter directly into repeated communication with God, himself.

Ultimately, Enoch is informed that there is a figure, the Son of Man, who is to judge the world (46.1-8; 48.2-3), separating out the righteous for salvation and the unrighteous for extermination. In that process this figure, whose name is secret since creation, will bring down the evil powers of this world and establish the destiny of the blessed reign of God in heaven and on earth (45.2-6). In the end, in the Enoch narrative, the name of this Son of Man is revealed to be Enoch, himself. He is the Son of Man and the Eschatological Judge, who will exercise the role and authority (ἐξουσία) of the exterminator of the wicked and the exonerator of the righteous (69.26–70.3; 71.14-17).

There are some elements that seem to indicate that the author of the Gospel of John knew of this tradition. John 3.13 may be read as a diatribe against the notion, apparently held by some apocalyptic Jews of the first century CE, that Enoch was *the* Son of Man, and the *unique* heavenly representative of God himself. In Jn 3.13, the gospel has Jesus declaring that no one ascends into heaven except the one who descended from heaven, namely, Jesus himself as Son of Man; and only he can rightly be designated the Son of Man, God's proper representative on earth. This is a broadside attack upon the Enochic traditions and their claim to be the proper tradition of Judaism. It throws down the gauntlet between Enochic Judaism, on the one hand, and the Jesus Movement, on the other. The gospel author is intending to stake

---

(1.6; 4.12-13). Thus, the glorification of the Johannine Son of Man corresponds with the Jewish apocalyptic and Synoptic interpretations of the 'one like a son of man' from Daniel 7'. It is interesting to note that Reynolds distinguishes between Jewish and Synoptic interpretations, though, of course, they are all Jewish and all forms of Second Temple Jewish Son of Man traditions.

30. George W.E. Nickelsburg and James C. VanderKam, *1 Enoch: A New Translation* (Minneapolis: Fortress Press, 2004), pp. 50-95.

out a bold position for the Jesus Movement as the authentic Judaism. It is the claim of the Fourth Gospel that the depiction of Jesus as the Son of Man represents the correct interpretation of the Danielic Son of Man tradition; so that while *1 Enoch* 37–71 has some of the data correct, it is in error in identifying Enoch as the true Son of Man.

Immediately following this claim in Jn 3.13 the author of that gospel launches into an extended narrative that further dismantles the Enochic tradition. John 3.14 indicates that the Son of Man is not a triumphal judge and is not enthroned in heaven with angelic status, but is rather the *Logos* incarnated in a man, in time and space, who will be lifted up (the suffering servant who will die) as was Moses' serpent in the wilderness. As a consequence he will not exercise his function (ἐξουσία) as Eschatological Judge, but he will instead carry out the divinely destined function of the Son of Man to be the savior of the world (Jn 3.16-18). John 4 then offers an illustration of the mission of Jesus as savior, as he visits with the Samaritan woman at Jacob's well, converts an entire Samaritan village, and declares himself *The* Messiah (4.26). He has set aside his function as the judge and condemner of the world (3.17; 5.27-47; 12.47). Obviously, Enoch cannot be the true Son of Man. Jesus makes the claim for a new kind of Son of Man (see again 12.47).

Enoch, as Son of Man, has a number of key characteristics. (1) He is a human whose odyssey begins on earth. (2) He ascends to heaven where he is enthroned as the heavenly Eschatological Judge. (3) As such, he is designated the Son of Man. (4) He is given angelic status though he does not become angelomorphic, and certainly not divine. (5) He is taught the revelation of all the secrets of heaven and eternity by his tour of the transcendental world. (6) He reveals these secrets to his descendants on earth. (7) He awaits the eschaton to carry out his divine commission of instituting the divine reign. Thus, in *1 Enoch* the Son of Man is both an historical and eschatological figure who becomes a heavenly figure, as well. He is a tangible individual actor and not a collective symbolic agent for God's enterprises.[31]

Burkett notes that many scholars such as Fuller,[32] Kümmel, Marshall, Nickelsburg, Collins, Slater, Caragounis, Witherington, and Barker, argue for the existence of numerous traditions on the Son of Man in Second Temple Judaism. They are persuaded that Daniel and *1 Enoch* play the primary

---

31. The Enochic Son of Man does not fit well the definition of Messiah in Isa. 61.1-9, or the oblique references in Pss. 2.6-10; 8; 110, or in the tradition of the royal messiah as Son of David seated on an earthly throne.

32. Reginald H. Fuller, 'The Son of Man: A Reconsideration', in *The Living Text: Essays in Honor of Ernest W. Saunders* (ed. Dennis E. Groh and Robert Jewett; Lanham, MD: University Press of America, 1985), pp. 207-17.

part in the influences of these traditions upon the gospels.[33] Burkett disagrees and comments upon the influence of *1 Enoch* upon the Synoptic Gospel narratives as follows.

> Despite the arguments of these scholars, it is not likely that the Similitudes can account for the origin of the Christian Son of Man. On the one hand, the apocalyptic sayings in the Synoptics emphasize the coming of the Son of Man, a coming that is practically absent from the Similitudes. On the other hand, a central feature of the Enochic Son of Man is his pre-existence, a feature that has no parallel in the Synoptic sayings. More plausibly, J. Theisohn... has argued that the Similitudes first influenced the Gospels at the level of Matthean redaction. The only close parallels between the Gospels and the Similtudes occur in material unique to Matthew. These include the motif of the Son of Man sitting on 'his throne of glory' (Mt. 19.28; 25.31; cf. *1 Enoch* 62.5; 69.27, 29), the depiction of the Son of Man as eschatological judge (Mt. 13.41-42; 16.27; 25.31-32), and the motif of a burning furnace into which rebellious angels and wicked humans are cast (Mt. 13.41-42, 49-50; 25.41; cf. *1 Enoch* 54.3-6). Theisohn's view is accepted by Mearns... Suter... and J.J. Collins.[34]

There are two flaws in Burkett's argument. First, he implies that if the traditions in Daniel or *1 Enoch* and those in the gospel narratives do not agree in detail, or depict the same worldview and stage scene for the Son of Man, they cannot be connected in any way. Daniel and *1 Enoch* cannot then

33. See Werner G. Kümmel, *The Theology of the New Testament according to its Major Witnesses* (Nashville: Abingdon Press, 1973), pp. 77-78; Kümmel, *Jesus der Menschensohn* (Stuttgart: Steiner, 1984), pp. 20-24; I. Howard Marshall, 'The Son of Man in Contemporary Debate', *Evangelical Quarterly* 42 (1970), pp. 67-87; Marshall, 'The Son of Man and the Incarnation', *Ex auditu* 7 (1970), pp. 29-43; Nickelsburg, 'Son of Man'; Nickelsburg, 'Review: J.T. Milik, *The Books of Enoch: Aramaic Fragments of Qumrân Cave 4*', *Catholic Biblical Quarterly* 40 (1978), pp. 411-19 (417-18); John J. Collins, 'The Son of Man in First-Century Judaism', *New Testament Studies* 38 (1992), pp. 448-66; Thomas B. Slater, 'One Like a Son of Man in First-Century CE Judaism', *New Testament Studies* 41 (1995), pp. 183-98; Caragounis, *Son of Man*; Ben Witherington, III, *The Christology of Jesus* (Minneapolis: Fortress Press, 1990), pp. 233-62; and Margaret Barker, *The Lost Prophet: The Book of Enoch and its Influence on Christianity* (Nashville: Abingdon Press, 1988), pp. 91-104.

34. Delbert Burkett, *The Son of Man Debate: A History and Evaluation* (Cambridge: Cambridge University Press, 1999), p. 78. See also Johannes Theisohn, *Der auserwählte Richter: Untersuchungen zum traditionsgeschichtlichen Ort der Menschensohngestalt der Bilderreden des Äthiopischen Henoch* (Göttingen: Vandenhoeck & Ruprecht, 1975), pp. 149-201; Christopher L. Mearns, 'The Parables of Enoch—Origin and Date', *Expository Times* 89 (1977–78), pp. 118-19; Mearns, 'Dating the Similitudes of Enoch', *New Testament Studies* 25 (1979), pp. 360-69; David Suter, 'Weighed in the Balance: The Similitudes of Enoch in Recent Discussion', *Religious Studies Review* 7 (1981), pp. 217-21; and Collins, *Apocalyptic Imagination*, pp. 178-93.

have influenced the depiction of the Son of Man in the gospels. However, historical themes and patterns influence subsequent concepts and world views in many ways, sometimes subtle and sometimes overt, in minor or major ways, slightly or definitively, often intuitively and sometimes pre-dominantly. Therefore, the influence of past ideas and narratives may have a variegated rather than an exact shaping influence upon subsequent world-views. The developing moments in human life tend to pick and choose the aspects of the past that they incorporate into the present. The ancient Son of Man traditions from Daniel and *1 Enoch* may have shaped the gospel nar-ratives by means of some of their aspects while the gospel authors ignored other parts of those same traditional stories or models. Moreover, secondly, Burkett points out that a central feature of the Son of Man in *1 Enoch* is that he is pre-existent, while there is none of that in the Synoptic Gospels.

Contrary to Burkett's claim most of the primary characteristics of the Son of Man in Daniel are also present in John, though a couple features are missing from that gospel. John has additional characteristics such as the descent and ascent of the Son of Man that are not in Daniel. The Synoptic Gospels have a human Son of Man who is, in the end, a heavenly Son of Man. Both of these are characteristics of the Danielic figure on the cloud before the Ancient of Days, though his humanness does not associate him directly with an earthly tenure. While the Son of Man in Daniel and the Syn-optic Gospels share significant features, they also differ in specific ways. It is evident that the authors of the gospels were formulating, in each case, their own individual picture of the Son of Man and freely adapting in their picture, elements that they had derived from the traditions in Daniel.

Similarly, the authors of both John and the Synoptic Gospels picked and chose from *1 Enoch*, each in his or her individual manner, source mate-rial that each could readily weave into his or her distinctive narrative of the nature and function of the Son of Man. Apparently they were dealing with a rich source of available material. Moreover, in specific gospel passages rather exact references are being made to the sources in Daniel and *1 Enoch*. John 3.13 and 5.27ff. confirm that the Gospel of John is referring to those sources. Burkett agrees with this very fact, at least regarding Matthew's use of the *1 Enoch* material in the references to the Son of Man's throne of glory and role of Eschatological Judge, as mentioned above. Regarding the refer-ences to the Eschatological Judge, Burkett should at least acknowledge the similar influences upon Mark and Luke.

Even more striking, of course, is Burkett's second point, namely, his ref-erence to the preexistence of the Son of Man in *1 Enoch*. He argues that the Synoptic Gospels cannot be dependent upon *1 Enoch* for their notion of the Son of Man because in Enoch he is preexistent, and not in those gospels. It is the case that most scholars refer to the Son of Man in *1 Enoch* as being preexistent. While Burkett and Reynolds disagree radically on whether the

Son of Man in Daniel, *1 Enoch*, and the gospels is apocalyptic, they agree that he is preexistent in Dan. 7.13 and in *1 Enoch*. In neither case, however, is there any warrant in the texts themselves for the preexistence of the Son of Man depicted.

Daniel's Son of Man appears without a time reference, except that he seems to present to the Ancient of Days during Daniel's vision, sometime around 535 BCE. In *1 Enoch* 37–71, only the name of the Son of Man is hidden from very early on, but Enoch arrives on the scene in the *Parables* sometime in history, presumably, since he is a biblical figure presented in Enochic tradition as having existed in history. So, it seems that a distinction must be made, as insisted upon by Manson and James VanderKam regarding the references in *1 Enoch* to the preexistence of the name (or election) of the Son of Man and of the Son of Man himself as having existed but hidden since creation.[35]

Thus, there is no indication anywhere in *1 Enoch* 37–71 that the Son of Man is preexistent to time or to the creation of the material world. Such preexistence references to the personification of Wisdom (Hochma/Sophia) may be noted in Proverbs 8–9 and Job 28, but in *1 Enoch* there is only reference to the *identity* of the Son of Man being hidden, presumably in the mind of God, since before the creation of the world. So, contrary to Hammerton-Kelly, Burkett, Reynolds, and numerous others, *1 Enoch* does not promote the idea of a preexistent Son of Man; but rather of the preexistence merely of the name, concept, or image of the Son of Man (48.1-3).[36]

> Paul Billerbeck asserted that 'pre-Talmudic Judaism knows nothing of a pre-existent Messiah' (Billerbeck 1905: 150). He argued that in the Similitdes of Enoch, the Messiah or Son of Man has ideal pre-existence in the thought world or world plan of God. He is chosen by God before the world's creation and his identity is kept a secret, but he does not have real pre-existence. He is a human being who has been taken to heaven to dwell and appointed to execute Judgment. Rudolf Otto...and Matthew Black... agreed that the son of man in *1 Enoch* has only ideal pre-existence, while T.W. Manson...similarly emphasized the human nature of the Danielic son of man.[37]

35. See again Thomas W. Manson, 'The Son of Man in Daniel, Enoch, and the Gospels', *Bulletin of the John Rylands Library* 32 (1950), pp. 171-93; and James C. VanderKam, 'Righteous One, Messiah, Chosen One, and Son of Man in 1 Enoch 37–71', in *The Messiah: Developments in Earliest Judaism and Christianity* (ed. James H. Charlesworth; Minneapolis: Fortress Press, 1992), pp. 169-91, 187. This is another case of Reynolds importing rather freely unrelated material into the text and interpreting it by eisegesis, not exegesis.

36. Robert G. Hamerton-Kelly, *Pre-existence, Wisdom, and the Son of Man: A Study of the Idea of Pre-existence in the New Testament* (SNTSMS, 21; Cambridge: Cambridge University Press, 1973), p. 100.

37. Burkett, *Son of Man Debate*, p. 29. See Paul Billerbeck, 'Hat die Synagoge einen

In any case, in *1 En.* 69.26-29, the Son of Man combines the role of enthronement and judgment, as does the Son of Man ultimately in the Synoptic Gospels. All of this stands in radical contrast with the nature of the Son of Man in the Gospel of John, as regards this issue. The Enochic scene is straight-forward. The hosts of heaven witness the exaltation and enthronement of the Son of Man and the judgment that is carried out by the Son of Man, namely Enoch himself.

In the Fourth Gospel, the Son of Man is a very different figure from the Enochic Son of Man in the *Parables* (*1 En.* 37–71). John's Son of Man:

(1) is not a man who begins his career on earth and is swept up into heaven by a whirlwind, as Enoch is. Instead, he is a divine figure whose journey begins in heaven (1.1-5), and is carried out on earth, both characteristics more like Daniel's Son of Man than Enoch's.

(2) John's Son of Man descends to earth to carry out his divinely designed function (1.14). This function is not to judge, as in Daniel, *1 Enoch*, and the Synoptic Gospels (5.27-47), but as savior (3.12-18).

(3) In John, as in Mark, Matthew, and Luke, he reveals himself on earth to be the Son of Man: to Nathanael and his companions (1.51ff.), to his disciples and the crowd (12.28), and to all humanity whom he will draw to himself (12.32). In *1 Enoch* he is announced the Son of Man by a special celestial decree from God to the angelic host in heaven.

(4) John's Son of Man is not raised to supra-angelic status, as in *1 Enoch* and the Synoptic Gospels, since in John he begins and remains superior to the angels, namely, divine.

(5) Moreover, he does not become angelomorphic; he manifests rather as anthropomorphic (1.14, 17ff.), as in Daniel, despite the fact that in John he is really theomorphic (Jn 1.1).

(6) John's Son of Man inherently knows all the wisdom and secrets of God, whereas Enoch needs to be given a celestial tour to be taught the mysteries he must reveal.

(7) John's Son of Man conveys these heavenly mysteries to humankind for the enlightenment and salvation of the whole world (1.4-5, 9-13), whereas in Daniel and *1 Enoch* he does so only for executing the eschatological judgment.

(8) In John he awaits no *eschaton* or final judgment, since for the Son of Man in John, as in Daniel, the judgment is already past. However, Enoch is commissioned to judge the world at some future

time and hence to bring in the *eschaton*, as is the Son of Man in the Synoptic Gospels.

(9) John's Son of Man is restored, in the end, to heavenly status by God himself (John 17), whereas Enoch is at best assigned to the angelic host and, though it is unclear, perhaps reassigned to earth in carrying out the final judgment (*1 En.* 70–71), as in the Synoptic Gospels.[38]

According to the Gospel of John, the judgment God pronounced upon the world in his pre-historic decision was the trascendental declaration that the entire world should be saved. Therefore, the ultimate destiny of the Son of Man in John is not a triumphalist *parousia* and eschatological judgment day; but a triumphant return to his heavenly *locus*, whence he had come. Jesus is reported to have described it: δόξασόν με σύ, πάτερ, παρὰ σεαυτῷ τῇ δόξῃ ᾗ εἶχον πρὸ τοῦ τὸν κόσμον εἶναι παρὰ σοί ('Father, glorify thou me in thine own presence with the glory which I had with thee before the world was made' [17.5]).

It seems likely that the author of the Fourth Gospel was well acquainted with the Enochic Son of Man tradition and set himself solidly against it. It is my sense that the author of John held an interpretation of Daniel 7–9 that proved to be radically different at almost every critical point from the Enochic interpretation of the Danielic tradition. The Fourth Gospel was written with an apologetic intent to make an aggressive statement against the Enochic tradition.

The gospel seems to know well and address directly all the key issues related to the identity of the Son of Man which are present in *1 Enoch* 37–71: the humanness of the Son of Man, ascent to heaven at the outset and presumed descent at the end, status with the angelic host, Eschatological Judge, non-preexistence, and so forth. Then the author of John turns each one of them on its head, presenting the Son of Man as: divine in nature,

---

38. It is apparent in *1 En.* 46.1 that this apocalyptic set of parabolic visions is influenced by the author's awareness of Dan. 7.13, in that the same metaphoric language is used in the former as in the latter, in reference to the Son of Man and God. In 46.1-7 we read, 'There I saw one who had the status of Head of Days, and his head was like white wool. And with him was another, whose countenance was like that of a human; [...] And I asked the one of the holy angels who went with me and showed me all the hidden things, about the son of man—who he was and whence he was (and) why he went with the Head of Days. And he answered [...] "This is the son of man who has righteousness, and righteousness dwells with him. And all the treasures of what is hidden he will reveal; for the Lord of Spirits has chosen him [...] And this son of man whom you have seen—he will raise the kings and the mighty from their couches and the strong from their thrones [...] because they do not exalt him or praise him, or humbly acknowledge whence the kingdom was given to them. [...] These are they who [...] raise their hands against the Most High"'.

descending at the outset and ascending at the end, supra-angelic status as divine, and judge who chooses instead to be the savior, preexistent, and so forth. Thus, the Son of Man concept of the Fourth Gospel reflects that there was an inverse influence upon it, derived from the impact of the Enochic apocalyptic tradition purveyed by *1 Enoch*. That is, the entire argument in John's perspective on the Son of Man contradicts the key elements of the Enochic Son of Man tradition. It demonstrates instead that in terms of what Jesus is as the Son of Man, Enoch could not possibly have been the true Son of Man.

Leslie Walck observes upon the similarities and contrasts between the Son of Man in the *Parables of Enoch* and in the Fourth Gospel and draws similar conclusions.[39] He confirms the point indicated above that, in contrast with *1 Enoch* 37–71, John's Gospel does not refer to the eschatological return of the Son of Man to execute final judgment. He sees a similarity, though a minimal one, between the two documents regarding the authority of the Son of Man to judge, forgive sins, and heal. He sees similarities in that both are ascending and descending Sons of Man, though he fails to notice that they do so in reverse order and that this becomes the critical and definitive dissimilarity, the watershed issue, for the author of the Fourth Gospel (3.13).

Another similarity Walck sees is that both figures are earthly and heavenly operatives, but he does not note the radical differences between these operations, precisely because he apparently overlooks the point of the sequence of their descent and ascent, or at least the weight of it. That is, he has not grasped, it seems, the essential character of John's apologetic. Walck also emphasizes the similarity in the fact that the Son of Man in Enoch and in John both feed the needy, in John with the multiplied loaves and fish, and in the *Parables* in the feasting that occurs at the reversal of the fortunes of the righteous. Both Son of Man figures also gather the lost, living and dead, restore wholeness to persons and the world, and dispose of the unrighteous.

However, Walck's assessment does not indicate the important details of action; and the import marking each of these aspects. It is essential that we do not overlook the fact that the Son of Man in John embraces the righteous, saves the sinners, and disposes of the unrighteous by saving them (3.16-17). As noted above, it is these details that indicate a radical difference of function on the part of the Son of Man in John and by the corollary figure in the *Parables of Enoch*. Nonetheless, Walck does see significant contrast between the two Son of Man figures:

39. Leslie W. Walck, 'The Son of Man in the Parables of Enoch and the Gospels', in *Enoch and the Messiah Son of Man, Revisiting the Book of Parables* (ed. Gabriele Boccaccini; Grand Rapids: Eerdmans, 2007), pp. 299-337.

> Where the exaltation and glorification of John's Son of Man include suffer-
> ing, the Son of Man in the *Parables* does not suffer, but rather acts as judge
> on behalf of the suffering righteous and elect. Where John's Son of Man func-
> tions as a link between heaven and earth [14.1-29], upon which the angels
> ascend and descend [1.51], in the *Parables* the angels are functionaries in
> the heavenly court and therefore are under the authority of the Son of Man.
> While the righteous and elect in the *Parables* will enjoy feasting in the pres-
> ence of a reigning Son of Man, their food is not miraculously multiplied as
> it was by Jesus [6.9-26], nor is what they eat put in terms of the flesh and
> blood of the Son of Man, as is found in John's sacramental description [6.51-
> 56]. And where the righteous and elect in the *Parables* are restored from the
> various places of being lost, in John health is restored to the sick (335-36).

Walck acknowledges that the 'similarities, then, are somewhat general',
but he contends, nonetheless that 'the dynamic of the Son of Man's authority is the same in both works'.[40] Walck's analysis is very helpful, so far as
it goes, but it is crucial to note further that, in the end, the Son of Man in
John sets aside the exercise of his authority and function as judge, in favor
of employing his authority and function as savior (3.15-18; 8.15; 12.47).
This stands in contrast to the model in the *Parables of Enoch* in which it is
precisely the authority and function of Eschatological Judge that dominates
the entire character and operation of the Son of Man. Nonetheless, Walck
concludes by observing that:

> The contrasts of suffering and sacramental terminology, it would seem,
> are necessary to the Christian, theological framework. Thus while precise,
> verbal similarities are few, the similarities…are striking. This suggests that
> possibly John knew the concepts and some of the characteristics of the
> Son of Man in the *Parables*, but he does not use them in such a way as to
> posit the direct influence of the *Book of Parables* on the Gospel of John…
> The sayings of John's Gospel show similarities in heavenly origins, author-
> ity, and the power to restore, but they are exemplified in ways different
> from the *Parables*. While these are fascinating similarities in the theologi-
> cal dynamics associated with the Son of Man and those he judges, they do
> not admit of direct, literary dependence.[41]

Walck's argumentation follows a somewhat different course than mine,
but he arrives at approximately the same conclusion as I do. The central
issue in the matter is the radical degree to which the Fourth Gospel disso-
ciates Jesus as the Son of Man from the function of judge in history, and
builds his character in the gospel narrative almost exclusively around the
function of the Son of Man as savior. This prompts the author of John to
set this gospel aggressively over against the model of the Son of Man in the
Parables of Enoch (Jn 3.13-18).

---

40. Walck, 'The Son of Man', p. 336.
41. Walck, 'The Son of Man', p. 336.

D. *Excursus:* 4 Ezra *and the Gospel of John*

The Book of *4 Ezra* is a narrative of seven dream visions that came to a man named Ezra. These night time visions, not unlike those of Daniel (7–12), indicate that an apocalyptic end to the world is near and a new age is about to be inaugurated.[42] They develop a picture of a Man rising from the sea with a large army in Ezra's penultimate vision (13.1-58), who will destroy the Roman Empire in vengeance and retribution for its destruction of Jerusalem in the Jewish revolt of 70 CE. The apocalyptic eschatology of *4 Ezra* comes to the conclusion that history is a dynamic ferment in which 'many have been created, but few will be saved' (8.3).

Like John's gospel, *4 Ezra* is a Jewish text written around 100 CE. Bruce Metzger contends that there are a number of resemblances between the two documents in terms of apocalyptic ideation and eschatological expectation, but no indication of interdependency.[43] What is of special interest in this Second Temple Judaism document is its apocalyptic and eschatological ideology, typical of competing traditions in Judaism of the time, including the gospels, particularly the Gospel of John. Metzger suggests some possibility of connection with Mt. 7.13; 22.14; and Luke 13.23ff., 21.7; but none with John.

Reynolds is confident that like John, *4 Ezra* also is shaped by what he sees as the apocalyptic character of the Danielic narratives: 11.1 has an eagle (Roman Empire) arising as in Dan. 7.3 (evil empire). The eagle is destroyed in 12.3 as in Dan. 7.11. Thereafter the Man rises from the sea in 13.1-12 as in Daniel's Man appearing on a cloud before the Ancient of Days (God) in heaven (7.13). This Man from the sea reveals the purposes of God in history. Further similarities between *4 Ezra* and Daniel are evident. *4 Ezra* refers to God as the Most High and Daniel refers to The People of the Holy Ones of the Most High (Dan. 7.22, 25, 27; *4 Ezra* 12.32; 13.29). Reynolds styles the human figures appearing in both of these apocalyptic 'revelations', and even more so the Son of Man in *1 Enoch*, as messianic personages that have a relationship of unique sonship to God. In *4 Ezra* 7.28-29 the Man from God is referred to by God as my son the Messiah, who will undertake the kingdom building ordeal and then die, be resurrected, and carry out the judgment.[44]

---

42. *4 Ezra* was written in Hebrew, though the texts available today are the ancient Ethiopic version (as in the case of *1 Enoch*, for example), ancient Armenian and Arabic, Latin, Georgian, ancient Syriac and Coptic versions.

43. Bruce M. Metzger, 'The Fourth Book of Ezra: A New Translation and Introduction', in *The Old Testament Pseudepigrapha, Apocalyptic Literature and Testaments* (ed. James H. Charlesworth; New York: Doubleday, 1983), pp. 517-59.

44. Raymond E. Brown, *An Introduction to the New Testament* (New York: Doubleday, 1997), p. 801.

Reynolds thinks the unique God-sent men in *4 Ezra* and Daniel 7–12 are depicted as having characteristics and actions as God himself. In this regard, the divine *Logos* as Son of Man in John's gospel comes to mind as reflecting a similar Second Temple tradition. The unique men in Daniel, *4 Ezra*, and the Synoptic Gospels are commissioned to take action in the human community for the judgment and extermination of the wicked and the salvation of a righteous remnant.[45] 'Not unlike the human-like figures of Daniel 7 and the *Parables of Enoch*, the man from the sea in *4 Ezra* 13 is described and acts in a manner analogous to the depictions of God in the OT. Also the people's responses to him are similar to responses that God receives'.[46] They are associated with clouds, extinguish enemies with a fiery breath, and melt humanity with a distinctive voice. Like the Son of Man in *1 Enoch*, the Man in *4 Ezra* is hidden for many ages but this does not inherently mean preexistence in either case. More likely, it is a reference to his identity being known pre-mundane but not his having a pre-creational existence.[47]

Like the Son of Man in both Daniel and *1 Enoch*, Ezra's Man from the sea is to bring the end to the world of destructive powers and evil empires as we know it; and by aggressive conquest institute instead the reign of God, joining earth and heaven in it. Reynolds concludes that the man in *4 Ezra*, *1 Enoch*, and Daniel 7–9 are all described as being pre-existent.[48] This notion, as we have repeatedly noticed, is readily challenged in all three cases. For example, in *1 Enoch*, only the name of the Son of Man is in the mind or heart of God from creation. In Daniel the Son of Man is presented to the Ancient of Days as an eschatological character. Equally, in *4 Ezra*, the prophet sees the man from the sea arise in a vision that is a prophecy of something that will happen in the future.

1 Enoch 37–71 and *4 Ezra* are both aware of and obviously interpret Daniel 7–9. Moreover, it is evident that *4 Ezra* is dependent upon both the Daniel and *1 Enoch* passages. Furthermore, it is worth noting that there is similarity between *4 Ezra* and the Son of Man in the Synoptic Gospels. However, there is no indication of any connection between *4 Ezra* and the Gospel of John. Indeed, it is quite obvious that they were not aware of one another, though they were contemporaneous. At least they were on mutually exclusive trajectories of Second Temple Judaism traditions.

There is similarity between *4 Ezra* and the Son of Man in the Synoptic Gospels. Both are human figures who are commissioned to establish the salvific reign of God on earth. Both are called to do so by extermination of the

---

45. Reynolds, *Apocalyptic Son of Man*, pp. 49-56.

46. Reynolds, *Apocalyptic Son of Man*, p. 53.

47. See Ulrich B. Müller, *Messias und Menschensohn in jüdischen Apokalypsen und in der Offenbarung des Johannes* (Gütersloh: Mohn, 1972), pp. 147-54.

48. Reynolds, *Apocalyptic Son of Man*, p. 54.

wicked and wickedness; and the assembling of the righteous into the divine kingdom. Similarities between *4 Ezra* and the Fourth Gospel are less obvious. They have in common the apocalyptic vision, the Man from God who reveals the heavenly mysteries, and the mission of establishing the reign of God on earth. Brown remarks that the similarities between the nature and function of the Son of Man in such documents as Daniel 7–9, *1 Enoch* 37–71, the Synoptic Gospels, *4 Ezra* and the Gospel of John indicates how well known such literature was in Second Temple Judaism after the First Jewish Revolt against the Romans in 70 CE.[49]

The theological questions raised in *4 Ezra* share similarities but also manifest marked differences from those in John's gospel. The unique Man in Ezra will only be recognized for who he really is on the moment when 'his day' arrives (13.4, 33), just as the Johannine Son of Man will be recognized for who he really is only in the day of his destiny, when he is lifted up on the cross, resurrected, and 'ascends to where he was before' (8.28 and 6.62). *4 Ezra* 5–6 and 8.4-36, lists the signs of the end of the age, similar to the 'Little Apocalypse' of Mark 13, and suggestive of the 'signs' structure of the Gospel of John.[50] *4 Ezra* 3.1–5.19 is concerned largely with the question of the origin of evil and suffering, an issue the Fourth Gospel takes for granted but does not overtly address. *4 Ezra* 5.21–6.34 is concerned with the eternal fate of those who died before God's uniquely redemptive Man appeared, whereas the Gospel of John asserts universal salvation and so is mainly focused upon the importance of the existential human response to the Son of Man.

There are dissimilarities between *4 Ezra* and the Gospel of John. In John the Son of Man descends from heaven. In *4 Ezra* the Man arises from the sea. In John he is the proclaimer of the divine reign to set things right by forgiveness and healing, while in *4 Ezra* he is the warrior to set things right on earth by conquest. In John he is the divine *Logos* and revealer of the heavenly mysteries of salvation through belief in the name of the Son of Man (3.15-18). In *4 Ezra* he is a Man and the revealer of the heavenly mysteries of judgment and extermination of the wicked majority, as well as, the salvation of those who are inherently righteous (6.35–9.25). Salvation comes by being a just person, not by faith in the divine forgiveness represented by the Son. In *4 Ezra* the Man cataclysmically ends history as we know it, as in *1 Enoch* and in Daniel 7–9. He does so by means of a universal judgment day. In John there is no judgment day, no coming judgment, no future expectation of the advent of the messianic man, and no end to history. The Son of Man in John has set aside his function as the Eschatological Judge in favor of mediating God's

---

49. Brown, *Introduction*, p. 8.

50. Paul N. Anderson, *The Christology of the Fourth Gospel: Its Unity and Disunity in the Light of John 6* (Tübingen: Mohr–Siebeck, 1996), pp. 268-69.

universal salvation. John's and *4 Ezra*'s Son of Man have little in common; they testify to two parallel and competing tradition of interpretation of the apocalyptic Son of Man in Second Temple Judaism. They have in common their apocalyptic expectation of a Man sent from God to reveal the heavenly mysteries of judgment and salvation, the vision of a new salvific age when God reigns universally on earth and in heaven, and a sense of the meaning of history as God's providentially unfolding economy.

4 Ezra and the Gospel of John afford us no warrant to perceive interdependency between them. Whether the two traditions were aware of each other may be impossible to determine. The significance of *4 Ezra* for Johannine Son of Man studies is that it illustrates the eschatological and apocalyptic mindset that prevailed at the end of the first century in the competing Second Temple Judaism traditions within which both arose. The contemporaneous Gospel of John and *4 Ezra* testify to two parallel and competing Jewish traditions of interpretation of the apocalyptic Son of Man.

E. *Conclusion: The Synoptic Gospels and the Gospel of John*

As detailed at length in Chapter 3 above, the Son of Man in the Synoptic Gospels is a human being, Jesus of Nazareth, and the forgiver of sins on earth. In those three gospels this Son of Man proclaims the impending divine reign on earth. He is ultimately exalted to the status of the heavenly Son of Man and is worshipped only in his exalted heavenly state. He is destined to return to earth in a dramatic *parousia*, as the heavenly Eschatological Judge of the living and the dead. As we have seen, he will bring in the divine kingdom on earth fully, gathering the righteous into the redeemed community of God's reign, and exterminating all of the unrighteous and all unrighteousness. This places the Son of Man in the Synoptic Gospels in relatively close alignment with the figure in *1 Enoch*, but competes with *1 Enoch* in that Jesus, not Enoch, is the Son of Man.[51]

---

51. In *1 En.* 37.3a Enoch indicates that the mysteries he learned in his heavenly journey he intends to 'recount to those who dwell on the earth'. In chap. 65 Enoch reveals the heavenly mysteries to his grandson, Noah, for publication to the earthly human community. Throughout *1 Enoch* he is constantly led by an archangel to survey the entire domain of heaven, including the dwelling places of the unrighteous, the righteous, and the angelic host. Throughout this pilgrimage Enoch encounters the Chosen One, also known as the Righteous One, who ultimately is identified as the Son of Man in 48.2. He in turn is finally announced as Enoch himself in 60.10, 70.1 and 71.14-17. This Chosen One is enthroned in 45.3, 51.3, 61.8. He is worshiped by the heavenly host repeatedly thoughout the *Parables of Enoch* but especially in 61.6-13. After his identification as the Chosen One and Son of Man, Enoch is worshipped with awe and praise by the redeemed righteous ones and with shame and fear by the condemned unrighteous people.

The careful explication of the texts that present the Son of Man logia in the Gospel of John compared with those of the Synoptic Gospels compels the following conclusions. Three qualities or characteristics dominate the description of the Son of Man, and hence the definition of Jesus of Nazareth, as the lead character in the story presented by John's Gospel. The Son of Man is presented in the Fourth Gospel primarily as (1) a divine figure who descends to earth from the heavenly sphere and will return thither. (2) As proclaimer of the impending divine kingdom, he is the revealer of the mysteries of God. (3) As that revealer, he is the savior of the world, who forgives sins on earth and in heaven. The Son of Man in John's Gospel is the *Logos*, who is described as taking up residence in Jesus of Nazareth, thus manifesting as the Son of Man. The person of the Son of Man in John is much less prominently associated with the roles of suffering servant and judge, though, as we have seen, those roles are both present in the Fourth Gospel.

In the Synoptic Gospels, however, the Son of Man is, throughout, a human agent named Jesus of Nazareth who, like Ezekiel the prophet, proclaims the impending reign of God on earth. He is a man who forgives sins on earth as part of his proclamation of the reign of God. This human agent endures the ordeal of Isaiah's Suffering Servant and so becomes the savior in the sense that he seeks the lost, as a shepherd seeks the strayed sheep. In the end, this man is exalted to heavenly status with the specific and exclusive role of being the Eschatological Judge. In the Synoptic Gospels, the progressively developing emphasis is upon this identity for the Son of Man. As the judge, he is the proclaimer of God's reign. As such, he is the one, moreover, who metes out vindication upon those who accept the divine reign. They will ultimately be gathered into God's kingdom. He will exterminate those who fail to accept the divine reign.

Thus it may be seen that the Son of Man in John's Gospel differs markedly from the Son of Man in the Synoptic Gospels; and the difference lies at the key points of the definition of this figure. In the Synoptic Gospels the Son of Man *is* the Eschatological Judge, while in John the role of judge is merely a *function* of the Son of Man. In John's Gospel the Son of Man repeatedly insists that he will not carry out this function of judge (Jn 5.27-47; 12.23ff.) but will carry out the function of savior (Jn 3.16-17).

A set of contrasts in Son of Man concepts is readily apparent between the Synoptic Gospels and the Gospel of John. It is the contrast (1) between a human being and the divine logos, (2) between the man from Mary's womb and the divine figure descended from heaven, (3) between the man who progressively becomes a heavenly figure and the deity whose true home always was and will always be in the heavenly sphere, (4) between a man ascending to heavenly status and the incarnate *Logos* returning there, whence he came, as glorified God, and (5) between the Eschatological Judge and the judge who abrogates that function in favor of his identity and role as savior. The synoptic Son of Man will (1) assign all humans their eternal status of salvation or damnation, (2) bring down the evil empires and powers of this world, and (3) terminate history as we know it. The Johannine Son of Man will allow to grow and flourish, through all time, the seed of love and grace that he has planted in the world during his tenure as incarnate Son of Man, so that history will forever be the matrix of salvation for all humans.

Thus, in the Synoptic Gospels the Son of Man *becomes* a heavenly figure over a human lifetime. This model is grounded in the assumption that he starts with his human birth and his earthly existence. There is no indication in these three gospels of any incarnation theology associated with his achieving heavenly status. He does not become divine, only heavenly. He shall come from heaven on the clouds with power and glory at the *eschaton*. Even in the mountain top experience of the transfiguration story the pattern of characters is Jesus and the disciples encamped there, on the one hand, and a visitation by the heavenly figures, on the other.

Moreover, those heavenly figures are all humans though heavenly, and while Jesus admittedly communes with those figures, they must descend to earth for that communication to happen. It is an earthly event. Even when Jesus uses 'I have come' statements in the Synoptic Gospels, those are phrases he uses to indicate that he is present in that moment and situation for a specific stated purpose, not an indication that he has arrived at that time and place from somewhere else or from a different kind of place. As in the ninety three times Ezekiel is called Son of Man and commissioned by divine authority to proclaim the advent of the divine kingdom, so also in the Synoptic Gospels, this commissioning does not imply incarnation, heavenly origin, preexistence, divinity, or heavenly destiny.

On the other hand, in the Fourth Gospel the Son of Man is a divine heavenly figure in his divine essence. He returns to his heavenly home as the divine *Logos*, never to return to earth. There is no second coming, no *parousia*, no dramatic appearance on the clouds of heaven, no termination of history, and no final judgment day. In John's Gospel God is the Judge. He judged the world before it was created. His judgment was that he would save the whole world, in spite of itself. The Son of Man descended from heaven to earth to reveal these mysteries of God. Thus the judgment has come into the world and is present in the person of the Son of Man in the sense that the destiny of humanity is cast in terms of whether people identify with or reject the Son of Man and the mysteries of salvation he reveals (Jn 3.15-18).

Chapter 5

SUMMARY AND CONCLUSION

As announced at the outset, this research project on the Son of Man has focused upon the definition of the conceptual and inter-textual features of that literary character in the Johannine story. The evidence generated in this work has made possible a number of summary conclusions, but has also suggested a number of corollary questions. Among these potentially important foci for future research are particularly three issues: Why? Why just then? and How much the Johannine stance affected the future of Jewish and Christian thought? That is, first, we have the question of why the Johannine Son of Man is of such special character as is presented in the Fourth Gospel, given the nature of the other Second Temple Judaism traditions; second, why this specially crafted Son of Man became possible and necessary in the ideology of this gospel at just that time in history; and finally, how much the Johannine approach affected, and was even directly responsible for, the mysterious and quite sudden disappearance of the concept and term of the apocalyptic Son of Man from the theological discourse in both Judaism and Christian traditions. In other words: which were the historical and sociological factors at play in the Jewish world and in the Christian community that prompted the author of John's Gospel to present its remarkable, distinctive view of the Son of Man just then and just in that way, and what were the consequences of the Johannine approach?

While the answers to these questions go beyond the limits of the present work, the questions themselves are a reminder of the immense potential of research in the subject, once one has parted from misleading theological assumptions and relocate the Gospel of John in its proper Jewish context.

As we have pointed out, research on the Son of Man in John has been neglected by New Testament scholars because their interest has been primarily in the historical Jesus, as if the theology of John were not in itself an important subject of analysis, regardless of whether the document is farther than the Synoptic Gospels from Jesus' *ipsissima verba* and from the events of Jesus actual life story with its description of his authentic activities.

The few New Testament scholars who have addressed the problem of the Son of Man in John and its relation to the Synoptic Gospels have done so in the narrow context of the development of early Christology, as if it were only a problem internal to Christian theology. None of these scholars is a specialist in Second Temple Judaism and so they could not fully recognize that the comparison of John's gospel with Mark, Matthew, and Luke–Acts is an intra-Judaism dialogue, not merely an intra-Christian debate. On the other hand, scholars in Second Temple Judaism have also neglected John's Gospel on the assumption that it was no longer 'Jewish' or was less 'Jewish' than the Synoptic Gospels.

Contemporary scholarship has shown that the tendency to construct the equation of Christian origins and early Christian documents as an opposition between Christian and Jewish texts at the end of the first century is a completely anachronistic model within the diverse world of first-century Judaism. Although the Gospel of John is an expression of a particular messianic movement, that of the disciples of Jesus, it is a thoroughly Jewish document. This present study has demonstrated that its concept of the Son of Man can be understood only in the broader literary context of Second Temple Jewish traditions. Even any sociological and historical analysis that would aim to contextualize the motivations of the theological development in the Gospel of John, here highlighted, will necessarily need to address not only the analysis of the sociology of the Johannine Community as an entity within the early Christian movement; but will need to see it in the broader context of the history and sociology of Judaism at the turn of the second century. Judaism is not merely the background but the context in which the Synoptic Gospels and the Gospel of John must be understood and compared.

By taking this approach of total immersion in the vibrant Jewish theological diversity of that time, and by shifting the emphasis from the historical Jesus to the theology of the Gospels, our analysis has shown that the perspective of the Son of Man in the Fourth Gospel differs significantly from that in the Synoptic Gospels. The differences are definitive and reflect the dissimilarities in the self-concept accorded the literary figure of Jesus in the first three gospels, on the one hand, and in the fourth gospel, on the other. As is described in detail in Chapter 3 above, Mark, Matthew, and Luke do not have the same list of Son of Man logia as John. Moreover the picture painted by those logia in the first three gospels is substantially different in definitive ways from the picture painted in the Fourth Gospel.

The Son of Man in the Synoptic Gospels is Jesus, the *man* from Nazareth, who proclaims the advent of God's kingdom to be established on earth. In that role he forgives sins, heals suffering persons, and in this way redeems humans. His odyssey leads him through the ordeal of the Suffering Servant to the exaltation to heavenly status as the Eschatological Judge. As such, he awaits an immediately impending *parousia* in which he will descend to judge the world, exterminate evil and the unrighteous, and gather the righteous into God's fully established kingdom on earth. That will end history as we know it and introduce a new salvific era.

Just as in the case of Ezekiel, so at the outset of the Synoptic Gospel narratives, this man is a mortal who is vested with the calling to proclaim the purposes and possibilities of God's reign on earth in pragmatic and operational ways. That divine reign establishes a world of forgiveness, of love that works and grace that heals and saves. The Son of Man carries out this work in the Synoptic Gospels mainly as the Forgiver of Sins on Earth.

In the Synoptic Gospels the Son of Man becomes the Suffering Servant Messiah as his story unfolds. The watershed event, as we have seen, was at Caesaria Philippi, as presented in Mk 8.31 and the synoptic parallels. In these gospels the ordeal of the suffering and death of the Son of Man is a stage in the progress toward his becoming the Eschatological Judge upon the occasion of his exaltation by resurrection from the dead and enthronement in heaven. During his earthly ordeal he not only forgives sins but fulfills the other messianic provisions of Isa. 61.1-4 and Isa. 53.

In John, on the other hand, the Son of Man is, from the outset, the divine *Logos* who descends from heaven and becomes incarnated in Jesus (Jn 1.1-3, 14). The title, Son of Man, is the title of the *Logos*, and secondarily defines the nature of Jesus of Nazareth as the human person in whom the *Logos* is incarnated. Jesus of Nazareth is a human in John as in Mark, Matthew, and Luke. However, for John the *Logos* in Jesus is defined as, and so defines Jesus as, the heavenly and divine Son of Man.

In John's gospel, Son of Man reveals all the heavenly mysteries about the divine reign which is already present on earth. This reign is the revelation and application of a divine judgment that occurred before the creation of the world and in which the Son of Man is the existential manifestation during his time on earth. God's superlapsarian judgment was to save utterly the world that he was going to create (Jn 3.16-17). He decided to erase evil by establishing everywhere in everyway the heavenly order. The ordeal of suffering endured by the Son of Man is the inevitable cost that attended this divine intervention into human history, from the descent of the *Logos* to the final ascent of the Son of Man to heaven. The entire process is a packaged divine economy, so to speak, that envelopes, as Iranaeus saw it, the entire divine program of creation, providence, and salvation for humankind.

Thus, in John, the advent of the Son of Man in Jesus is the watershed event. His descent from heaven and presence in history is the issue before which all humans, institutions, and powers stand. Their salvation or destruction depends upon their response to his existential presence. Neither he nor God judges anyone. Humans judge themselves if they fail to identify with the Son of Man and his cause. For John he is the divine light in the darkness of human history (Jn 1.4-5, 9), and humans have a standing invitation to come to the light or experience the lostness of 'loving darkness more than light' (Jn 3.18-21).

Moreover, as we have noted, the emphasis in the three Synoptic Gospels is, in the end, upon the exaltation of the Son of Man to the heavenly status of Eschatological Judge, whence he will descend to judge the righteous and unrighteous. In radical contrast, the Fourth Gospel emphasizes that the glorification of the Son of Man, which returns him permanently to his original home and inherent divine status, is an exaltation of the Son of Man as God. In this exaltation, God as the *Logos*, is glorified. In John there is no anticipation of a glorious return of the Son of Man to earth as Eschatological Judge. There is no *eschaton*, no final judgment, and hence, no *parousia*. The Son of Man is the Eschatological Judge in John because that is the function of the Son of Man (Jn 5.27), but he chooses not to judge or prosecute since the judgment of the world was to save it. The advent of the Son of Man is for the purpose of revealing that he is God's agent of that salvation (3.12, 16-17).

The purpose of this study has been to discern what the Son of Man is in John's Gospel. I have done this by assessing the message of the thirteen Johannine Son of Man logia in comparison with other Son of Man traditions within Second Temple Judaism: Ezekiel, Daniel, *1 Enoch*, and the Synoptic Gospels, with brief glances, when relevant, to *4 Ezra*, and the *Testament of Abraham*.

From the outset this study was structured to determine (1) the identity of the Son of Man in John, in comparison with the Son of Man in the Synoptic Gospels, (2) the relationship between the Son of Man in John and in other Second Temple Son of Man traditions, and (3) the nature of the Son of Man in John compared with the traditions of the Son of Man as Judge and Suffering Servant. The following conclusions are possible and relevant.

1. The distinctive message of the Gospel of John is focused in the claim that the divine *Logos* became flesh and enacted in human history the role of the historic Son of Man, but enacted it in a unique and unprecedented manner that demonstrates that Enoch could not possibly be the true Son of Man of the Hebrew prophecies in the Psalms, Ezekiel and Daniel. In the Johannine Son of Man the author connects the redemptive messiah of Isaiah 61, the suffering servant of Isaiah 53, and the new idea of a universal savior.

2. The author of the Fourth Gospel was influenced in varying degrees and in differing details, by Second Temple Judaism Son of Man traditions. These shaped his understanding of the nature and function of the Son of Man as heavenly figure, proclaimer of the impending divine reign, savior of the world, revealer of the mysteries of God, and eschatological judge. The Ezekiel tradition of the Son of Man as a human proclaimer of the impending divine reign, which so profoundly influenced the Synoptic Gospels, is not significantly reflected in the concept of the Son of Man in John's gospel.

3. However, the Son of Man in the Fourth Gospel reflects quite clearly the four major features of the Danielic Son of Man. He has heavenly status with

God. He manifests in human form. He holds power and authority invested in him by God to destroy evil and bring the world under God's reign. He is never enthroned as or accorded the *identity* of Eschatological Judge, does not act in the *function* of judge, but carries out the mission of God's work on earth as savior. This strongly inclines us toward the conclusion that the author of the Fourth Gospel was well acquainted with the Danielic Son of Man tradition and took key aspects of it seriously as the framework for his narrative regarding the Son of Man.

4. This strong correlation between the two traditions is not undermined by the fact that Daniel's Son of Man never descends to earth but commands operations from the heavenly headquarters; while John's Son of Man visits the theater of operations on earth. This latter factor is, of course, central to the Johannine Son of Man message and model.

5. The *Parables of Enoch* are very much on the mind of the author of John's gospel, but the influence of the Enochic Son of Man tradition upon the Fourth Gospel is a reverse influence. John's gospel is a broadside attack against any possibility that the Son of Man as represented in *1 Enoch* 37–71 could ever be the true Son of Man. Enoch's Son of Man is a human who starts on earth, ascends to heaven, is nominated the Eschatological Judge, and carries out that mission. This is not much different from the way the Synoptics portray *their* Son of Man, Jesus of Nazareth. John escalates the competition with Enoch by moving the concept of the Son of Man to a superior and unreachable level. The Fourth Gospel represents the Son of Man as a divine figure who starts in heaven, descends to earth, takes on the role of a human, and then functions as savior instead of judge. He returns to his heavenly *locus* as God, in triumphant exaltation.

Moreover, the Fourth Gospel claims that no one can ascend to heaven except the heavenly figure that descended thence. Enoch is out. Moreover, God's business on earth, by means of the Son of Man, is saving and not judging. Like the Enochic Son of Man, John's Son of Man knows the secret mysteries of God. However, while Enoch must learn them by his tour of heaven, and then relay them to another earthly agent, his grandson Noah, John's Son of Man inherently knows the divine mysteries, and visits this world to instruct the human community himself. Enoch thinks the heavenly mysteries are about extermination of the wicked and gathering up the righteous, but John's Son of Man knows that the secret wisdom is the mystery of forgiving grace and salvation of the whole world.

6. The author of the Fourth Gospel was well acquainted with the Enochic tradition and saw it as the primary counterforce in Second Temple Judaism to Jesus as the Son of Man. Therefore the author of John's gospel engaged the Enochic tradition with a frontal attack, discrediting it on its key points: first, the notion that Enoch had ascended into heaven to acquire the secret knowledge of God; and, second, that he revealed that knowledge to Noah

and subsequently will reveal or enact it in the form of the eschatological judgment, ending time and history.

7. There seems little reason to conclude that the Synoptic Gospels influenced the Johannine notion of the Son of Man or that the author of John's gospel was aware of Mark, Matthew, and Luke–Acts.

The remarkable achievement of the Fourth Gospel, therefore, lies in the fact that it constitutes a vigorous *apologia*, placed in the mouth of Jesus himself, to the effect that God judged that his intention and desire is to save the whole world, and that, in consequence, the Son of Man in John will not exercise his function as Eschatological Judge, but will rather deploy his role and exercise his *exousia* in the world as the forgiver of sins and the divine savior (3.13-18).

BIBLIOGRAPHY

A. *Monograph Sources Specific to the Son of Man in the Gospel of John (in chronological order)*

Ainger, William (1822), *Christ's title, 'The Son of man', elucidated from its application in the Gospel according to St John: a sermon preached before the University of Cambridge, on the commencement Sunday, June 30, 1822.* Cambridge: Deightons & Nicholsons.

Dieckmann, Hermann (1927), 'Der Sohn des Menschen, im Johannesevangelium', *Scholastik* 2, pp. 229-47.

Preiss, Théo (1953), 'Le fils de l'homme dans le IVᵉ Evangile', *ETR* 28, pp. 7-61.

Beus, Charles de (1955–56), 'Het gebruik en de betekenis van de uitdrukking "de Zoon Des Mensen" in het Evangelie van Johannes', *Nederlands theologisch tijdschrift* 10, pp. 237-51.

Schulz, Siegfried (1957*), Untersuchungen zur Menschensohn-Christologie im Johannesevangelium, zugleich ein Beitrag zur Methodengeschichte der Auslegung des 4. Evangeliums* (Göttingen: Vandenhoeck & Ruprecht).

Sidebottom, Ernest M. (1957a), 'The Son of Man as Man in the Fourth Gospel', *Expository Times* 68, pp. 231-35, 280-83.

Sidebottom, Ernest M. (1957b), 'The Ascent and Descent of the Son of Man in the Gospel of St. John', *ATR* 39, pp. 115-22.

Meeks, Wayne A. (1963), 'The Man from Heaven in Johannine Sectarianism', *JBL* 91, pp. 44-72.

Schnackenburg, Rudolf (1964-65), 'Der Menschensohn im Johannesevangelium', *NTS* 11, p. 123.

Freed, Edwin D. (1967), 'The Son of Man in the Fourth Gospel', *JBL* 86, pp. 402-409.

Kinniburgh, Elizabeth (1968), 'The Johannine "Son of Man"', *SE* 4, pp. 64-71.

Smalley, S.S. (1968–69), 'The Johannine Son of Man Sayings', *NTS* 15, pp. 278-301.

Ruckstuhl, Eugen (1972), 'Die johanneische Menschensohnforschung, 1957–69', in J. Pfammatter and F. Furger (eds.), *Theologischer Berichte*, I (Eindsiedeln: Benziger), pp. 171-284.

Lindars, Barnabas (1973), 'The Son of Man in the Johannine Christology', in B. Lindars and S.S. Smalley (eds.), *Christ and Spirit in the New Testament: Studies in Honour of Charles F. Digby Moule* (Cambridge: Cambridge University Press), pp. 43-60.

Maddox, Robert (1974), 'The Function of the Son of Man in the Gospel of John', in *Reconciliation and Hope: Festschrift for L.L. Morris* (ed. Robert J. Banks; Exeter: Paternoster Press), pp. 186-204.

Coppens, Joseph (1976), 'Le fils de l'homme dans l'evangile johannique', *ETL* 52, pp. 28-81.

Moloney, Francis J. (1976a), 'The Johannine Son of Man Debate', *BTB* 6, pp. 177-89.

Moloney, Francis J. (1976b), *The Johannine Son of Man* (Rome: Pontificial Biblical Press).

Moloney, Francis J. (1977), 'A Johannine Son of Man Discussion?', *Salesianum* 39, pp. 93-102.

Borgen, Peder (1977), 'Some Jewish Exegetical Traditions as Background for Son of Man Sayings in John's Gospel (Jn 3.13-14 and context)', in M. de Jonge (ed.), *L'Evangile de Jean* (Gembloux: Duculot), pp. 243-58.

Painter, John (1977), 'Review: F.J. Moloney, *The Johannine Son of Man*', *ABR* 25, pp. 43-44.

Neyrey, Jerome (1982), 'The Jacob Allusions in John 1.51', *CBQ* 44, pp. 586-605.

Pamment, Margaret (1985), 'The Son of Man in the Fourth Gospel', *JTS* 36/1, pp. 56-66.

Roth, Wolfgang (1985), 'Jesus as the Son of Man: The Scriptural Identity of a Johannine Image', in D.E. Groh and R. Jewett (eds.), *The Living Text: Essays in Honor of Ernest W. Saunders* (Lanham, MD: University Press of America), pp. 11-26.

Meeks, Wayne A. (1986), 'The Man from Heaven in Johannine Sectarianism', in John Ashton (ed.), *The Interpretation of John* (IRT, 9; Philadelphia: Fortress Press and London: SPCK), pp. 141-73.

Rhea, Robert (1990), *The Johannine Son of Man* (Zurich: Theologischer Verlag Zürich).

Burkett, Delbert (1991), *The Son of the Man in the Gospel of John* (JSNTSup, 56; Sheffield: Sheffield Academic Press).

Müller, Mogens (1991), 'Have You Faith in the Son of Man? (John 9.35)', *NTS* 37, pp. 291-94.

Pazdan, Mary M. (1991), *The Son of Man: A Metaphor for Jesus in the Fourth Gospel* (Collegeville, MN: Liturgical Press).

Pryor, John W. (1991), 'The Johannine Son of Man and the Descent–Ascent Motif', *JETS* 34, pp. 341-51.

Painter, John (1992), 'The Enigmatic Johannine Son of Man', in F. van Segbroeck, C.M. Tuckett, G. van Belle, and J. Verheyden (eds.), *Four Gospels 1992, Festschrift Frans Neirynck* (BETL, 100; 3 vols.; Louvain: Peeters), pp. 1869-87.

Bauckham, Richard (1993), 'Review: Delbert Burkett, *The Son of Man in the Gospel of John*', *Evangelical Quarterly*, pp. 266-68.

Létourneau, Pierre (1993), *Jésus, fils de l'homme et fils de Dieu: Jean 2, 23–3,35 et la double christologie johannique* (Montreal: Bellarmin).

Moloney, Francis J. (1993), 'Review: Delbert Burkett, *The Son of Man in the Gospel of John*', *JTS* 44, pp. 259-61.

Pazdan, Mary M. (1993), 'Review: Delbert Burkett, *The Son of Man in the Gospel of John*', *Interpretation* 47, pp. 312-13.

Fossum, Jarl E. (1995), 'The Son of Man's Alter Ego: John 1.51, Targumic Tradition and Jewish Mysticism', in his *The Image of the Invisible God* (Göttingen: Vandenhoeck & Ruprecht), pp. 135-51.

Moloney, Francis J. (1995), 'Review: Delbert Burkett, *The Son of Man in the Gospel of John*', *ABR* 43, pp. 85-87.

Ham, Clay A. (1998), 'The Title "Son of Man" in the Gospel of John', *Stone–Campbell Journal* 1, pp. 67-84.

Ramos, F.F. (1999), 'El hijo del hombre en el cuarto evangelio', *Studium legionense* 40, pp. 45-92.

Sasse, Markus (2000), *Der Menschensohn im Evangelium nach Johannes* (TANZ, 15; Tübingen: Francke).

Wink, Walter (2001), '"The Son of Man" in the Gospel of John', in R.T. Fortna and T. Thatcher (eds.), *Jesus in the Johannine Tradition* (Louisville, KY: Westminster/ John Knox Press), pp. 117-23.

Moloney, Francis J. (2002), 'Review: M. Sasse, *Der Menschensohn im Evangelium nach Johannes*', *JTS* 83, pp. 210-15.

Moloney, Francis J. (2005), 'The Johannine Son of Man Revisited', in G. van Belle, J.G. van der Watt, and P Maritz (eds.), *Theology and Christology in the Fourth Gospel: Essays by the Members of the SNTS Johannine Writings Seminar* (BETL, 184; Leuven: University of Leuven Press), pp. 177-202.

Casey, Maurice (2007), *The Solution to the 'Son of Man' Problem* (LNTS, 343; New York: T. & T. Clark), pp. 274-313.

Ensor, P. (2007), 'Glorification of the Son of Man: An Analysis of John 13.31-32', *Tyndale Bulletin* 58/2, pp. 229-52.

Reynolds, Benjamin E. (2008), *The Apocalyptic Son of Man in the Gospel of John* (Tübingen: Mohr–Siebeck).

B. *General Sources on the Son of Man in Second Temple Judaism*

Abbott, Edwin A. (1909), *The Message of the Son of Man* (London: Black).

Abbott, Edwin A. (1910), *'The Son of Man' or Contributions to the Study of the Thought of Jesus* (Diatessarica, 8; Cambridge: Cambridge University Press).

Albertz, Rainer (2001), 'The Social Setting of the Aramaic and Hebrew Book of Daniel', in John J. Collins and Peter W. Flint (eds.), *The Book of Daniel, Composition and Reception* (Leiden: E.J. Brill), pp. 171-204.

Alting, Jakob (1685), *Commentarius in loca quaedam selecta Novi Testamenti*, cited in Scholten (1809), pp. 203-204.

Appel, Heinrich (1896), *Die Selbstbezeichnung Jesu: Der Sohn des Menschen* (Stavenhagen: Beholtz).

Aretius, Benedict (1577), *Commentarii in quatuor evangelistas* (Lausanne).

Ashton, John,(ed.) (1986), *The Interpretation of John* (IRT, 9; Philadelphia: Fortress Press).

Ashton, John (1991, 2007), *Understanding the Fourth Gospel* (Oxford: Oxford University Press).

Barclay, William (1975), *The Gospel of John* (rev. edn; 2 vols.; Philadelphia: Westminster Press).

Barker, Margaret (1988), *The Lost Prophet: The Book of Enoch and its Influence on Christianity* (Nashville: Abingdon Press).

Barrett, Charles Kingsley (1955), *The Gospel according to St John* (New York: Macmillan).

Barrett, Charles Kingsley (1975), *The Gospel of John and Judaism* (London: SPCK).

Barrett, Charles Kingsley (1978), *The Gospel according to St John: An Introduction with Commentary and Notes on the Greek Text* (2nd edn; Philadelphia: Westminster Press).

Barrett, Charles Kingsley (ed.) (1989), *The New Testament Background, Writings from Ancient Greece and the Roman Empire That Illuminate Christian Origins* (San Francisco: Harper).

Barth, Karl (1922), *Der Römerbrief* (München: Kaiser Verlag).

Bartlet, Vernon (1892), 'Christ's Use of the Term "Son of Man"', *Expositor*, series 4, VI, pp. 400, 422-43.

Bauer, Walter (1924), *Jesus, der Galiläer* (Tübingen: Mohr–Siebeck).

Bauernfeind, O. (1957), *Die Apostelgeschichte* (Religion in Geschichte und Gegenwart, 4; Tübingen: Mohr–Siebeck).

Beasley-Murray, George R. (1987), *John* (Word Biblical Commentary, 36; Waco, TX: Word Books).

Becker, Jürgen (1979), *Das Evangelium nach Johannes* (2 vols.; OTKNT, 4/1–2; Gütersloh: Mohn).

Beiler, Irwin R. (1936), *Studies in the Life of Jesus* (New York: Abingdon–Cokesbury).

Ben-Chorin, Schalom (1967), *Bruder Jesus: Der Nazarener in jüdischer Sicht* (Munich: List).

Beyerle, Stefan (2001), 'The Book of Daniel and its Social Setting', in John J. Collins and Peter W. Flint (eds.), *The Book of Daniel, Composition and Reception* (Leiden: E.J. Brill), I, pp. 205-28.

Beyschlag, Willibald (1891–92), *Neutestamentliche Theologie* (Halle: Strien).

Beza, Theodore de (1557), *Annotations in Volume 3 of Novum D. N. Iesu Christi Testamentum* (Geneva).

Billerbeck, Paul (1905), 'Hat die Synagoge einen präexistenten Menschensohn gekannt?', *Nathanael* 21, pp. 89-150.

Black, Matthew (1948–49), 'Unsolved NT Problems: The 'Son of Man' in the Old Biblical Literature', *Expository Times* 60, pp. 11-15.

Black, Matthew (1948–49), 'Unsolved NT Problems: "The Son of Man" in the Teaching of Jesus', *Expository Times* 60, pp. 32-36.

Blank, Joseph (1981), *The Gospel According to St John* (NTSR, 8–9; New York: Crossroad).

Boccaccini, Gabriele (1991), *Middle Judaism: Jewish Thought 300 BCE to 200 CE* (Minneapolis: Fortress Press).

Boccaccini, Gabriele (1992), *Portraits of Middle Judaism in Scholarship and Arts: A Multimedia Catalog from Flavius Josephus to 1991* (Turin: Zamorani).

Boccaccini, Gabriele (1998), *Beyond the Essene Hypothesis: The Parting of the Ways between Qumran and Enochic Judaism* (Grand Rapids: Eerdmans).

Boccaccini, Gabriele (2002), *Roots of Rabbinic Judaism: An Intellectual History, from Ezekiel to Daniel* (Grand Rapids: Eerdmans).

Boccaccini, Gabriele (ed.) (2005), *Enoch and Qumran Origins: New Light on a Forgotten Connection* (Grand Rapids: Eerdmans).

Boccaccini, Gabriele (ed.) (2006), *Enoch and the Messiah Son of Man: Revisiting the Book of Parables* (Grand Rapids: Eerdmans).

Boccaccini, Gabriele (ed.) (2009), *Enoch and the Mosaic Torah: The Evidence of Jubilees* (Grand Rapids: Eerdmans).

Bornkamm, Günther (1960), *Jesus of Nazareth* (London: Hodder & Stoughton).

Borsch, Frederick H. (1963), 'The Son of Man', *ATR* 45, pp. 174-90.

Borsch, Frederick H. (1967), *The Son of Man in Myth and History* (NTL; Philadelphia: Westminster Press).

Borsch, Frederick H. (1970), *The Christian and Gnostic Son of Man* (Studies in Biblical Theology, 2/14; London: SCM Press).

Borsch, Frederick H. (1992), 'Further Reflections on "The Son of Man": The Origins and Development of the Title', in James H. Charlesworth (ed.), *The Messiah:*

Developments in Earliest Judaism and Christinaity (Minneapolis: Fortress Press), pp. 130-44.

Bowker, John (1977), 'The Son of Man', *JTS* 28, 19-48.

Braun, Herbert (1959), 'The Meaning of New Testament Christology', *Journal for Theology and the Church* 5, 89-127.

Brown, Raymond E. (1966), *The Gospel According to John I–XII, and XIII–XXI, Translation with an Introduction and Notes* (2 vols.; Anchor Bible; Garden City, NY: Doubleday).

Bucer, Martin (1527), *Ennarrationum in evangelia Matthaei, Marci, et Lucae* (Argentorati: Hervag).

Bullinger, Heinrich (1542), *In sacrosanctum Iesu Christi Domini nostri evangelium secondum Matthaeum, commentariorum libri xii* (Tiguri: Froschover).

Bultmann, Rudolf (1921) *Die Geschichte der synoptischen Tradition* (Göttingen: Vandenhoeck & Ruprecht).

Bultmann, Rudolf (1934), *Jesus and the Word* (trans. L.P. Smith and E.H. Lantero; New York: Scribner's).

Bultmann, Rudolf (1951), *Theology of the New Testament* (trans. K. Grobel; 2 vols.; New York: Scribner's).

Bultmann, Rudolf (1963), *History of the Synoptic Tradition* (trans. J. Marsh; Oxford: Blackwell).

Bultmann, Rudolf (1964), 'The Primitive Christian Kerygma and the Historical Jesus', in Carl E. Braaten and R.A. Harrisville (eds.), *The Historical Jesus and the Kerygmatic Christ* (Nashville: Abingdon Press).

Bultmann, Rudolf (1971), *The Gospel of John: A Commentary* (trans. G.R. Beasley-Murray; Oxford: Blackwell).

Burkett, Delbert (1999), *The Son of Man Debate: A History and Evaluation* (Cambridge: Cambridge University Press).

Caird, G. B. (1968–69), 'The Glory of God in the Fourth Gospel: An Exercise in Biblical Semantics', *NTS* 15, pp. 265-77.

Calvin, John (1961), *The Gospel according to St John, Part One, A New Translation 1–10* (trans. T.H.L. Parker; *Calvin's New Testament Commentaries*; Grand Rapids: Eerdmans), pp. 153-72.

Caragounis, Chrys C. (1986), *The Son of Man: Vision and Interpretation* (WUNT, 38; Tübingen: Mohr–Siebeck).

Casey, Maurice (1996), *Is John's Gospel True?* (London: Routledge).

Casey, Maurice (2007), *The Solution to the 'Son of Man' Problem* (LNTS, 343; New York: T. & T. Clark).

Charlesworth, James H. (ed.) (1991), *John and the Dead Sea Scrolls* (New York: Crossroad).

Chialà, Sabino (2007), 'The Son of Man: The Evolution of an Expression', in Gabriele Boccaccini (ed.), *Enoch and the Messiah Son of Man: Revisting the Book of Parables* (Grand Rapids: Eerdmans), pp. 153-78.

Case, Shirley J. (1927a), *Jesus: A New Biography* (New York: Greenwood), pp. 366-67, 370-71.

Case, Shirley J. (1927b), 'The Alleged Messianic Consciousness of Jesus', *JBL* 46, pp. 1-19.

Chilton, Bruce D. (1981), 'The Transfiguration: Dominical Assurance and Apostolic Vision', *NTS* 27, pp. 115-24.

Collins, John J. (1984, 1998), *The Apocalyptic Imagination, An Introduction to Jewish Apocalyptic Literature* (Grand Rapids: Eerdmans).

Collins, John J. (1992), 'The Son of Man in First-Century Judaism', *NTS* 38, pp. 448-66.

Collins, John J. (1993), *Daniel* (Hermeneia; Minneapolis: Fortress Press).

Collins, John J. (2000), *Between Athens and Jerusalem: Jewish Identity in the Hellenistic Diaspora* (Grand Rapids: Eerdmans).

Collins, John J. and Peter W. Flint (eds.) (2001), *The Book of Daniel: Composition and Reception* (2 vols.; Leiden: E.J. Brill).

Collins, John J. and George W.E. Nickelsburg (1980), *Ideal Figures in Ancient Judaism: Profiles and Paradigms* (Chico, CA: Scholars Press).

Collins, Raymond F. (1990), *These Things Have Been Written: Studies on the Fourth Gospel* (Louvain Theological and Pastoral Monographs, 2; Louvain: Peeters).

Colpe, Carsten (1969–72), 'Der Begriff "Menschensohn" und die Methode der Erforschung messianischer Prototypen', *Kairos* 11/4 (1969), pp. 241-263; 12/2 (1970), pp. 81-112; 13/1 (1971), pp. 1-17; 14/4 (1972), pp. 241-57.

Colpe, Carsten (1969), 'ὁ υἱὸς τοῦ ἀνθρώπου', in *Theological Dictionary of the New Testament* (trans. Geoffrey W. Bromiley; Grand Rapids: Eerdmans), VIII, pp. 400-77.

Colwell, Ernest C. (1933), 'A Definite Rule for the Use of the Article in the Greek New Testament', *JBL* 52, pp. 12-21.

Conzelmann, Hans (1961), *The Theology of St Luke* (trans. Geoffrey Buswell; New York: Harper).

Dahl, Nils A. (1969), 'The Atonement—An Adequate Reward for the Akedah? (Rom 8.32)', in E. Earle Ellis and Max Wilcox (eds.), *Neotestamentica et semitica: Studies in Honour of Matthew Black* (Edinburgh: T. & T. Clark), pp. 15-29.

Daube, David (1956), *The New Testament and Rabbinic Judaism* (London: Athlone Press).

Davies, William D., and Dale C. Allison (1991), *A Critical and Exegetical Commentary on the Gospel according to Saint Matthew* (2 vols.; ICC; Edinburgh: T. & T. Clark).

Davis, Francis H. (1961), 'The Son of Man. I. The Image of the Father', *The Furrow* 12, pp. 39-48.

De Boer, Martinus C. (1996), *Johannine Perspectives on the Death of Jesus* (CBET, 17; Kampen: Kok Pharos).

Dieckmann, Hermann (1927), 'Der Sohn des Menschen im Johannesevangelium', *Scholastik* 2, pp. 229-47.

Dieckmann, Hermann (1927), 'ὁ υἱὸς τοῦ ἀνθρώπου', *Biblica* 2, pp. 69-71.

Dodd, Charles H. (1953), *The Interpretation of the Fourth Gospel* (Cambridge: Cambridge University Press).

Dorner, Isaak A. (1845), *Entwicklungsgeschichte der Lehre von der Person Christi* (2nd edn; 3 vols.; Stuttgart: Leisching).

Dougall, Lily, and Cyril W. Emmet (1922), *The Lord of Thought* (London: SCM Press).

Downing, F. Gerald (1988), *Christ and the Cynics, Jesus and the Other Radical Preachers in First-Century Traditions* (Sheffield: Sheffield Academic Press).

Driver, Samuel R. (1902), 'Son of Man', in James Hastings (ed.), *A Dictionary of the Bible* (Edinburgh: T. & T. Clark).

Drummond, James (1877), *The Jewish Messiah* (London: Longmans).

Drummond, James (1901), 'The Use and Meaning of the Phrase, 'The Son of Man', in the Synoptic Gospels', *JTS* 11, pp. 350-58, 539-71.

Dunn, James D. G. (1992), 'Christology (NT)', in David N. Freedman (ed.), *The Anchor Bible Dictionary* (New York: Doubleday), I, pp. 978-91.

Ebrard, Johannes H. A. (1862–63), *Christliche Dogmatik* (2nd edn; 2 vols.; Königsberg: Unzer).

Ehrman, Bart D. (1992), *The Orthodox Corruption of Scripture: The Effect of Early Christological Controversies on the Text of the New Testament* (New York: Oxford University Press).

Eissfeldt, Otto (1943), *Einleitung in das Alte Testament* (Tübingen: Mohr–Siebeck).

Fitzmyer, Joseph A. (1981), *The Gospel according to Luke I–IX* (Anchor Bible, 28; Garden City, NY: Doubleday).

Flusser, David (1988), *Judaism and the Origins of Christianity* (Jerusalem: Magnes Press).

Foakes-Jackson, Frederick J., and Kirsopp Lake (eds.) (1920), *The Beginnings of Christianity* (5 vols.; London: Macmillan).

Fossum, Jarl E. (1995), *The Image of the Invisible God: Essays on the Influence of Jewish Mysticism on Early Christology* (Novum Testamentum et orbis antiquus, 3; Freiburg: Universitätsverlag Freiburg).

Fuchs, Ernst (1964), 'The Quest of the Historical Jesus', in *Studies of the Historical Jesus* (London: Oxford University Press), pp. 11-31.

Fuller, Reginald H. (1985), 'The Son of Man: A Reconsideration', in Dennis E. Groh and Robert Jewett (eds.), *The Living Text: Essays in Honor of Ernest W. Saunders* (Lanham, MD, University Press of America), pp. 207-17.

Geldenhuys, Norval (1954), *Commentary on the Gospel of Luke* (The International Commentary on the New Testament; Grand Rapids: Eerdmans).

Godet, Frédéric (1872), *Commentaire sur l'Evangile de saint Luc* (2nd edn; Neuchâtel: Sandoz).

Goguel, Maurice (1904), *L'apôtre Paul et Jésus-Christ* (Paris: Fischbacher).

Gould, George P. (1917), 'The Son of Man', in James Hastings (ed.), *A Dictionary of Christ and the Gospels* (Edinburgh: T. & T. Clark), II, pp. 659-65.

Grotius, Hugo (1679), 'Annotationes in libros evangeliorum', in *Opera omnia theologica* (Amsterdam).

Grundmann, Walter (1966), *Das Evangelium nach Lukas* (THKNT; Berlin: Evangelische Verlagsanstalt).

Haenchen, Ernst (1984), *John 1. A Commentary on the Gospel of John, Chapters 1–6* (trans. Robert Funk; Hermeneia; Philadelphia: Fortress Press).

Hamerton-Kelly, Robert G. (1973), *Pre-existence, Wisdom, and the Son of Man: A Study of the Idea of Pre-existence in the New Testament* (SNTSMS, 21; Cambridge: Cambridge University Press).

Hammond, Henry (1639), *A Paraphrase and Annotations upon All the Books of the New Testament* (repr. 4 vols.; Oxford: Oxford University Press, 1865).

Hampel, Volker (1990), *Menschensohn und historischer Jesus: Ein Rätselwort als Schlüssel zum messianischen Selbstverständnis Jesu* (Neukirchener–Vluyn: Neukirchener Verlag).

Hanson, Anthony T. (1991), *The Prophetic Gospel: A Study of John and the Old Testament* (Edinburgh: T. & T. Clark).

Hare, Douglas R. A. (1990), *The Son of Man Tradition* (Minneapolis: Fortress Press).

Head, Peter M. (1990), 'Some Observations on Early Papyri of the Synoptic Gospels: Especially Concerning Scribal Habits', *Biblica* 71, pp. 240-47.

Head, Peter M. (2004), 'The Habits of New Testament Copyists: Singular readings in the Early Fragmentary Papyri of John', *Biblica* 85, pp. 399-408.

Higgins, Angus J.B. (1964), *Jesus and the Son of Man* (London: Lutterworth).

Hofmann, Johann C.K. von (1886), *Biblische Theologie des Neuen Testaments* (Nordlingen: Beck).

Hooker, Morna D. (1967), *The Son of Man in Mark: A Study of the Background of the Term 'Son of Man' and its Use in St Mark's Gospel* (Montreal: McGill University Press).

Hooker, Morna D. (1979), 'Is the Son of Man Problem Really Insoluble?', in E. Bes and R.M. Wilson (eds.), *Text and Interpretation: Studies in the New Testament, Presented to Matthew Black* (Cambridge: Cambridge University Press), pp. 155-68.

Hooker, Morna D. (1986), *Continuity and Discontinuity: Early Christianity in Its Jewish Setting* (London: Epworth Press).

Hoskyns, Edwin C. (1947), *The Fourth Gospel* (2nd edn; London: Faber & Faber).

Howard, Wilbert F., and Arthur J. Gossip (1952), *The Gospel according to St John* (The Interpreter's Bible, 8; Nashville: Abingdon Press), pp. 488-90.

Hunter, Archibald M. (1951), *Interpreting the New Testament, 1900–1950* (London: SCM Press).

Hunter, Archibald M. (1957), *Introducing New Testament Theology* (Philadelphia: Westminster Press).

Hunter, Archibald M. (1965, 1986), *The Gospel according to John* (The Cambridge Bible Commentary on The New English Bible; Cambridge: Cambridge University Press).

Jansen, Cornelius (1576), *Commentariorum in suam concordiam, ac totam historiam evangelicam partes quatuor* (Louvain: Sangrium).

Jansen, Cornelius (1639), *Tetrateuchus, sive commentarius in sancta Iesu Christi evangelia* (Louvain: Zeger).

Jeremias, Joachim, and Walter Zimmerli (1954), *The Servant of God* (2nd edn; Studies in Biblical Theology, 20; London: SCM Press).

Juel, Donald (1977), *Messiah and Temple: The Trial of Jesus in the Gospel of Mark* (Missoula, MT: Scholars Press).

Kanagaraj, Jeyaseelan J. (1998), *'Mysticism' in the Gospel of John: An Inquiry into its Background* (JSNTSup, 158; Sheffield: Sheffield Academic Press).

Käsemann, Ernst (1969), *Jesus Means Freedom* (London: Trinity Press International).

Keener, Craig S. (2003), *The Gospel of John: A Commentary* (Peabody, MA: Hendrickson).

Kittel, Gerhard (ed.) (1964–74), *Theological Dictionary of the New Testament* (trans. Geoffrey W. Bromiley; 9 vols.; Grand Rapids: Eerdmans).

Klausner, Joseph (1929), *Jesus of Nazareth* (London: Lutterworth).

Kocher, Johann C. (1766), *Analecta philologica et exegetica in quatuor ss. evangelia* (Altenburg: Richter).

Kraft, Robert A., and George W.E. Nickelsburg (eds.) (1986), *Early Judaism and its Modern Interpreters* (Philadelphia: Fortress Press).

Kratz, Reinhard (2001), 'The Visions of Daniel', in John J. Collins and Peter W. Flint (eds.), *The Book of Daniel: Composition and Reception* (Leiden: E.J. Brill), I, pp. 91-113.

Kühl, Ernst (1907), *Das Selbstbewusstsein Jesu* (Berlin: Runge).

Kümmel, Werner G. (1957), *Promise and Fulfillment: The Eschatological Message of Jesus* (Studies in Biblical Theology, 23; Naperville, IL: Allenson).

Kümmel, Werner G. (1969/1973), *The Theology of the New Testament according to its Major Witnesses* (Nashville: Abingdon Press).

Kümmel, Werner G. (1984), *Jesus der Menschensohn* (Stuttgart: Steiner).

Kvanvig, Helge S. (1981), 'An Akkadian Vision as Background for Daniel 7', *SitTh* 35, pp. 85-89.

Kvanvig, Helge S. (1988), *Roots of Apocalyptic: The Mesopotamian Background of the Enoch Figure and of the Son of Man* (WMANT, 61; Neukirchen–Vluyn: Neukirchener Verlag).

Leaney, Alfred R.C. (1991), 'The Johannine Paraclete and the Qumran Scrolls', in James H. Charlesworth (ed.), *John and the Dead Sea Scrolls* (New York: Crossroad).

Leivestad, Ragnar (1972), 'Exit the Apocalyptic Son of Man', *NTS* 18: 243-67.

Létourneau, Pierre (1993), *Jésus, fils de l'homme et fils de Dieu: Jean 2.23–3.36 et la double christologie johannique* (Paris: Cerf).

Lightfoot, Robert H. (1966), *St John's Gospel: A Commentary* (rev. edn by C.F. Evans; Oxford: Oxford University Press).

Lindars, Barnabas (1983), *Jesus Son of Man: A Fresh Examination of the Son of Man Sayings in the Gospels* (Grand Rapids: Eerdmans).

Loisy, Alfred (1903), *La quatrième Évangile* (Paris: Picard).

Luthardt, Christoph E. (1875–76), *Das johanneische Evangelium nach seiner Eigenthumlichkeit geschildert und erklärt* (2 vols.; Nuremberg: Geiger).

Lutz, Johann L.S. (1861), *Biblische Dogmatik* (2nd edn; Pforzheim: Flammer).

Luz, Ulrich (2001), *Matthew 8–20* (trans. J.E. Crouch; Hermeneia; Minneapolis: Fortress Press).

Mack, Burton (1997), 'Q and a Cynic-Like Jesus', in William E. Arnal and Michel Desjardins (eds.), *Whose Historical Jesus?* (Studies in Christianity and Judaism, 7; Waterloo, Ontario: Wilfrid Laurier University).

Mann, Christopher S. (1986), *Mark: A New Translation with Introduction and Commentary* (Anchor Bible, 27; Garden City, NY: Doubleday).

Manson, Thomas W. (1950), 'The Son of Man in Daniel, Enoch, and the Gospels', *BJRL* 32, pp. 171-95.

Manson, Thomas W. (1959), *The Teaching of Jesus: Studies in its Form and Content* (Cambridge: Cambridge University Press).

Marshall, I. Howard (1970), 'The Son of Man in Contemporary Debate', *Evangelical Quarterly* 42, pp. 67-87.

Marshall, I. Howard, (1991), 'The Son of Man and the Incarnation', *Ex auditu* 7, pp. 29-43.

Martyn, James Louis (1968), *History and Theology in the Fourth Gospel* (New York: Harper & Row).

McGrath, James F. (2001), *John's Apologetic Christology: Legitimation and Development in Johannine Christology* (Cambridge: Cambridge University Press).

McGrath, James F. (1998), 'Change in Christology: New Testament Models and the Contemporary Task', *ITQ* 63/1, pp. 39-50.

Mearns, Christopher L. (1977–78), 'The *Parables of Enoch*—Origin and Date', *Expository Times* 89, pp. 118-19.

Mearns, Christopher L. (1978–79), 'Dating the Similitudes of Enoch', *NTS* 25, pp. 360-69.

Meeks, William A. (1967), *The Prophet-King, Moses Traditions and the Johannine Christology* (NovTSup, 14; Leiden: E.J. Brill).

Metzger, Bruce M. (1983), 'The Fourth Book of Ezra: A New Translation and Introduc-
    tion', in James H. Charlesworth (ed.), *The Old Testament Pseudepigrapha* (New
    York: Doubleday), pp. 517-59.
Metzger, Bruce M. (1998), *A Textual Commentary on the Greek New Testament* (2nd
    edn; New York: United Bible Societies).
Michaelis, Johann D. (1790–92), *Anmerkungen für Ungelehrte zu seiner Uebersetzung
    des Neuen Testaments* (4 vols.; Göttingen: Vandenhoeck & Ruprecht).
Moloney, Francis J. (1998), *The Gospel of John* (Sacra Pagina Series, 4; Collegeville,
    MN: Liturgical Press).
Moloney, Francis J. (2005), *The Gospel of John: Text and Context* (Leiden: E.J. Brill).
Morris, Leon (1995), *The Gospel of John* (rev. edn; Grand Rapids: Eerdmans).
Mosche, Gabriele C.B. (1788–90), *Erklarung aller Sonn- und Festtags-Episteln* (2nd
    edn; 2 vols.; Frankfurt: Fleischer).
Müller, Mogens (1977), 'Uber den Ausdruck 'Menschensohn' in den Evangelien', *ST*
    31, pp. 65-82.
Müller, Mogens (1984a), *Der Ausdruck 'Menschensohn' in den Evangelien: Vorausset-
    zungen und Bedeutung* (Leiden: E.J. Brill).
Müller, Mogens (1984b), 'The Expression "the Son of Man" as Used by Jesus', *ST* 38,
    pp. 47-64.
Müller, Ulrich B. (1972), *Messias und Menschensohn in jüdischen Apokalypsen und in
    der Offenbarung des Johannes* (SENT, 6; Gütersloh: Mohn).
Munoa, Phillip B., III (1998), *Four Powers in Heaven: The Interpretation of Daniel 7
    and the Testament of Abraham* (Sheffield: Sheffield Academic Press).
Münster, Sebastian (1537), *Torat hammashiach: Evangelium secundum Matthaeum
    in lingua hebraica, cum versione latina aeque succinctis annotationibus* (Basel:
    Petrus).
Nestle, Eberhard, Erwin Nestle, Barbara Aland, Kurt Aland, Johannes Karavidopou-
    los, Carlo M. Martini, and Bruce M. Metzger (eds.) (1996), *Novum Testamentum
    graece* (27th edn; Stuttgart: Deutsche Bibelgesellschaft).
Neusner, Jacob (1986), *Judaism and Scripture: The Evidence of Leviticus Rabbah*
    (Chicago: University of Chicago Press).
Neusner, Jacob, William S. Green, and Ernest S. Frerichs (eds.) (1987), *Judaisms and
    their Messiahs at the Turn of the Christian Era* (Cambridge: Cambridge Univer-
    sity Press).
Nickelsburg, George W.E. (1978), 'Review: J.T. Milik, *The Books of Enoch*', *Catholic
    Biblical Quarterly* 40, pp. 411-19.
Nickelsburg, George W.E. (1992), 'Son of Man', in David N. Freedman (ed.), *Anchor
    Bible Dictionary* (New York: Doubleday), VI, pp. 137-50.
Nickelsburg, George W.E. (2001), *1 Enoch 1* (Hermeneia; Minneapolis: Fortress
    Press).
Nickelsburg, George W.E. and James C. VanderKam (2004), *1 Enoch: A New Transla-
    tion* (Minneapolis: Fortress Press).
Nicholson, Godfrey C. (1983), *Death as Departure: The Johannine Descent–Ascent
    Schema* (SBLDS, 63; Chico, CA: Scholars Press).
Noesgen, Karl Friedrich (1869), *Christus der Menschen- und Gottessohn* (Gotha:
    Perthes).
Odeberg, Hugo (1929), *The Fourth Gospel Interpreted in its Relation to Contemporane-
    ous Religious Currents in Palestine and the Hellenistic-Oriental World* (Uppsala:
    Argonaut).

Otto, Rudolf (1951), *The Kingdom of God and the Son of Man: A Study in the History of Religion* (trans. Floyd V. Filson and Bertram Lee-Woolf; London: Lutterworth).

Otto, Rudolf (1958), *The Idea of the Holy: An Inquiry into the Non-rational Factor in the Idea of the Divine and its Relation to the Rational* (trans. John W. Harvey; New York: Oxford University Press).

Owen, Paul L. (2009), 'Review: M. Casey, *The Solution to the 'Son of Man' Problem*', *RBL*.

Owen, Paul L., and David Shepherd (2001), 'Speaking up for Qumran, Dalman and the Son of Man', *JSNT* 81, pp. 81-122.

Painter, John (1991, 1993), *The Quest for the Messiah: The History, Literature and Theology of the Johannine Community* (Edinburgh: T. & T. Clark).

Pamment, Margaret (1983), 'The Son of Man in the First Gospel', *NTS* 29, pp. 116-29.

Perrin, Norman (1974), *A Modern Pilgrimage in New Testament Christology* (Philadelphia: Fortress Press).

Porter, Stanley E. (1992), *Idioms of the Greek New Testament* (Sheffield: Sheffield Academic Press).

Porter, Stanley E. (2006), 'Scripture Justifies Mission: The Use of the Old Testament in Luke–Acts', in Porter (ed.), *Hearing the Old Testament in the New Testament* (Grand Rapids: Eerdmans), pp. 102-26.

Rad, Gerhard von (1952), *Theologisches Wörterbuch zum Neuen Testament* (Göttingen: Vandenhoeck & Ruprecht).

Reicke, Bo (1973), 'Jesus in Nazareth—Luke 4.14-30', in Horst R. Balz and Siegfried Schulz (eds.), *Das Wort und die Wörter: Festschrift G. Friedrich zum 65. Geburtstag* (Stuttgart: Kohlhammer), pp. 47-55.

Reim, Gunter (1974), *Studien zum alttestamentlichen Hintergrund des Johannesevangeliums* (SNTSMS, 22; Cambridge: Cambridge University Press).

Reuss, Edouard (1860), *Histoire de la théologie chrétienne au siècle apostolique* (2nd edn; 2 vols.; Strasburg: Treuttel & Wurtz).

Roberts, Alexander, and James Donaldson (eds.) (1967), *The Ante-Nicene Fathers: Translations of the Writings of the Fathers down to A.D. 325* (Grand Rapids: Eerdmans).

Robinson, James M. (1994), 'The Son of Man in the Sayings Gospel Q', in Christoph Elsas (ed.), *Tradition und Translation: Zum Problem der interkulturellen Übersetzbarkeit religiöser Phänomene: Festschrift für Carsten Colpe zum 65. Geburtstag* (Berlin: de Gruyter).

Rodgers, Peter (2009), 'Luke 4.18, to Heal the Brokenhearted', in J. Harold Ellens (ed.), *The Healing Power of Spirituality: How Religion Helps Humans Thrive* (3 vols.; Westport, CT: Praeger), I, pp. 162-69.

Ross, John M. (1991), 'The Son of Man', *JBS* 13, pp. 186-98.

Royce, James R. (2007), *Scribal Habits in Early Greek New Testament Papyri* (Leiden: E.J. Brill).

Sacchi, Paolo (1976), *Storia del mondo giudaico* (Turin: Società Editrice Internationale).

Sacchi, Paolo (1994), *Storia del Secondo Tempio: Israele tra VI secolo a C. e I secolo d. C.* (Turin: Società Editrice Internationale).

Safrai, Shmuel and Moritz Stern (eds.) (1977), *The Jewish People in the First Century: Historical Geography, Political History, Social, Cultural and Religious Life and Institutions* (2 vols.; Philadelphia: Fortress Press).

Sanday, William (1891), 'On the Title, "Son of Man"', *Expositor* 4/3, pp. 18-32.

Sanders, E. P. (1977), *Paul and Palestinian Judaism: A Comparison of Patterns of Religion* (Philadelphia: Fortress Press).

Schleiermacher, Friedrich (1830–31), *Die christliche Glaube* (2nd edn; Halle an der Saal: Hendel).

Schmithals, Walter (1979), 'Die Worte vom leidenden Menschensohn: Ein Schlüssel zum Lösung des Menschensohns-Problem', in C. Andreson and G. Klein (eds.), *Theologia crucis—signum crucis: Festschrift fur Erich Dinkler zum 70. Geburtstag* (Tübingen: Mohr–Siebeck).

Schnackenburg, Rudolf (1982), *The Gospel according to St John* (trans. K. Smith; 3 vols.; New York: Crossroad; Freiburg: Herder).

Scholten, Wessel (1809), *Specimen hermeneutico-theologicum: De appellatione tou huiou tou anthropou, qua Jesus se Messiam professus est* (Trajecti ad Rhenum: Paddenburg & Schoonhoven).

Schürer, Emil (1874), *Lehrbuch der neutestamentlichen Zeitgeschichte* (Leipzig: J.C. Hinrichs).

Schürer, Emil (1973), *The History of the Jewish People in the Age of Jesus Christ* (rev. edn by Geza Vermes, Fergus Millar, Martin Black, and Martin Goodman; 3 vols.; Edinburgh: T. & T. Clark).

Schürmann, Heinz. (1969), *Das Lukasevangelium* (THKNT; Freiburg: Herder).

Schweizer, Eduard (1959), 'Der Menschensohn (Zur eschatologischen Erwartung Jesu)', *ZNW* 50, pp. 185-209.

Segal, Alan F. (1981), 'Ruler of This World: Attitudes about Mediator Figures and the Importance of Sociology for Self-Definition', in Albert I. Baumgarten and Alan Mendelson (eds.), *Jewish and Christian Self-Definition. II. Aspects of Judaism in the Graeco-Roman Period* (London: SCM Press), pp. 255-56.

Segal, Alan F. (1986), *Rebecca's Children: Judaism and Christianity in the Roman World* (Cambridge, MA: Harvard University Press).

Sidebottom, Ernest M. (1957), 'The Ascent and Descent of the Son of Man in the Gospel of *St* John', *ATR* 39, pp. 115-22.

Sidebottom, Ernest M. (1961), *The Christ of the Fourth Gospel in the Light of First-Century Thought* (London: SPCK).

Sidebottom, Ernest M. (1961), *The Christ of the Fourth Gospel* (London: SPCK).

Slater, Thomas B. (1995), 'One like a Son of Man in First-Century CE Judaism', *New Testament Studies* 41, pp. 183-98.

Sloyan, Gerard S. (1988), *John* (Interpretation; Atlanta: John Knox).

Stalker, James (1899), *The Christology of Jesus* (New York: Armstrong).

Stevens, George B. (1899), *The Theology of the New Testament* (New York: Scribner's).

Stephenson, T. (1917–18), 'The Title "Son of Man"', *Expository Times* 29, pp. 377-78.

Stott, Wilfrid (1972), '"Son of Man": A Title of Abasement', *Expository Times* 83, pp. 278-81.

Strachan, Robert H. (1917), *The Fourth Gospel: Its Significance and Environment* (London: SCM Press).

Strack, Hermann L., and Paul Billerbeck (1928), *Kommentar zum Neuen Testament aus Talmud und Midrasch* (München: Beck).

Strathmann, Hermann (1968), *Das Evangelium nach Johannes* (NTD, 4; Göttingen: Vandenhoeck & Ruprecht).

Stuhlmacher, Peter (1992), *Biblische Theologie* (2 vols.; Tübingen: Mohr–Siebeck).

Stuhlmacher, Peter (ed.) (1973), *Das Evangelium und die Evangelien* (Tübingen: Mohr–Siebeck).

Suggs, Jack M. (1970), *Wisdom, Christology, and Law in Matthew's Gospel* (Cambridge, MA: Harvard University Press).

Suter, David (1981), 'Weighed in the Balance: The Similitudes of Enoch in Recent Discussion', *Religious Studies Review* 7, pp. 217-21.

Talbert, Charles H. (1977), *What Is a Gospel? The Genre of the Canonical Gospels* (Philadelphia: Fortress Press).

Taylor, Vincent (1952), *The Gospel according to St Mark* (New York: Macmillan).

Taylor, Vincent (1959), *Jesus and his Sacrifice: A Study of the Passion-Sayings in the Gospels* (London: Macmillan).

Tenney, Merrill C. (1981), *The Gospel of John* (The Expositor's Bible Commentary, 9; Grand Rapids: Zondervan).

Theisohn, Johannes (1975), *Der auserwählte Richter: Untersuchungen zum traditionsgeschichtlichen Ort der Menschensohngestalt der Bilderreden des Äthiopischen Henoch* (Göttingen; Vandenhoeck & Ruprecht).

Theissen, Gerd, and Annette Merz (1998), *The Historical Jesus: A Comprehensive Guide* (trans. John Bowden; Minneapolis: Fortress Press).

Tholuck, Augustus (1827), *Commentar zu dem Evangelio Johannis* (Hamburg: Perthes).

Thomasius, Gottfried (1857), *Christi Person und Werk: Darstellung der evangelisch-lutherischen Dogmatik vom Mittlepunkte der Christologie aus* (2nd edn; Erlangen: Blasing).

Thüsing, Wilhelm (1960), *Die Erhöhung und Verherrlichung Jesu im Johannesevangelium* (Münster: Aschendorff).

Tödt, Heinz E. (1965), *The Son of Man in the Synoptic Tradition* (London: SCM Press).

Trench, Richard C. (1882), *Notes on the Parables of our Lord* (14th edn; London: Clarendon Press).

Tuckett, Christopher (1982), 'The Present Son of Man', *JSNT* 14, pp. 48-81.

Vermes, Geza (1973*)*, *Jesus the Jew: A Historian's Reading of the Gospels* (London: Collins).

Vielhauer, Philipp (1957), *Gottesreich und Menschensohn in der Verkündigung Jesu* (Tübingen: Mohr–Siebeck).

Vielhauer, Philipp (1963), 'Jesus und der Menschensohn: Zur Diskussion mit Heinz Eduard Tödt und Eduard Schweizer', *Zeitschrift fur Theologie und Kirche* 60, pp. 133-77.

Walck, Leslie W. (2007), 'The Son of Man in the *Parables of Enoch* and the Gospels', in Gabriele Boccaccini (ed.), *Enoch and the Messiah Son of Man: Revisiting the Book of Parables* (Grand Rapids: Eerdmans), pp. 299-337.

Weiss, Bernard (1868), *Lehrbuch der biblischen Theologie des Neuen Testaments* (Berlin: Hertz).

Wellhausen, Julius (1899), 'Des Menschen Sohn', in *Skizze und Vorarbeiten* (Berlin: Reimer), VI, pp. 187-215.

Westcott, Brooke F. (1908), *The Gospel according to St John: The Greek Text with Introduction and Notes* (2 vols.; London: Murray).

Witherington, Ben (1990), *The Christology of Jesus* (Minneapolis: Fortress Press).

Wolf, Johann C. (1725), *Curae philologicae et criticae in IV. ss. evangelia et actus apostolicos* (2 vols.; Hamburg).

Wolzogen, Johan L. von (1656), *Commentaria in evangelium Matthaei* (Irenopolis).

Zahn, Theodor (1903), *Das Evangelium des Matthäus* (Leipzig: Deichert).

Zwingli, Ulrich (1531), *Annotationes in quatuor evangelia ac epistolas* (Tiguri: Froschover).

OTHER ANCIENT LITERATURE

INDEX OF SUBJECTS*

---

* The terms, Jesus, Son of Man, Fourth Gospel or Gospel of John, and Kingdom have not been included in this index because they all appear on nearly every page.

CPSIA information can be obtained
at www.ICGtesting.com
Printed in the USA
BVOW06*0454211117
500893BV00012BA/225/P

9 781906 055998